Studying Human Resource Management

Edited by Stephen Taylor and Carol Woodhams

The only textbooks mapped to the CIPD Intermediate level learning outcomes: *Studying Human Resource Management*, *Developing People and Organisations*, and *Managing People and Organisations*, together cover all of the learning outcomes for the core and optional units in Human Resource Management and Human Resource Development.

Series editors:

Stephen Taylor is a Senior Lecturer in Human Resource Management at the University of Exeter. He is also a Chief Examiner for the CIPD.

Carol Woodhams is a Senior Lecturer in Human Resource Management at the University of Exeter. She is CIPD National Examiner for Designing and Delivering Training.

Jim Stewart is Professor of HRD at Coventry University. He is also Chief Examiner of Learning and Development for CIPD, as well as Visiting Panel Chair and External Moderator.

Studying Human Resource Management, edited by Stephen Taylor and Carol Woodhams
Contributors: Ted Johns, Graham Perkins, Krystal Wilkinson

Developing People and Organisations, edited by Jim Stewart and Patricia Rogers
Contributors: Jill Ashley-Jones, Susan Barnes, Terrence Wendell Brathwaite, Gary Connor, Amanda Lee, Rosalind Maxwell-Harrison, Michael McFadden, Sharon McGuire, Michelle McLardy, Ian McLean, Sophie Mills, Graham Perkins, Krish Pinto, Raymond Rogers, Dalbir Sidhu, Kirsten Stevens, Carol Woodhams

Managing People and Organisations, edited by Stephen Taylor and Carol Woodhams
Contributors: Cecilia Ellis, Ted Johns, Graham Perkins, Gail Swift, Krystal Wilkinson

The Chartered Institute of Personnel and Development is the leading publisher of books and reports for personnel and training professionals, students, and all those concerned with the effective management and development of people at work. For details of all our titles, please contact the publishing department:
tel: 020 8612 6204
email: publishing@cipd.co.uk
The catalogue of all CIPD titles can be viewed on the CIPD website:
www.cipd.co.uk/bookstore

Studying Human Resource Management

Edited by Stephen Taylor and Carol Woodhams

Chartered Institute of Personnel and Development

Published by the Chartered Institute of Personnel and Development,
151, The Broadway, London, SW19 1JQ

This edition first published 2012

Typeset by Fakenham Prepress Solutions, Fakenham, Norfolk NR21 8NN
Printed in Great Britain by Bell & Bain, Glasgow

British Library Cataloguing in Publication Data
A catalogue of this publication is available from the British Library

ISBN 978 1 84398 312 5

Chartered Institute of Personnel and Development, CIPD House,
151, The Broadway, London, SW19 1JQ
Tel: 020 8612 6200
Email: cipd@cipd.co.uk
Website: www.cipd.co.uk
Incorporated by Royal Charter
Registered Charity No. 1079797

Contents

List of Figures and Tables

Contributor Biographies

Stephen Taylor is a Senior Lecturer in Human Resource Management at the University of Exeter Business School and also Chief Examiner for the Chartered Institute of Personnel and Development (CIPD). He previously taught at Manchester Business School, at Manchester Metropolitan University Business School, and worked in a variety of HR management roles in the hotel industry and in the NHS. He is the author/co-author of several books on HRM and employment law. He regularly represents parties in employment tribunals and undertakes HR consultancy and training work.

Dr Carol Woodhams is a Senior Lecturer in Human Resource Management at the University of Exeter Business School. She has held a number of positions within the CIPD, including National Examiner for Designing and Delivering Training, External Moderator for the Advanced Qualification, and editor of the flexible learning materials at Intermediate and Advanced levels. She previously taught at Plymouth University and Manchester Metropolitan University. Her specialist teaching subjects are employee resourcing and equality and diversity. Her research topics include studies of gender and disability discrimination in the UK and China. Prior to her academic career she held posts in management in the hospitality sector.

Ted Johns has been – and continues as – a Chief Examiner first for the IPM, then the IPD and now the CIPD, for over 30 years. He was responsible for the adoption of the Big Idea of the Thinking Performer as the strategic vision for HR professionalism, and was recently delighted to be elected as a Companion Member of the Institute. He has written or co-authored books on ethical leadership, organisational change, customer care, world-class customer service excellence and time management. Ted was a founder director of the Institute of Customer Service and officiated as its Chairman for seven years before retiring in 2009. He is a noted conference and seminar speaker not only in the UK but also in many other parts of the world.

Graham Perkins is a PhD student at Plymouth University. His PhD is focused on how idea generation can best be enabled within SMEs. Alongside his studies Graham works as an HR consultant for a variety of organisations and has a broad spectrum of experience from learning and development projects through to facilitating and analysing staff surveys.

Krystal Wilkinson is currently a Doctoral Student at Leeds University Business School, in the Division of Work and Employment Relations, and is also an Associate Lecturer at both Leeds University and Manchester Metropolitan University Business Schools. She has been on CIPD exam marking teams for several years and has recently been involved in authoring Workbooks for the CIPD Flexible Learning resource. Prior to returning to academia, Krystal had several years' operational HR experience in a range of sectors including construction, hospitality and retail.

CHAPTER 1

Studying HRM

Stephen Taylor and Carol Woodhams

CHAPTER CONTENTS

- Studying HRM at Levels 5 and 6
- What is HRM?
- Evidence-based HRM
- Core HRM debates

KEY LEARNING OUTCOMES

By the end of this chapter, you should be able to:

- Appreciate the requirements necessary to gain the CIPD's intermediate-level qualifications.

- Define the term 'human resource management' and explain how it has evolved in recent years.

- Distinguish between 'nuts and bolts' HR activities and those which have a more strategic character.

- Understand the importance of using robust third-party evidence when making HR decisions and justifying arguments.

- Access significant research findings in the HR field.

- Explain the key ways in which thinking about HR is influenced by different frames of reference and sets of assumptions.

This is the first in a series of three textbooks that the Chartered Institute of Personnel and Development (CIPD) is publishing for students who are studying towards achieving its intermediate-level qualifications in Human Resource Management (HRM) and Human Resource Development (HRD). Whether you have enrolled on a discrete programme provided by a college or are looking to gain your CIPD award as part of an undergraduate business degree, you will find that these books provide you with a sound introduction to your studies.

This first book covers the learning outcomes for the four core units that everyone aiming to achieve the intermediate diploma must successfully complete. The second and third books in the series, entitled *Developing People and Organisations* and *Managing People and Organisations*, cover the learning outcomes that make up the optional units, at least four of which you will be studying in order to complete your qualification.

Our aim in this chapter is to introduce you to the study of HRM at undergraduate level, defined by the Quality Assurance Agency for Higher Education (QAA) as being at Levels 5 and 6. We start by explaining exactly what level 5 and level 6 study involves and what you will need to do in order to achieve it. After this we discuss the meaning of the term 'human resource management' before going on to explain how effective HR managers base their decisions and their thinking on solid evidence. Finally, we introduce you to a range of tensions and differences of perspective which underlie the study and practice of HRM and which you will find helpful to understand as you embark on your programme of study.

STUDYING HRM AT LEVELS 5 AND 6

The UK's **QAA for Higher Education** has the role of setting definitive, generic standards which all awarding bodies and institutions of higher education must observe when developing courses, as well as teaching and assessing their students. This is therefore a good place to start understanding what you will be expected to achieve on your programme. The CIPD's intermediate-level awards are set at level 5, but if you are studying them as part of a bachelor's honours degree programme you will be required to meet the level 6 expectations. The level 5 standards and the level 6 standards are set out below.

Descriptor for a higher education qualification at level 5: foundation degree

The descriptor provided for this level of the FHEQ is for any **foundation degree**, which should meet the descriptor in full. This qualification descriptor can also be used as a reference point for other level 5 qualifications, including diplomas of higher education, higher national diplomas, and so on.

Foundation degrees are awarded to students who have demonstrated:

- knowledge and critical understanding of the well-established principles of their area(s) of study, and of the way in which those principles have developed

- the ability to apply underlying concepts and principles outside the context in which they were first studied, including, where appropriate, the application of those principles in an employment context

- knowledge of the main methods of enquiry in the subject(s) relevant to the named award and ability to evaluate critically the appropriateness of different approaches to solving problems in the field of study

- an understanding of the limits of their knowledge and how this influences analyses and interpretations based on that knowledge.

Typically, holders of the qualification will be able to:

- use a range of established techniques to initiate and undertake critical analysis of information, and to propose solutions to problems arising from that analysis
- effectively communicate information, arguments and analysis in a variety of forms to specialist and non-specialist audiences, and deploy key techniques of the discipline effectively
- undertake further training, develop existing skills and acquire new competences that will enable them to assume significant responsibility within organisations.

And holders will have:

- the qualities and transferable skills necessary for employment, requiring the exercise of personal responsibility and decision-making.

Descriptor for a higher education qualification at level 6: bachelor's degree with honours

The descriptor provided for this level of the FHEQ is for any **bachelor's degree with honours**, which should meet the descriptor in full. This qualification descriptor can also be used as a reference point for other level 6 qualifications, including bachelor's degrees, graduate diplomas, and so on.

Bachelor's degrees with honours are awarded to students who have demonstrated:

- a systematic understanding of key aspects of their field of study, including acquisition of coherent and detailed knowledge, at least some of which is at, or informed by, the forefront of defined aspects of a discipline
- an ability to deploy accurately established techniques of analysis and enquiry within a discipline.
- conceptual understanding that enables the student:
  - to devise and sustain arguments, and/or to solve problems, using ideas and techniques, some of which are at the forefront of a discipline
  - to describe and comment upon particular aspects of current research, or equivalent advanced scholarship, in the discipline
- an appreciation of the uncertainty, ambiguity and limits of knowledge
- the ability to manage their own learning and to make use of scholarly reviews and primary sources (for example, refereed research articles and/or original materials appropriate to the discipline).

Typically, holders of the qualification will be able to:

- apply the methods and techniques that they have learned to review, consolidate, extend and apply their knowledge and understanding, and to initiate and carry out projects
- critically evaluate arguments, assumptions, abstract concepts and data (that may be incomplete), to make judgements, and to frame appropriate questions to achieve a solution – or identify a range of solutions – to a problem
- communicate information, ideas, problems and solutions to both specialist and non-specialist audiences.

And holders will have the qualities and transferable skills necessary for employment requiring:

- the exercise of initiative and personal responsibility
- decision-making in complex and unpredictable contexts
- the learning ability needed to undertake appropriate further training of a professional or equivalent nature.

You can see from this that a great deal of emphasis is placed at both levels on being able to demonstrate knowledge and understanding of core, well-established principles across the student's field of study. However, the standards go beyond this, requiring students also to demonstrate the following:

- an ability to analyse these principles critically
- an ability to apply the principles in the workplace
- a capacity to evaluate the evidence on which the principles are founded, including academic research
- an appreciation of the limits to our knowledge in any area of study
- an ability to communicate the principles to a variety of audiences
- the capacity to undertake further professional development independently in the future
- skills associated with effective decision-making, problem-solving and exercising personal initiative in their field of study.

WHAT DOES ALL OF THIS MEAN AS FAR AS STUDYING HRM IS CONCERNED?

First of all, it means that you will need to study how HR managers apply the principles of their management discipline across a wide range of settings. If you have studied HRM previously, it is likely that you were encouraged to focus your attention primarily on your own organisation, perhaps evaluating what it did and discussing what improvements it might make. You now need to widen your perspective very considerably. A key point about studying HRM at this level is the way that it requires you to gain a good understanding of the variety of different approaches that are used to manage people in different organisations, industries and also in different countries.

Secondly, it means that you must be able not just to advocate an approach to use or to take a decision in the field of HRM, but also to justify your approach or decision with good, robust, evidence-based arguments. The same is true of practical problem-solving. So you need to become familiar with the most important and influential contemporary research studies that have been published in the field of HRM. It also requires you to develop a good understanding of the business environment in which HRM is carried out and of ways in which this is changing and evolving.

Thirdly, it means that you need to develop a good understanding of the major contemporary, professional debates that exist in HRM, and to be in a position to engage in these debates yourself. This means thinking beyond some of the rather simplistic prescriptions of 'good practice HRM' that are often advanced and to develop a more sophisticated appreciation of the complex and sometimes messy realities of practical people management in a workplace.

Finally, you need to be able to communicate your ideas, together with the evidence that underpins them, effectively to a variety of potential audiences. This presents a range of challenges. Communicating to a specialist audience with a significant understanding of HRM is straightforward insofar as a lot of prior understanding and familiarity with terms can be assumed, but sophisticated arguments must be developed, backed up by credible evidence, if you are to be persuasive. By contrast, a non-specialist audience that does not have extensive understanding of HRM often requires as much (if not more) convincing, but will only be persuaded if you can communicate the more basic ideas and arguments effectively.

STRUCTURING YOUR STUDIES

A key to successful study at all levels and across all subjects is the ability to organise yourself and to plan your course effectively. Studying HRM is no exception. Your tutors will help you to do this by guiding you through a structured course of study that they have designed, step by step. At each point readings will be recommended, learning exercises provided and key points underlined.

However, there are also additional things you can do to help structure your studies effectively. These involve making use of two key documents that have been published by the CIPD and also, more generally, exploring the wealth of resources that are available to you on the CIPD's extensive website (www.cipd.co.uk).

The first of the key documents is the CIPD's guide to its intermediate-level qualifications. Hard copies are widely available, but you can also download the contents from the qualifications area of the Institute's website. Here you will find for each unit of study (core or optional) a summary of the main learning outcomes that you need to work towards being able to demonstrate, together with short summaries setting out what each encompasses in practice. The document also sets out the CIPD's 'rules of combination', which allows you to see which core units and which optional units can be combined to make up a programme of study.

The second key document you will find it useful to refer to when structuring your studies is the **CIPD's HR Profession Map**. This can also be found in a prominent position on the Institute's website in the section called 'CIPD and the HR profession'. The Map is an extensive tool which can be used for many purposes. It sets out the following in a user-friendly format:

- eight behaviours that HR professionals need to develop in order to carry out their roles effectively in the contemporary business world

- ten areas of professional practice which help define the typical boundaries around generalist and specialist career paths in both HRM and HRD
- four bands and transitions which provide broad guidelines for career development across the HR field, from 'delivering fundamentals' (band 1) to 'Leadership colleague, client confidante and coach'.

You will read more about the CIPD's HR Profession Map in Chapter 6, 'Proceeding with your Learning about Human Resource Management'.

WHAT IS HRM?

The term **human resource management** was first coined in the early 1960s in the USA. For a number of years before this, academics and policy-makers had been using the term 'human resources' alongside 'natural resources' when talking about a nation's economic assets (see Ginzberg 1958), but the word 'management' was only added later. An academic journal entitled *Human Resource Management* was launched in 1961 at Michigan University, but it was not until the 1980s that the term became widely used all over the world in the context of employment in organisations.

At first HRM signified a new way of managing people that was clearly distinct from traditional personnel management: more strategic, less reactive and more firmly focused on achieving organisational objectives. However, before long, at least for most people, HRM started to be used simply to describe a body of management activities rather than any particular approach to carrying them out. During the 1990s in particular, people who had previously been called personnel directors, personnel managers, personnel officers, personnel advisers and personnel assistants re-labelled themselves as human resource professionals. At the same time organisations tended to rebrand training activities under the banner of human resource development. 'Industrial relations' became 'employment relations', while 'pay and benefits' tended to be renamed 'reward management'.

HRM has thus now come to be the most commonly used label for a group of activities that are all, one way or another, related to the management of an organisation's relationship with the people who work for it. These people may be employees working under contracts of employment, but they are also increasingly self-employed persons, casual staff, agency workers and employees of partner organisations.

On one level, therefore, professional HR managers are concerned with the nuts and bolts of day-to-day people management. Alongside line managers they design jobs and organisational structures, recruit and select new staff, issue contracts, lead induction processes, ensure that everyone is paid correctly and on time, run training courses, develop succession plans, reward good performance, seek to improve poor performance, negotiate and consult with staff representatives, develop management careers, discourage absence, administer retirements and resignations, and, as and when necessary, ensure that dismissals are carried out legally.

Increasingly, however, HRM is becoming a strategic activity. HR managers are not just concerned with achieving the nuts and bolts tasks efficiently; they are also both integral to the delivery of an organisation's longer-term strategic objectives and leading figures in the development of business strategies. Central to this side of their work is active involvement in the management of both structural and cultural change. They help ensure that the crucial people management side of change is given proper attention alongside its legal, financial and technical aspects. HR managers help to plan change management episodes and to communicate the need for them, as well as being centrally involved in their implementation and subsequent evaluation.

In order that an organisation's strategic objectives can be achieved, supportive and deliverable HR strategies need to be developed, communicated and implemented. Remuneration arrangements have to be designed so that they reward behaviours which increase the chances that the organisation will meet its objectives and diminish the chances that it won't. The same goes for resourcing, development and employee relations strategies, all of which also need to reinforce one another.

Another aspect of strategic HR activity is the management of an organisation's reputation as an employer. Here we increasingly see the use of marketing language (for example, employer branding, segmentation, employee value propositions) being used as organisations seek to position themselves strategically in the labour market. Central to this development is a keen understanding that recruiting and retaining effective performers is a highly competitive business, and that there is a need to differentiate what we offer potential recruits from that which our chief competitors offer.

Reputation-building is a long-term project which managers can influence, but cannot control. The same is true of other strategic HRM initiatives, such as organisation development (OD), the development of effective knowledge management systems, the promotion of employee well-being and other activities that one way or another involve building up an organisation's human capital. Developing an actively and positively engaged workforce which demonstrates initiative and discretionary effort is another crucial HR activity that can neither be achieved overnight nor introduced by management diktat.

Importantly, all of this – both the nuts-and-bolts activities and those which are more strategic in character – has to be carried out against the backdrop of an increasingly volatile, unpredictable, competitive, highly regulated and complex global business environment. Effective HR managers thus have to keep more than half an eye on the future, always seeking to ensure that their organisations are better placed than others to meet coming challenges. More often than not, this means thinking about multiple, alternative, possible future scenarios and planning for as many as possible. A premium thus has to be placed on developing organisational agility, along with a capacity for flexible working and for the swift and productive implementation of change.

EVIDENCE-BASED HRM

A key part of studying HRM seriously as part of a degree-level qualification involves getting into the habit, wherever you can, of justifying your views on the subject using robust and credible evidence. This approach is called **evidence-based HRM**. This will not only help you to secure your qualification, but it should also mean that you carry your 'habit' over into the workplace. In the future you will take decisions, develop policies and, when debating with colleagues, take up positions which are informed by robust evidence.

You may think it strange that this point has to be made at all. Surely all successful managers base their decisions on robust and credible evidence? Of course many do, or at least take account of it. But decisions, policies and debating positions are also often informed by hunches, limited anecdotal evidence, singular personal experience, widely believed myths of various kinds and sometimes by raw prejudice. Even quite senior managers with successful careers behind them commonly dismiss published research on human resource management matters as being overly theoretical and largely irrelevant to their line of business. More often they are simply disinclined to take account of it because they prefer to manage by instinct, or take on board from the research only the points which match their own pre-existing beliefs.

Pfeffer and Sutton (2006, pp1–12) coined the phrase **'the knowing–doing gap'** to describe this phenomenon. All over the world, including in major public sector organisations and international corporations, they found examples of managers implementing policies that 'often clashed with, and at times were the opposite of what we know about organisations and people'. Instead of basing thinking and decision-making on evidence, there is a preference for 'casual benchmarking', 'doing what seems to have worked in the past' and 'following deeply held unexamined ideologies'. The result, at best, is sub-optimal performance in the field of HRM and, at worst, business failure and wholly avoidable job losses.

In other fields of professional endeavour this casual approach to evidence would never be tolerated. Imagine how we would react if a doctor was to prescribe treatments which were not wholly informed by robust scientific research or if an engineer built a bridge using hunches and myths when drawing up the designs. Government policy also has to be informed by robust research as well as by the results of consultation exercises, and is only implemented after regulatory impact assessments have been carried out, not to mention extensive scrutiny by Parliament and the media. Yet for some reason the same philosophy has yet to permeate fully into the realm of management decision-making.

A major aim of the CIPD is to actively encourage evidence-based management in the HR field. It does this partly by undertaking and sponsoring major research projects and then disseminating the results as widely as possible, and partly by promoting good practice through its professional education activities.

MAKING USE OF ROBUST EVIDENCE

When studying at undergraduate level you are not going to be expected to gain an in-depth understanding of contemporary research that has been published in your field of study. You are, however, going to be expected to justify any arguments that you make in assignments and when answering exam questions, and to do so reasonably convincingly. While you may well sometimes want to justify a point of view with an ethical argument or with reference to your own experience, you will also need to tap into published research when it is available. Moreover, especially when debating contentious professional issues, you will need to evaluate pieces of published research that reach different conclusions about the same issue.

Academic research

Academic writers publish the findings from their research projects in books, but more commonly in learned journals. These are excellent sources of research data because, in order to get published, any article is first subjected to peer review. That means that it must first be scrutinised anonymously by reviewers who are specialists in the field. They typically suggest that amendments must be made before publication is possible. As a result, before you read an account of any research findings, the article concerned will have been rewritten, resubmitted to the journal and re-reviewed, often extensively and on a number of occasions. You will find a list of recommended journals providing credible evidence in Chapter 6.

It is important, however, not to restrict yourself to findings that are published in UK-based HR or HR-related journals. Most of the most important recent research has been published in international HRM journals, in those which have a more general management focus and, sometimes, in journals that are not management-focused at all. This is particularly true of developments in the wider business environment which are of general significance, but which happen also to be important from a practical HRM perspective.

 REFLECTIVE ACTIVITY 1.1

An example of an academic journal article that has had considerable influence on thinking among HR professionals in the UK was published in 2007 in *The Review of Economics and Statistics*, an economics journal published by the Massachusetts Institute for Science and Technology. The authors were Maarten Goos and Alan Manning and their article was called 'Lousy and lovely jobs: the rising polarization of work in Britain'. This took forward research that they originally published a few years earlier and an analysis that they subsequently applied across the EU (see Goos and Manning 2003; Goos et al 2009).

In their article Goos and Manning demonstrate, using detailed statistical analysis, that over three decades in the UK there has been strong growth both in the number of jobs which are highly skilled in nature and in the number of lower-paid, low-skilled jobs in the service sector. By contrast, the proportion of jobs that fall between these two stools – skilled manual work and clerical jobs, for example – has been in long-term decline. They conclude that the major cause of this trend has been the development of technologies which can carry out the jobs in 'the disappearing middle' more cost-effectively than people can.

Their article was published in an American journal whose readership consists mainly of economists, while the conclusions are aimed primarily at government policy-makers. The findings are, however, hugely relevant to HRM, not least because they strongly suggest that further polarisation of our labour market is likely in the future. This means that organisations are likely to struggle to recruit higher-skilled people in the coming decades, labour markets tightening as demand for the relatively few appropriately qualified people increases. By contrast, recruitment for people to do less skilled work will become less problematic. Finding people to do these jobs will get easier, but in many cases people seeking and holding these jobs will be overqualified.

Questions:

1 How would you go about accessing copies of Goos and Manning's articles on the polarisation of labour markets?

2 Based on your reading here, consider the following: what is the significance of their findings for managers who are charged with undertaking long-term human resource planning (HRP) activities for their organisations?

Indeed, one of the things that makes studying HRM interesting is the way that in doing so we draw on research findings that come from a wide variety of fields. The following are the main examples:

- occupational psychology
- sociology of work
- labour market economics
- employment law
- business ethics
- human geography.

People who specialise in each of these disciplines have a tendency to come at their subjects with different sets of assumptions, diverse perspectives and, in some cases, widely divergent views on the appropriate approaches to use when carrying out research. While this makes tracking down and evaluating research of relevance to practical HRM fascinating, it also complicates matters (see Coyle-Shapiro et al 2004). Sometimes, for example, research will have great potential relevance for practical HRM, but this will not be apparent from the conclusions reached by the author, whose focus is elsewhere.

Edited books provide good summaries of recent academic research, setting out the key findings and debating different interpretations.

Finally, of course, textbooks written for students, such as this one, aim to provide good introductions to and overviews of key findings from the academic research. Following up the references that the authors of textbooks cite is often the best starting point when seeking out robust research on key contemporary HR issues.

Other sources of robust research

Academic research published in peer-reviewed journals is generally the most authoritative. But it is sometimes written in an inaccessible style and often assumes a great deal of prior knowledge on the part of its readers. The focus can also be overly theoretical for students who are just starting their studies at level 5 or level 6. Moreover, it is the case that some areas of HRM activity which have a great deal of practical significance for organisations have not attracted much interest from academic researchers. The field of recruitment and selection provides a good example. If you are researching methods of selection (interviews, personality tests, aptitude tests, assessment centres, and so on), their relative utility and their capacity to predict future job performance, you will find hundreds of peer-reviewed articles of a very high quality reporting research findings from all over the world. Employee selection is a very well-researched field. By contrast, the process of recruitment (that is, actively encouraging applications from would-be employees), despite being just as significant practically, has never been the focus of much academic research internationally, and almost none at all of any serious value in the UK. You will also search in vain for any robust academic research on company car schemes, for example, or on the practical impact of much recent UK employment law.

Fortunately these gaps are filled pretty effectively by other sources of published research. You will, for example, find a great deal of highly relevant HR-related research published on the CIPD's website. The Institute has a substantial Public Policy and Research (PPR) division, which both carries out its own research projects and sponsors research from leading teams of academics and consultants. Indeed, some of the most significant and influential UK-based research has been carried out under the auspices of the CIPD. Examples are the well-known **'black box studies'** carried out by John Purcell and his colleagues (see Purcell et al 2003) and much of the most important recent research on the state of the psychological contract in the UK pioneered by David Guest and his colleagues (see Guest and Conway 2001).

Government departments also commission and publish excellent research which has considerable practical relevance for HRM. A great deal is freely available to download from websites, while the number of publications that is made available increases each year. Some of the best examples are the following:

- **Workplace Employment Relations Survey:** a huge nationwide study that is carried out every few years into many aspects of employment practice in UK workplaces, including the very smallest. Summaries of the findings are published on the Department for Business, Innovation and Skills (DBIS) website.

- **Leitch Review:** a comprehensive government-sponsored investigation into the state of skills in the UK, carried out between 2004 and 2006, which has informed government policy since. The final report is published on the HM Treasury website along with much of the research which informed its key findings.

- **Macleod Report on Employee Engagement:** published by the BIS in 2009, it has been hugely influential (see Macleod and Clarke 2009).

- The **Office for National Statistics** (ONS) publishes a vast amount of data on employment matters on its website. This includes regularly collected statistics alongside articles and larger research reports on particular topic areas.

And you will find other examples listed in Chapter 6.

Finally, you will in addition find that some commercially produced research is also relevant and useful to you. Companies such as Incomes Data Services (IDS) and Industrial Relations Services (IRS) are both well-established and very well-respected publishers of HR-related research whose publications are widely available both in libraries and, at a fee, online. Major consultancies such as PricewaterhouseCoopers, Towers Perrin and Hay also undertake important research which is published online.

CORE HRM DEBATES

Aside from the need to develop a capacity for evidence-based thinking about HRM, in order to succeed in your level 5 or level 6 study of HRM, you also need to grasp the idea that HRM is a heavily contested field. That is to say that different people have very different ideas about it and, in particular, approach its study with different perspectives and different sets of assumptions. In short, there are competing schools of thought about HRM which tend to give rise to considerable tensions between people. In fact, it is often the case that neither side in a debate is either wholly right or wholly wrong. Both hold positions which are readily defended and entirely credible.

From a student's point of view the key is not to take up one position or another, but simply to appreciate the different perspectives and to be aware of how they necessarily infuse what you read on the subject of HRM. In this final section of the chapter we are going to introduce you to some of the major rival sets of perspectives. Some are of greatest relevance to HR practitioners looking to improve the effectiveness of their function's activities; others tend more to preoccupy the thinking of researchers.

BEST PRACTICE VS BEST FIT

Underlying many contemporary debates about the contribution made by HR to the achievement of organisational objectives is the ever-present division between **best practice thinking** and **best-fit thinking**.

This division at root concerns the extent to which it is ever really possible to identify a clear 'best way' of carrying out HR activities which is universally applicable. Adherents of a best practice perspective argue that there are certain HR practices and approaches to their operation which will invariably help an organisation in achieving competitive advantage. There is therefore a clear link between HR activity and business performance, but the effect will only be maximised if the 'right' HR policies are pursued.

While there are differences of opinion on questions of detail, all strongly suggest that the same basic bundle of human resource practices tends to enhance business performance in all organisations, irrespective of the particular product market strategy being pursued.

The main elements of the **best practice bundle** include the use of the more advanced selection methods, a serious commitment to employee involvement, substantial investment in training and development, the use of individualised reward systems and harmonised terms and conditions of employment as between different groups of employees.

The alternative **best fit** school also identifies a link between human resource management practice and the achievement of competitive advantage. Here, however, there is no belief in the existence of universal solutions. Instead, all is contingent on the particular circumstances of each organisation.

What is needed is HR policies and practices which 'fit' and are thus appropriate to the situation of individual employers. What is appropriate (or best) for one will not necessarily be right for another.

Key variables include the size of the establishment, the dominant product market strategy being pursued and the nature of the labour markets in which the organisation competes.

? REFLECTIVE ACTIVITY 1.2

Some fields of HRM practice are dominated by best practice thinking, while others broadly accept best fit assumptions.

A good example of the former is employee selection. Academics and consultants who undertake research in this field overwhelmingly share a best practice perspective on their work. They often disagree about exactly which method of selection is best and about how much better than its rivals it is, but they agree that there is 'out there', somewhere, a method which is more effective than all the others. The idea that some approaches to employee selection are most appropriate in one setting while others are best in other settings is only very rarely articulated in their work.

By contrast, research in the field of reward management has long been dominated by best-fit thinking. Whether or not there is a single, universal approach to the management of pay and benefits which trumps all the others never seems to be considered. The idea of even asking such a question does not seem to occur to those who research in this field. Instead the aim is always to establish what set of reward practices, used in combination, is most appropriate in different types of settings.

Questions:

1 Why do you think that the frame of reference used by researchers focusing on employee selection and reward management varies so much?

2 Do you tend towards 'best fit' or 'best practice' when thinking about HRM practices? Why do you think that is the case?

TAYLORISM VS HUMANISM

Two distinct traditions to the management of people in organisations, based on totally opposing principles, can be identified.

The first is known as the **scientific management**, or **Taylorist**, approach (the two terms are used interchangeably), after Frederick W. Taylor, who pioneered these principles when designing jobs in the first factories to make use of large-scale production lines. The second is often referred to as the humanist approach, pioneered by managers who saw that a fundamental flaw in Taylorist principles was their tendency to dehumanise work.

The scientific management approach is systematic and very logical. It involves examining in great detail all the individual tasks that need to be carried out by a team of workers in order to achieve an objective.

The time it takes to accomplish each task is calculated and jobs are then designed so as to maximise the efficiency of the operation. In short, an analyst works out on paper how many people need to be employed, carrying out which tasks and using which machinery. Waiting time and duplication of effort is minimised to reduce costs.

Principles of scientific management, or Taylorism, allow tasks to be designed so as to minimise the number of more-skilled people the organisation requires. This is done by packaging all the specialised tasks to form one kind of job, which is then graded more highly than others made up of less specialised, lower-skilled tasks. The workforce is thus deployed with machine-like efficiency. Each plays a carefully defined role in a bigger process that is overseen, supervised, controlled and maintained by managers.

While originally developed for use in engineering and car assembly plants, the principles of Taylorism live on and are still widely deployed. For example, call centres are very much organised along Taylorist principles, each employee having a tightly defined role and being responsible for hitting targets of number of calls made or answered in each hour of work. As a result, it is planned that costs are kept as low as possible given the expected throughput of work.

The public sector also makes heavy use of Taylorist principles in designing and redesigning jobs so as to maximise efficiency. In recent years many skill mix reviews have been carried out in hospitals, schools and in the police, the aim being to allocate duties between staff by seeking to ensure that highly qualified (and highly paid) staff spend 100% of their time carrying out duties that only they can perform. Lower-skilled activities are then packaged together into jobs carried out by support workers.

The major criticism made of scientific management is that it is dehumanising and, therefore, ultimately bad for business. The adoption of Taylorist principles leads to the creation of jobs which are tedious, repetitive and unpleasant to perform. The result is a disengaged workforce and, hence, absence, high staff turnover and the development of adversarial industrial relations. It also often creates resentment among people forced into workplace straight-jackets, which leads to low motivation, low commitment and low performance.

Moreover, because of this, more supervisors are needed than would be the case if people are positively motivated by the content of their jobs. Taylorism can thus be criticised for being a relatively inefficient approach over the long term.

An alternative **humanist** approach evolved in the middle of the twentieth century that draws on notions of intrinsic motivation and involves designing jobs and managing work in ways which engage and even excite people.

The alternative principles start with the idea that employees achieve higher levels of motivation, satisfaction and performance if the jobs they do are made more interesting and challenging. The key is to maximise the enjoyment, satisfaction and well-being that job-holders derive from their work. While it must be accepted that many jobs are never going to be highly enjoyable, it can be argued that managers should nonetheless try to design them and manage people in such a way as to maximise the satisfaction that job-holders derive from their work. This then in turn leads to:

- an organisation which is able to attract and retain good performers
- reduced levels of absence, stress and burnout
- a high-trust industrial relations environment
- highly motivated and engaged staff
- discretionary effort.

Humanism is associated with HR practices that seek to enrich jobs, to reward hard work, to manage performance positively and to involve people in the management of their areas of work. In recent years there has been a particular focus placed on teamworking, on partnership approaches to management and on the development of emotionally intelligent leaders. A key tool used in this approach to management is the staff survey. This enables organisations to measure levels of work satisfaction, to identify areas of under-performance and to track progress over time.

PLURALIST VS UNITARIST

This difference in perspective is particularly associated with the management of employee relations in organisations and infuses much of what is written about employee relations. The implications are profound because those who come at issues with unitarist perspectives invariably advocate different managerial approaches than those whose outlook is pluralist in nature.

Put simply, a **unitarist** assumes that, for the most part, employers and employees share the same fundamental, long-term objectives as far as their relationship with one another is concerned. Both, for example, have an economic interest in the financial success of their organisation: the employer in order to maximise profit and the employee in order to maximise job security and career opportunity. It follows that any conflict between staff and management is solvable and short term in nature. Once the 'correct' policies and practices are put in place, a good relationship can be restored and maintained. Harmonious relations between employer and employee is the norm, conflict is abnormal.

None of these assumptions is held by **pluralists**. Pluralists believe that not only do employers and employees have different interests; they have multiple different interests. What employees seek (high wages, limitations on hours, control over their work, maximisation of health and safety, generous benefits, job security, and so on) are an inevitable source of conflict. This is because employers are looking for something rather different from the employment relationship (flexibility, low labour costs, a high degree of management control, improved productivity, and so on). The result, inevitably, is tension between 'two sides of industry'. A situation in which, for example, trade unions maintain a low-trust relationship with management is seen by people with a pluralist perspective as being entirely normal and expected. Pluralists see HRM as a process by which two parties with divergent interests continually negotiate the terms of their relationship.

BUREAUCRATIC VS PRAGMATIC

In some organisations HRM is characterised by the presence of **bureaucracy**. The HR function tends to direct people management activities through the issuing of written policies and by requiring line managers to complete documentation to demonstrate that they are putting policies into action.

Such approaches have the advantage of ensuring that people are treated equally and that 'the rule of law' effectively applies across an organisation. This helps to reduce perceptions of unfairness, which is a major source of demotivation in organisations. At its worst, however, it means that process replaces thought in the way that people are managed. For example, completing performance appraisal documentation can become more important than actually managing individual performance effectively.

The alternative approach, known as **pragmatism**, is to cut back as far as possible on rules, form-filling and written policies. Managers are able to treat good performers more favourably than poor performers and are free to manage their teams by 'gut instinct'. The result can be considerable diversity of practice across an organisation. This may work well for some, but also tends to lead to inequity.

CENTRALISED VS DECENTRALISED

The way the HR function is organised always seems to be a problem in organisations, changes occurring regularly as senior managers search in vain for the ideal situation.

The traditional approach is **centralised**, with an HR director to whom all other HR staff report directly or indirectly. Some aspects of HR work are carried out by officers who carry responsibility for the people in particular departments, while others (typically payroll, recruitment and training) are managed centrally by specialists on behalf of the whole organisation.

By contrast, the **decentralised** approach locates most HR staff in departments, reporting to local managers and making the effective management of their teams the priority.

In recent years the so-called **three-legged stool model** associated with Dave Ulrich (1997) has become fashionable. This involves the creation of three distinct types of HR specialist. Much administrative work is carried out in call-centre-type, centralised teams who provide 'shared services' across the whole organisation. The second group are specialists in areas of HR work who provide advice as and when necessary to managers. They typically cover employment law, training and development and all strategic HR issues. The final, third group are labelled 'business partners'. They tend to be generalists who work alongside line managers and are concerned primarily with the management of case work and dealing with individual employee issues in departments. The three-legged stool model thus seeks to blend centralisation with decentralisation so as to maximise both efficiency and effectiveness.

INTERNALLY FOCUSED VS EXTERNALLY FOCUSED

This division in approach relates primarily to the relationship an organisation has with its labour markets – a crucial aspect of effective HRM.

Externally focused approaches involve looking outside the organisation when new people are required, hiring people who have gained their experience and skills in other organisations. This approach requires that pay rates are set at or above the going market rate and that the organisation spends plenty of money advertising jobs and promoting its image in the labour market as a desirable employer to work for. The benefits derive from the wide field of talent the organisation has to choose from when recruiting staff and the diversity of professional experience that tends to infuse senior management teams.

By contrast, the internally focused approach involves developing internal labour markets. People tend to be hired early in their careers, often as school-leavers or graduate recruits, and brought into organisations with a strong commitment to HRD. They are then developed internally and promoted up the organisation when they are ready for new challenges and responsibilities. It is relatively rare in such organisations for senior people to be recruited from outside the organisation. Pay rates are primarily set with reference to internal fairness and the need to maximise effort among staff who are invited to compete for promotion up an organisational hierarchy.

The approach has the advantage of being highly motivating to existing staff, but inevitably it also means that the range of talent that the organisation has to choose from when filling senior posts is both limited and lacking in diversity.

STAKEHOLDER VS STOCKHOLDER ORIENTATIONS

This is another fundamental difference of perspective that can be observed in different organisations. An organisation that is heavily stockholder-oriented is one which is managed almost entirely in the interests of its owners. Shareholder value is the only really significant management target, and this increasingly means 'short-term shareholder value'. In other words, the organisation's sole purpose (in its own managers' eyes) is to gain for its owners a quicker and more substantial financial return on their investment than their competitors are able to achieve. As far as employees are concerned, this perspective tends to be associated with job insecurity, the intensification of work and approach to management that is sometimes described as 'asinine' in its approach. This means that people are treated in an unsophisticated manner, being motivated via the use of financial incentives on the one hand and tight discipline on the other. If you work really hard and deliver the stockholders' objectives, you are well rewarded. If you don't, you are likely to be dismissed rapidly without sentiment.

The alternative stakeholder orientation is far more pleasant from an employee perspective, but can mean that the organisation is less competitive and financially successful – at least in the short term. Stakeholder thinking recognises that a number of groups of people have a legitimate stake in an organisation's long-term success and that there is therefore a shared interest between owners, managers, staff, suppliers, customers and the wider community. All will pull together and work collaboratively in the organisation's interests if they are all treated fairly. As far as employees are concerned, this stakeholder perspective means that managers are interested in their long-term development, in retaining their skills in the organisation and in providing them with the opportunity to thrive. Not only will they benefit, but the organisation will too.

REFLECTIVE ACTIVITY 1.3

Questions:

1 Think about an organisation you, your friends or relatives have worked for. Would you say that the approach to management was characterised more by a stockholder or by a stakeholder perspective?

2 Why might it be in the long-term financial interests of an organisation to move towards a stakeholder perspective and away from a stockholder perspective?

3 In what circumstances might the reverse be the case?

Our aim in this chapter has been to introduce you to the area of human resource management at level 5. We have reviewed what constitutes a level 5 approach to the area of study and how this is integrated with the CIPD's framework of professional development. One of the requirements of HR professionalism is that we are well prepared to offer the best advice and on the basis of the most solid evidence available. This necessitates having the skills, knowledge and sufficient curiosity to keep up to date with developments in the field, critically evaluating their application in practice. To this end we introduced the discipline of human resource management, exploring as we did so its development and some of its key debates. We trust that we have given you sufficient understanding of the field that you are able to embark on the rest of your programme of study from a solid base.

FURTHER READING

CIPD (2010) *Next generation HR: time for change – towards a next generation for HR*. This is the outcome of the CIPD's future–focused research that examines the future of the role. It positions HR leaders as building sustainability and equity by being 'insight-driven provocateurs' who are assured and confident in influencing.

PURCELL, J., KINNIE, K., HUTCHINSON, S., RAYTON, B. and SWART, J. (2003) *Understanding the people and performance link: unlocking the black box*. London: Chartered Institute of Personnel and Development. The CIPD's seminal study that examines the nature and contribution of people management to organisation performance.

TYSON, S. (2006) *Essentials of human resource management*. 5th ed. Oxford: Butterworth-Heinemann. Chapters 3 and 4. Reviews the development of the profession, the goals of specialist HR professionals and how the function assists in the achievement of organisation goals. Also explores in more depth the debates aired in this chapter.

REFERENCES

COYLE-SHAPIRO, J., TAYLOR, S., SHORE, L. and TETRICK, L. (2004) Commonalities and conflicts between different perspectives of the employment relationship: towards a unified perspective. In: COYLE-SHAPIRO, J., TAYLOR, S., SHORE, L. and TETRICK, L. (eds) *The employment relationship: examining psychological and contextual perspectives*. Oxford: Oxford University Press.

FAYOL, H. (1949) *General and industrial management* [translated from the French edition (Dunod) by Constance Storrs]. London: Pitman.

GINZBERG, E. (1958) *Human resources: the wealth of a nation*. New York: Simon & Schuster.

GOOS, M. and MANNING, A. (2003) McJobs and MacJobs: the growing polarisation of jobs in the UK. In: DICKENS, R., GREGG, P. and WADSWORTH, J. (eds) *The labour market under New Labour*. Basingstoke: Palgrave.

GOOS, M. and MANNING, A. (2007) Lousy and lovely jobs: the rising polarization of work in Britain. *The Review of Economics and Statistics*. Vol 89, No 1. pp118–33.

GOOS, M., MANNING, A. and SALOMONS, A. (2009) Job polarisation in Europe. *The American Economic Review*. Vol 99, No 2. pp58–63.

GUEST, D. E. and CONWAY, N. (2001) *Public and private sector perceptions on the psychological contract*. London: CIPD.

MACLEOD, D. and CLARKE, N. (2009) *Engaging for success: enhancing performance through employee engagement*. A report to government. London: Department for Business, Innovation and Skills.

MAYO, E. (1933) *Human problems of an industrialised society*. New York: Harpers.

PFEFFER, J. and SUTTON, R. I. (2006) *Hard facts: dangerous half-truths and total nonsense: profiting from evidence-based management.* Boston: Harvard Business School Press.

PURCELL, J., KINNIE, N., HUTCHINSON, S., RAYTON, B. and SWART, J. (2003) *Understanding the people and performance link: unlocking the black box.* London: CIPD.

ULRICH, D. (1997) *Human resource champions: the next agenda for adding value and delivering results.* Boston: Harvard Business Press.

WEBER, M. (1947, reissued 1964) *A theory of social and economic organization.* New York: Free Press.

CHAPTER 2

Managing and co-ordinating the HR function

Krystal Wilkinson and Stephen Taylor

CHAPTER CONTENTS

- Introduction
- Purpose and key objectives of the HR function
- How HR objectives are delivered in different organisations
- How the HR function can be evaluated
- The HR contribution to change management
- Ethical HRM
- HR and organisational performance

KEY LEARNING OUTCOMES

By the end of this chapter, you should be able to:

- Explain the purpose and key objectives of the HR function in contemporary organisations, and how the focus of the function has evolved over time.

- Understand the various ways in which the HR function can be structured, and the common choices in different types of organisation.

- Explain the importance of considering cultural and institutional variance when dealing with HR across national borders.

- Understand how the HR function can be evaluated in terms of value added and contribution to sustained organisational performance.

- Understand the contribution of HR to effective change management.

- Explain the role of ethics and professionalism in HR management and development.

- Understand the relationship between HR activities and broader organisational performance.

INTRODUCTION

The purpose of this chapter is to introduce you to human resources (HR) activity and to the role of the HR function in organisations in general terms. It covers the aims and objectives of the function and the ways that these are evolving; different ways of delivering HR objectives; emerging developments in the management of the employment relationship; and methods that can be used to demonstrate how the function adds value to its organisation. The chapter also covers the role and requirements of contemporary HR professionals – in terms of the key contribution they can make to organisational change programmes, and the importance of professionalism and ethics in all activities. You will also be alerted to published research which links HR activity with positive outcomes at an organisational level, in terms of increased performance and reputation.

PURPOSE AND KEY OBJECTIVES OF THE HR FUNCTION

The purpose of the HR function is to support the delivery of the organisation's strategy and objectives through the effective management of people and performance. As such, an organisation's HR strategy and all activities should be clearly aligned with the strategy and activities of the business.

The CIPD website foregrounds the centrality of the function and the professionals working within it to their organisation's success:

> Today HR is at the centre of business performance. HR professionals have an important role to play in driving decisions that enable their organisations to thrive in both the short and the longer term. Where in the past the function delivered the fundamentals that underpinned the employee lifecycle (such as recruitment, induction and salary administration), supporting organisation performance is now the theme running through HR's work.
>
> Recognising that HR is a business discipline – and encouraging managers to view business as a 'people' discipline – is crucial. This partnership approach is vital in order for HR professionals to be able to deliver maximum benefit to their organisations.
>
> To ensure that HR professionals can deliver to this wider agenda, we're seeing greater specialism ... We're also seeing an increasing globalisation of the profession, and an increasing number of CIPD members with overseas responsibilities.

In the rest of this section we explore some of these trends in more detail, including key objectives and areas of focus for HR professionals; how objectives and areas of focus have evolved over time, and where the future is seen to lie; the relationship with line management; and key issues in international HRM.

KEY OBJECTIVES AND HOW THEY HAVE EVOLVED

In terms of what are seen to be the key objectives and activities of the HR function, a 2007 CIPD survey of 787 HR professionals reported that the following were considered the most important: to recruit and retain key staff (cited by 70% of respondents); to develop employee competencies (62% of respondents); to improve the management of people performance (61%); to maximise employee involvement and engagement (59%).

In recent years, due to the problematic economic climate, the focus of HR, together with most other business functions, has been on cost saving; maximising return on investment; and demonstrating value added. We will cover these issues later in the chapter when we consider HR function evaluation. Over the longer term, the objectives of the function have evolved considerably, from a purely welfare focus back at its inception to the current focus on strategy and performance. There are also different issues being highlighted as important for the HR function of the future. Let us explore this evolution in more detail.

The birth of the function: personnel management

The evolution of people management as a distinct profession can be seen to date back to the Industrial Revolution, when factories established personnel departments to look after the wages and welfare of workers. Key activities were employee record-keeping; adherence to policies regarding recruitment, training and wage administration; welfare-oriented initiatives such as providing medical care or housing; attempts to increase productivity via wage increases and training; dealing with trade unions; and basic report-card performance appraisal.

The move to human resource management

Towards the end of the twentieth century, increasing attention was being given in the industrial world to the notion that non-monetary factors could have a bigger influence on worker productivity and motivation than wages. There was a new importance assigned to behaviour, and so people management was required to develop its passive and administrative approach into something more dynamic – human resource management – where people are seen as a valuable resource to be developed rather than as mere cogs in the company machine. The main concerns became recruitment and development that was directed towards increasing worker commitment and loyalty; efforts to provide employees with a challenging work environment and a range of benefits; behaviourally driven training and development activities; more sophisticated performance appraisal; and an emphasis on leadership.

The move to strategic human resource management (SHRM)

The evolution of the field took a further turn at the end of the century when new power was given to the function. Due to increased free market competition at a global level and the growth of technology and knowledge-based industries, the importance of people to company success was elevated. The workforce, having previously been promoted from 'cogs' to 'resources', were now to be viewed as 'assets' – a valuable source of competitive advantage. This marked the elevation of the HR function to a strategic player in the organisation, responsible for aligning individual and team goals with organisation objectives, facilitating a participative culture, and even directly shaping organisation strategies. Activities of the SHRM department include the following:

- linking HR practices to organisation strategy
- fostering a healthy psychological contract in a context of short-term employment rather than job security
- the linking of compensation to contribution
- training and development linked to encouraging innovation
- knowledge management and talent development planning
- employee participation
- motivation through enriching the work experience
- performance and talent management as opposed to appraisal
- cross-cultural issues
- measuring the value added by HR activities.

The evolution of the HR function is unlikely to have finished, and speculation is already being made about future developments in focus. In the CIPD's 2010 *Next Generation HR* report – which was based on a substantial research project conducted in 2009 into the changing nature of the HR function – two key objectives were highlighted as priorities for HR moving forwards:

1 **Future-proofing the organisation.** The report notes a new focus on building 'future-fit cultures', which go beyond being healthy (engaged employees), to become agile and changeable – a culture for always staying one step ahead of the game. Key concepts here are trust and transparency, and treating employees in the same way that we treat customers. The report goes on to talk about the need for HR to become organisation guardians and commentators: managing brand risk; designing processes that support progressive ways of doing business; and being prepared to challenge behaviour (even of the most senior leaders) when it breaches what the organisation stands for.

2 **Being insight-driven.** The report states that 'the best HR functions understand exactly how their organisation in their market facing their specific challenges can respond in a way unique to it'. It goes on to clarify that 'organisation insight' requires an understanding of both context (market, stage of evolution) and culture (what really make things happen here – in terms of people and politics).

HOW HR OBJECTIVES ARE DELIVERED IN DIFFERENT ORGANISATIONS

The HR function can be organised in several different ways: in small to medium-sized organisations, there can be one individual (HR sole practitioner) who works closely with operational managers to manage and deliver the people agenda. In larger organisations, there are likely to be a team, or teams, of HR professionals. In this section we will consider generalist and specialist HR roles; the role of line managers in HR delivery; different delivery options such as shared-service centres, HR outsourcing and the use of consultants; and the Ulrich model for HR provision. We will also consider how HR tends to be delivered in different organisational and national contexts.

GENERALIST AND SPECIALIST ROLES

HR generalists have knowledge of, and involvement in, all areas of the HR function. Sole practitioners will always tend to be generalists as they need to be able to deal with every part of the HR remit on their own. However, sometimes a whole HR team will be made up of generalists – each member may have main areas of responsibility, but they are all capable of handling activities in all areas. Such a structure can be very useful when there are peaks in demand (large recruitment drives) or when the business operates on a 24/7 basis (so that training sessions and employee relations meetings that are out of hours, for example, can be spread around the team). The workload is likely to consist of a variety of tasks – working with managers to determine people needs; taking part in activities; developing policies, procedures and information systems.

Recruitment, resourcing and talent planning specialists are responsible for managing the people in the organisation in order to meet the changing needs of the business – focusing on the company's short-term and long-term objectives. They need to understand and plan around changing demographics, supply and demand, staff turnover and scarce skills. They then need to be able to identify, attract and select the sort of individuals who can create a competitive advantage for the organisation. Finally, they have an important role in developing processes to identify talent across the organisation and integrating them with succession planning and other HR activities such as performance management.

Learning and talent development specialists are responsible for ensuring that the company has employees who possess the skills that it needs now and who are developing the skills that it will need in the future. They do this by producing a learning and development strategy that is in alignment with the overall organisation strategy, and then utilising a broad range of appropriate provisions in order to deliver the strategy – often including structured development programmes, off-the-job training events, on-the-job training provisions, coaching and mentoring schemes, and online provisions. They are also required to evaluate the effectiveness of all provisions.

Organisation development specialists are responsible for ensuring the health of the business itself in the long term. It is widely acknowledged that 'change-ready' and agile businesses are best placed to cope with the challenges of a fast-changing external environment, and OD specialists have a key role in building this capability – working on the organisation's culture, improving the capability of employees, or altering the focus of an organisation (towards quality or customer service, for example).

Employee engagement specialists are responsible for issues such as internal communications, employee relations and the employer brand. It is about what motivates employees to turn up to work each day, and then what makes them go the extra mile. Specialists will design a range of quantitative and qualitative mechanisms to gain information, analyse the results and develop action plans for improving engagement. They will also be responsible for managing procedures to deal with any conflict in the organisation.

Performance and reward specialists are responsible for monitoring the contribution that individuals and teams are making to the business; taking action to improve performance when it is lagging; and ensuring that positive employee skills, behaviours, attitudes and contributions are effectively rewarded – in the forms of salary, allowances, benefits and more intrinsic ways (autonomy, recognition, and so on). Specialists must ensure that reward is managed in a way that is fair, market-based and cost-effective.

THE ROLE OF LINE MANAGERS

As you are aware, the whole purpose of the HR function is the effective management of people and performance issues in the business. The HR team, however, are not the only people who have an involvement in this. Each and every individual employee will have their own line manager (or several people to whom they report) who is responsible for allocating work and monitoring performance. As the line managers have day-to-day contact with employees, they are also likely to be the first point of call when an employee has any questions or concerns about any aspect of the employment experience, or has a personal issue that may have an impact on their work.

It is essential, therefore, that the HR department and line managers work together to manage people issues effectively and consistently. HR managers need to make sure that key HR information, policies and procedures are communicated to line managers; that line managers receive regular training on the implementation of policies and procedures; and that line managers are aware of the importance of seeking HR advice when they are unsure of how to proceed or are faced with complex issues. There is also another reason for HR partnership with line management. If many of the operational people activities can be devolved to the line, more HR time can be devoted to strategic issues, which should in turn elevate the status of the HR function within the organisation.

In the 2007 CIPD survey, the extent to which the allocation of HR-related tasks is divided between the HR function and line management was found to vary substantially between organisations. There were, however, some general trends.

It seems that the responsibility for pay and benefits, employee relations, training and development, and implementing redundancies tends to be retained by the HR team; while responsibilities for work organisation and for recruitment and selection lie mainly with line managers.

SHARED SERVICES, OUTSOURCING AND HR CONSULTANCY

Some organisations opt for a **shared service centre** for their HR provision. Such centres are also used for other support functions (such as finance, IT) and are seen as a way to provide a corporate service across a large organisation or, sometimes, across several partner organisations (such as a group of NHS trusts or local councils).

There are two distinctive features of HR shared service centres: they offer a common service provision of routine HR administration and sometimes more complex HR activities; and they are service-focused, enabling the customers of the shared service to specify the level and nature of the service.

The benefits that can be gained from a move to shared service include the following:

- reducing costs and avoiding duplication of effort
- benefiting from economies of scale (when securing training provisions, benefits provisions, and so on)
- improving the quality of service to customers – the use of more efficient processes can deliver greater consistency, and more timely and accurate information and advice to the customers of the service (individual employees or line managers)
- shared knowledge
- as a possible profit centre (if services are sold to third-party organisations)
- as a precursor to outsourcing.

Outsourcing

The practice of **HR outsourcing** refers to purchasing a service from an external source rather than performing it in-house. In factories and hospitals, for example, support services such as catering and cleaning are often outsourced – because this proves cheaper than employing people directly and the quality is often better (the company that provides the service being experts in the field).

In recent years, the practice has been more evident in office functions, with companies deciding to outsource entire support functions (HR, finance and IT being common targets) to expert providers, or to outsource parts of a function – such as payroll or recruitment – so that those employed by the company can focus on strategic issues and work which requires specific company know-how.

Consultancy

Some organisations may choose to hire specialist HR consultants to provide advice on certain issues or develop specific strategies or policies (but not usually implement them). A consultant would work for a consultancy firm or be self-employed, and would be contacted by an organisation to enter the business, perform a specific task and then leave. As consultants engage with multiple and changing clients, they can bring deeper levels of expertise than a company could hope to have in-house, and each client only has to purchase as much service as they need.

For each individual assignment, a contract should be drawn up between the client and the consultant. Cope (2003, pp78–9) suggests the following general model:

- background (client area, situation under consideration, business context)
- outcome (goals and objectives, measurement)
- engagement plan (timeframe, methodology, resource allocation, key milestones, initial known data requirements)
- responsibilities (client, consultant, stakeholders)
- boundaries and scope (areas for inclusion and exclusion, potential risk)
- specifics (payment, terms and conditions)
- confidentiality (termination process, liability, disclosure policy)
- review process
- closure (process and review dates).

If outsourcing or HR consultants are used, it is extremely important to ensure that regular evaluation occurs to ensure that the services received are as agreed and effective.

THE ULRICH MODEL

US business academic David Ulrich proposed a pioneering new model for HR service delivery, which has since become known as the 'three-legged stool' model for HR. It is based on three different types of HR professionals in an organisation, each working in distinct ways:

- **HR business partners:** senior HR professionals working closely with business leaders or line managers, usually embedded in the business unit, influencing and steering strategy and strategy implementation
- **centres of excellence:** small teams of HR specialists – developing and delivering innovative HR solutions in areas such as reward, learning, engagement and talent management
- **shared service centre:** as cited above, a large unit that handles the routine 'transactional' services across the business.

Despite the intense interest surrounding the Ulrich model and business partnering, there is little empirical evidence to illustrate how many companies actually structure their HR function in this way. In the CIPD's 2010 *HR Outlook* survey, 30% of survey respondents from large organisations described their structure and the 'three-legged model', although far fewer did so in medium and small organisations.

APPROACH TO THE FUNCTION IN DIFFERENT CONTEXTS

It should be noted that different types of organisation are likely to organise their HR function in different ways, and that the function will have different primary objectives in different contexts. We will not spend too long on this issue as there is undoubtedly a lot of variation in approach within each type of organisation, but it is important to be aware of key traits and differences. You will also find more discussion of some of these issues in Chapter 3:

- **Large private sector companies:** as the company is privately owned, the key objective for all functional departments will be revenue generation (making money for the shareholders) and proving that the function adds value. The function itself is likely to be large, and may be made up of mainly generalists, mainly specialists, or something akin to the Ulrich model.

- **Public sector:** as the company is a public body, the key objectives will be linked to enhancing the service provision to the public. Revenue generation is likely to be less of an issue, but maximising efficiency to save public money will be a key objective. The HR team are likely to have more constraints on how they design and deliver certain activities due to government stipulations and expectations surrounding best practice in issues of equality of opportunity and diversity, and so on. The function itself is likely to be structured in a similar way as in large private sector companies.

- **Voluntary sector:** as the company is likely to be limited in terms of funds, the focus on all functions will be to operate in a cost-effective way, but to try to attract new investment and volunteer staff. HR activities will be based on trying to attract individuals with a certain value stance and make them feel valued and appreciated in the company (as financial rewards are likely to be minimal or non-existent). The size of the HR function will depend on the size of the organisation.

- **Small and medium-sized enterprises (SMEs):** as the size of the workforce and resources of the company are likely to be small, the HR function is likely to consist of a sole practitioner working in partnership with operational management, or there might not be any direct HR presence at all – with basic people management issues being conducted by an office manager or operations manager, and HR consultants being brought in only when there are specific issues to deal with or new policies/practices are required.

- **Networked organisations:** this refers to organisations working in collaboration to develop products or deliver services. HR may well be delivered through a shared service centre that covers all of the organisations in the network, or each organisation may have its own HR people who are required to work collaboratively with their counterparts throughout the network.

- **Multinational organisations (MNCs):** as most MNCs are privately owned, one key objective for all functions will be revenue generation, but an additional objective will be ensuring the smooth running and effective operation of the company across national borders. We will consider this issue further in the next section.

You may wish to consider such organisation type variations – in terms of HR priorities, available resources and team structure – when you are thinking about personal job transitions and how you want your HR career to progress. Different contexts come with different experiences and opportunities, and not every type of organisation is likely to be equally appealing.

CULTURAL AND INSTITUTIONAL VARIATIONS ACROSS NATIONAL BORDERS

When considering HR in the global context, there are a number of different issues to bear in mind:

- Different countries have different cultures, which can affect employee expectations and behaviours in work.
- Different countries have different employment legislation frameworks. UK immigration legislation is also a key issue.
- Different countries have different tax arrangements, and different provisions for things such as medical cover.
- Different countries have different labour markets – as a result of economic factors (whether the markets are tight/loose) and welfare provisions (whether parents, etc, are better off in work or at home).
- Different countries have different standards of living – which affects pay expectations.
- Different countries have different education systems – which affects the age at which individuals enter the labour markets and the skill sets they have.

Cultural variations across national borders are especially important to be aware of, as they will have an impact on all aspects of HR activities. One of the most famous authors on national culture variations is Hofstede (1991), who initially developed four main factors of culture differentiation:

- **Power distance:** this refers to the extent to which people believe that power should be distributed equally or unequally. In work terms, it relates to the centralisation of authority within an organisation. Countries with a 'high power distance' (such as the Philippines, Singapore, France and Greece) tend to have hierarchical organisations in which it is accepted that the more senior employees have more power. Countries with a 'low power distance' (such as the UK, Sweden and New Zealand) tend to have flatter organisation structures and a less autocratic style of management.
- **Uncertainty avoidance:** this refers to the extent to which people feel

uncomfortable with ambiguous situations. Countries such as France, with a 'high uncertainty avoidance', tend to have lots of rules and regulations in organisations and employees are not expected to take risks.

- **Individualism/collectivism:** this refers to the extent to which people operate on an individual basis or as part of a group. In a 'high individualism' culture, such as the USA, people tend to look out for themselves, preferring individual objectives, individual performance assessment and reward based on individual performance. In 'low individualist' or 'high collectivist' cultures, such as Japan, people prefer to work in teams, have team-based assessment and have collectively negotiated reward.

- **Masculinity/femininity:** this refers to the extent to which people demonstrate what are seen to be masculine or feminine traits. The former include aggressiveness and assertiveness, the latter caring and emotional intelligence.

Cultural and institutional variations across national borders will be relevant not only when an HR professional wants to work in a different country themselves, but when they work in any company that is international, or where employees may be posted for overseas assignments.

When it comes to developing an HR strategy in an international company, one of the key decisions to be made will be the extent to which national variations in the above factors are taken into consideration. There are several options:

- **Ethnocentric:** the home-country strategy and practices are rolled out across the company; key decisions are made by the home-country headquarters; and employees from the home country tend to fill important jobs.

- **Polycentric:** strategy and practices are adapted to each national context; local managers usually head up each subsidiary and decide how things should be done.

- **Geocentric or global:** the most effective policies and procedures from around the business are implemented and the most effective individuals selected for key roles and to make key decisions. For example, the vacuum cleaner company Electrolux has recruited and developed a group of international managers from a range of different countries. They now have a mobile base of managers that can be deployed in different locations as the need arises, and who can learn from each placement and spread that knowledge as they move on.

The decision over which approach to follow for the HR strategy may well be linked to the approach adopted at the organisational level, but this is not always the case. Furthermore, even where a company decides to operate a specific approach at both the company and departmental level, certain processes may well need to be adapted somewhat to ensure things such as legal compliance and effectiveness (with the ethnocentric approach) or the development of a unified company identity (with the polycentric approach).

HOW THE HR FUNCTION CAN BE EVALUATED

In order for the HR function to demonstrate that it adds value, it must have in place robust systems for the evaluation of its activities – both at an individual level and cumulatively.

COMMON METHODS AND METRICS

Traditionally, HR evaluation has focused on the efficiency and effectiveness of the range of practices operated by the function. Efficiency concerns establishing that each activity is as cost-effective as possible in terms of time and money; effectiveness concerns establishing that the activity is meeting its objectives. A range of techniques are available for evaluating individual HR activities on these grounds and also for assessing the cumulative effect.

The most commonly used evaluation tools include the following:

- **HR statistics:** this refers to things such as recruitment spend; number of job applications; number of new recruits; absence figures; turnover levels; disciplinary and grievance stats; training and development spend; training hours per employee; and so on. While they may not tell the company much if gathered in isolation, they can be very useful in terms of benchmarking – either internal (comparing current performance with previous years, or comparing different departments to target problem areas) or external (comparing the company with others in the industry and/or local area).

- **Key performance indicators (KPIs):** this refers to identifying the aspects of HR performance that are the most critical for the achievement of business objectives, often including a target for each activity, and then assessing the performance against this target. The ideal for KPIs is that they are specific, measurable, achievable, performance-relevant and time-bound (have a deadline).

- **Balanced scorecard:** this is a document that lists an agreed set of performance measures in a series of tables, along with a 'high-level strategy map' showing how these measures relate to each other and the firm's strategic objectives. The scorecard's measures are grouped under four 'perspectives': customer; financial; internal business process; and learning and growth. All departments would have their own scorecard, with the specific measures under each of the perspectives tailored to their own specific functional activities. This enhances the sense that all departments are working to the same objectives and enables cross-company comparisons.

MEETING THE NEEDS OF THE CUSTOMERS

As well as assessing the efficiency and effectiveness of HR activities, another way in which the function can be evaluated concerns the extent to which the HR department are seen to be meeting the needs of their customers.

In order to do this, the function first needs to consider who their customers are.

This can be done by conducting a stakeholder analysis – where you identify all of the parties that require some sort of service from the department and then you consider what the specific requirements are of each.

REFLECTIVE ACTIVITY 2.1

Who are the different 'customers' of the HR department in your own organisation or one you are familiar with? What do they require from the HR function?

EVALUATING EMERGING HR GOALS AND PURPOSES

As mentioned above, in the context of the evolution of people management, key areas of focus for the profession moving forward are seen to be future-proofing the organisation and ensuring that HR is 'insight-driven'. This refers to a new emerging purpose for the function – going beyond the traditional people–performance remit and focusing instead on contributing to overall long-term organisational performance. In one *People Management* feature, 'A new way of seeing HR: insight-led HR', some pioneering HR leaders were seen to display new capabilities, including the ability to 'read' the health of the organisation as a whole and operate considerably 'off piste' if required.

This also means new requirements for evaluation. HR professionals need to look beyond people–performance metrics to assess their own abilities and consider whether they personally possess the 'three savvies' that are required for being 'insight-driven':

- **contextual savvy:** being alert to the external factors and macro trends that affect the organisation now and in the future
- **organisational savvy:** having a sophisticated understanding of the people and cultural aspects of the organisation – how to get things done with these unique individuals in our very particular context
- **business savvy:** having a true understanding of how the organisation makes money and what most matters when looking at its current and future commercial health.

This requires self-evaluation and perceptiveness to the responses given by key organisational stakeholders. For example, are HR included at board level, are they involved in key organisation strategy-making, are they respected?

As summarised by Jackie Orme, former CIPD chief executive:

> We need to change the unspoken currency of success in HR. Too often we get stuck in a cycle of measuring ourselves on the volume of activities and initiatives, and on the multiple demands we are responding to. We feel this is what is necessary to demonstrate value and be recognised accordingly. We need to unlock our curiosity and realise that having a unique viewpoint and a clear sense of what matters in light of this has to be a much bigger part of our definition of success.

THE HR CONTRIBUTION TO CHANGE MANAGEMENT

Change is a key, and unavoidable, issue in the modern organisational world. All sorts of things cause organisational change – the challenges of growth, especially global markets; challenges of economic downturns and tougher trading conditions; changes in strategy; technological changes; competitive pressures, including mergers and acquisitions; customer pressure and shifting markets; new legislation and government initiatives. Research indicates that organisations are undergoing major change approximately once every three years, while smaller changes are occurring almost continually (CIPD 2011). As the old saying goes, the only constant in life is change.

Effective change management is hugely important, as despite the extent of change faced by modern business, evidence suggests that a considerable number of organisation change initiatives fail. CIPD research suggests that less than 60% of reorganisations meet their stated objectives.

If a change management is to be successful, the HR function usually has a vital part to play. This is because effective change management concerns more than just the controllable (business processes that can be designed and implemented) – it also concerns the uncontrollable (people, and the meanings that people attach to such processes).

THE HR CONTRIBUTION TO THE CONTROLLABLE

HR professionals can contribute to the development of change programmes in the following ways:

- involvement at the initial stage in the project team
- advising project leaders in skills available within the organisation – identifying any skills gaps, training needs, new posts, new working practices, and so on
- balancing out the narrow/short-term goals with broader strategic needs
- assessing the impact of change in one area/department/site on another part of the organisation
- balancing the interests of different stakeholder groups
- understanding stakeholder concerns to anticipate problems
- understanding the appropriate medium of communication to reach each group
- evaluating and reporting on the impact of change initiatives on human resources – this can include absence levels; turnover figures; number of grievances raised; internal moves; training spend; employee feedback (satisfaction survey scores); and so on.

THE HR CONTRIBUTION TO THE UNCONTROLLABLE

Individuals and their reactions to proposed changes are 'uncontrollable' because everyone is different. Each employee will have their own personality (more or less comfortable with change); their own history (experience of changes in the past);

and their own unique position in terms of the change under consideration (it might or might not affect them, and if it does, this might be positive or negative).

The HR department can help to deal with the somewhat uncontrollable human element of change by being aware of the more typical reactions and being aware of the interpersonal activities they can instigate to facilitate the change initiative.

It has been established that most people pass through a typical cycle of emotions as they deal with change and its consequences – a sort of emotional roller-coaster. This is illustrated in Figure 2.1:

Figure 2.1 Approaches to change

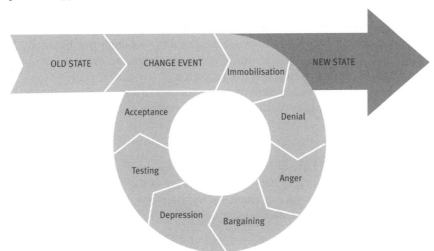

Here are some thoughts that might be expressed by someone passing through the change cycle in relation to something they see as bad news:

- What? Oh no!
- It can't be true!
- You cannot be serious!
- Can we sort this out some other way?
- That's it – after 20 years of service they want me to …
- Am I going to be part of this?
- Yes, I can live with this – it's not bad really. I can now …

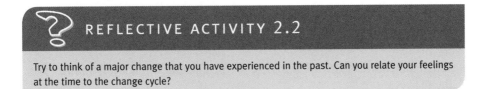

REFLECTIVE ACTIVITY 2.2

Try to think of a major change that you have experienced in the past. Can you relate your feelings at the time to the change cycle?

Research has also found that certain types of organisation change will be more emotive than others. The findings of one CIPD survey on organisational change (Guest and Conway 2001) suggest that, contrary to popular opinion, employees generally have a positive view of change and will often see it as helping them do their jobs better. Changes in job design, new technology and products thus tend to be welcomed by employees. The types of change that were perceived more negatively, and therefore require more careful handling, were the following: those that might affect job security, prospects or careers; changes to reward, pay or appraisal; changes to information, communication, involvement and relationships; and changes to policies affecting how, when and where work is done. Unfortunately, these are just the sort of changes that you are likely to be involved in.

So what is HR's role in dealing with the uncontrollable? While there can be no magic formula to ensure that everyone will react positively, there are some general elements that will improve the likelihood of employee buy-in. This includes: an organisational culture that embraces change; appropriate communication; ensuring employee participation in any change; HRD interventions; and the management of expectations and conflict. We will now explore some of these issues in more depth, focusing on HR's role in each.

Change-ready culture

Different organisations have different 'cultures' when it comes to receptiveness to change. The HR team can gain an understanding of the culture of the organisation by holding informal employee focus groups, including questions on change initiatives in staff satisfaction surveys, or holding interviews with a range of company stakeholders.

You can also think about how changes have been carried out and conducted in the past. If you can answer yes to the following questions, adapted from the Positive Employee Practices Institute, then the culture is likely to be more receptive to new change initiatives:

- Does the company take time to thoroughly plan for each change?
- Do the people affected by a change get to take part in the planning and implementation?
- Are the goals, purposes and potential benefits of change efforts clearly communicated to everyone in the organisation?
- When changes are announced, is there open dialogue about the disruptions they may create and the difficulties that may need to be addressed in order to make the changes successful?
- When people have problems implementing changes, do they communicate freely about them and ask for help?
- When people express negative feelings about change, are they listened to and are their concerns addressed?
- When difficulties or disruptions arise, are people quick to address and fix them?

- Has the company experienced recent successes in implementing major changes?
- Does the company take time to learn from efforts at change that do not succeed?
- Are successful change efforts recognised and celebrated?

Communication

The importance of internal communication throughout any change process is cited time and again in management literature. If the vision of the future is clear and is clearly communicated, people will be less confused and less likely to offer resistance. In the absence of this, the informal company grapevine is likely to spring into action, based on assumptions and individual fears. It tends to be the responsibility of the HR department to ensure that appropriate communication mechanisms are in place and that they are operating effectively.

Appropriate methods of communication during change initiatives include the following:

- **Top-down channels:** this is for the dissemination of accurate information. Ideally the managing director or senior managers should take the time to speak directly to employees. They could hold a formal meeting in a central location (small company) or could visit the different company sites. Regular official information bulletins should also be publicised (in letters to staff; via the intranet; on bulletin boards; and via line managers in team meetings).
- **Bottom-up channels:** this is to allow employee participation and idea generation. There could be collective consultation, change workshops, and so on.
- **Two-way discussion:** there should be one-to-one meetings between employees and their line managers and/or the HR department to discuss the personal implications of change initiatives and any concerns that individuals may have.

The skills and attributes that the HR department needs to exercise include the following:

- **Stakeholder awareness and the ability to influence at all levels:** HR professionals need to be aware not only of the employees during change initiatives, they may also need to persuade senior management of the importance of commitment to communication activities, and/or coach line managers in effective communication.
- **Honesty:** 'users, management and other stakeholders will demand honest, consistent and up-to-date information whether the news is good, bad or unremarkable' (CIPD 2005).
- **Thoroughness and patience:** it is important that communication provides all of the information that stakeholders need, including the following:
  - the need for, the nature and the scope of the change
  - who will be affected

– training, retraining and/or redeployment implications
– implications for quality of work/life
– implications for staffing and work patterns
– the proposed rate and timing of implementation
– the expected benefits and adverse effects of the change.

This can take some time, and the same message may need to be delivered several times.

- **The ability to listen:** providing information is only half of the process; the key is to ensure that communication is two-way and that employees have the opportunity to ask questions and express their opinions/concerns.
- **Empathy and concern for stakeholder reactions** to change and the ability to ensure stakeholder understanding.
- **Monitoring of the effectiveness of communication channels.**

HRD interventions

Training and development initiatives can help with change management in a number of areas, including:

- **enhancing employee responsiveness to change:** employees can be instructed on the importance of being aware of what is happening externally (the business environment) and how to be more responsive to the views and experiences of suppliers and customers; they can also be given development opportunities where they are expected to be creative and innovative
- **enhancing the ability of employees to adapt to change:** by addressing any skills gaps that arise as a result of a change initiative
- **coaching and mentoring activities** for those finding it difficult to cope with change.

PUBLICISING SUCCESS

One crucial activity throughout any organisational change programme, and in the aftermath, is the widespread publicising of success stories. This includes not only the overall impact of the programme (that is, company performance), but also individual success stories – examples of employees whose actions or attitudes have had a significant positive impact on the success of the change; and also employees who have gained from it. This will help 'bed in' the change, support a change-ready culture and put employees in a more positive frame of mind in the event of future change initiatives.

ETHICAL HRM

The *Oxford English Reference Dictionary* defines the terms as follows:

- Ethics is 'the rules of conduct recognised as appropriate to a particular profession or area of life'.

- Professionalism is 'the qualities or typical features of a profession or of professionals, especially competence, skill, etc'.

Here we are going to focus on thinking about ethics in HR practice. In Chapter 3 you will find a discussion on professionalism in HRM.

THE BUSINESS CASE FOR AN ETHICAL APPROACH TO HR MANAGEMENT

Kew and Stredwick (2010, p351) make reference to a definition of ethics that has three core elements: fairness; deciding what is right and wrong; and the practices and rules which underpin responsible conduct between individuals and groups.

It is absolutely vital that the HR function takes an ethical approach in all its actions. As we will see below, ethical behaviour is a core element of the required standards of an HR professional. There is also a clear business case for ethical HR management, covering several areas:

- Ethical behaviour is essential in the development and maintenance of positive relationships with the workforce. The workforce needs to trust the HR function and this is only possible if the function acts fairly and decently at all times.

- Ethical standards are a key determinant of the employer brand and reputation. Ethics is a hot topic in society in general and individuals are increasingly considering ethical factors when they are deciding which companies they are willing to work for. It is certainly clear that individuals are unlikely to want to work for a company with a reputation of unethical treatment towards its employees.

- Role-modelling – if the department is going to champion ethical behaviour in the workforce as a whole, it must practise what it preaches.

Furthermore, there is even evidence to suggest that ethical practice can improve overall business performance. Kew and Stredwick (2010, pp381–2) cite a study carried out by the Institute of Business Ethics in 2003, which compared a number of FTSE-350 companies that met certain ethical criteria (including having a long-standing code of ethics and scoring highly on certain league tables) with a control sample. It was found that the ethical companies scored more highly on three different measures of financial performance.

Taylor (2011) notes the irony in HR taking a leading role in ethical issues, however – after having spent years and years trying to distance itself from its 'pink and fluffy' welfare roots to gain credibility as a strategic player:

> It is a paradox, given the centrality of ethics to so much HR activity that our function has generally sought, at least in recent years, to distance itself from perceptions that it plays a significant ethical role…. Since the 1980s the emphasis has been on shedding our image as a management function concerned with employee welfare or even one which seeks to represent the interests of employees…. Instead a very deliberate attempt has been made to craft a vision of HRM as being 100% business-focused, delivering key

strategic objectives on behalf of the organisation and adding financial value. In the future it is likely that there will be some reversal of this established trend…. HR managers will have to rediscover an interest in ethics, actively promote ethical behaviour across the organisation and take care that they apply ethical approaches towards the management of people themselves.

CODES OF ETHICS

As well as having a personal responsibility for ethical decision-making and acting as role-models for others, the HR team often has a leading role to play in the promotion of ethical behaviour for all. One of the ways they can do this is via the development and publicising of a corporate code of ethics. This is a form of code of conduct that can be defined as 'written, distinct, formal document(s), which consists of moral standards which help guide employee or corporate behaviour' (Schwartz 2001, p27).

Such codes can be of three different types: educational (aimed at increasing moral awareness and behaviour within the company); regulatory (detailing rules for behaviour providing help on the resolution of moral conflicts); or aspirational (laying down general values and communicating ideals to individuals).

Good codes of ethics recognise the importance of relationships with all major stakeholders (both internal and external). The specific content will vary from company to company, but they tend to have an introduction to the purpose of the document, followed by sections detailing the expected behaviour of all employees in relation to a range of specific topics.

THE HR ROLE IN PROMOTING KEY PHILOSOPHIES

Just as the HR function was seen to have a responsibility for both demonstrating and promoting ethical decision-making and good communication in relation to change management, there are several other issues that HR has primary responsibility for championing and promoting throughout the workplace. These include the following:

- **Equality of opportunity:** HR professionals should ensure:
  - that all policies, procedures and activities guarantee fairness to all (fair access, fair treatment, and so on)
  - that decisions about things such as recruitment, promotion, training and redundancy are made in relation to job requirements (and other fair and objective criteria) and are in no way discriminatory
  - that channels are available for employees to raise their concerns if they feel they have been treated unfairly
  - that equal opportunity training is delivered to all employees, especially those in management positions.
- **Diversity:** HR professionals should:
  - monitor levels of diversity in the workplace and take action to promote the interests of under-represented groups (via targeted recruitment campaigns, targeted training and development activities, and so on)

- provide training for all management staff on the importance of diversity at work, including the business case.

- **Dignity at work:** HR professionals should ensure:
  - that there is a clear policy relating to dignity at work
  - that the policy is clearly communicated to all employees at the time of induction
  - that training is provided for all employees on the importance of respect and dignity at work
  - that channels are available for employees to raise their concerns if they feel they have been the victim of bullying or harassment at work
  - that full investigations take place in relation to allegations of bullying or harassment and that appropriate action is taken if allegations are proven.

- **Work–life balance:** HR professionals should:
  - ensure that the company is meeting legal expectations in the field of work–life balance; this includes monitoring compliance with the Working Time Directive and clearly communicating employee rights
  - champion the importance of work–life balance to senior management and try to secure funding for work–life balance provisions
  - consider the usefulness (versus costs) of different work–life balance provisions
  - develop suitable work–life balance policies and provisions
  - communicate the importance of work–life balance to all line management staff and provide training in the various policies and provisions available
  - be prepared to coach on personal work–life balance with some management staff. If senior staff work extremely long hours, they might be communicating an expectation of this to junior employees, the result of which can be a long-hours culture. Managers should be encouraged to change – both for their own well-being and for that of those they manage
  - communicate work–life balance provisions to all employees
  - monitor the take-up of work–life balance provisions and evaluate their effectiveness.

- **Health and well-being:** HR professionals should:
  - champion the importance of employee health and well-being to senior management and try to secure funding for provisions
  - develop a policy around health and well-being at work
  - ensure that all line management staff receive training on monitoring the health and well-being of their staff, and on providing the first level of support if team members have problems (with things such as stress, for example)
  - consider the usefulness (versus costs) of different health and well-being provisions
  - communicate the selected health and well-being provisions to all managers and employees.

THE SIGNIFICANCE OF LEGAL COMPLIANCE

It is essential that HR practitioners comply with employment legislation. At times, it is possible that the requests of senior management (based on operational concerns) may contradict the stipulations of employment law, which can put HR professionals in a difficult position. For example, management may try to dismiss an employee on the grounds of capability, when the real reason is that they don't like the individual or they want to avoid having to pay a redundancy settlement. In such situations, it is essential that professional integrity and legal obligations are adhered to. The HR professional should argue the business case for compliance and ensure that senior managers are aware that lawful remedies are more beneficial to the company in the long run (avoiding tribunal costs, ensuring that the reputation of the company is not damaged).

Having said this, it is important to be aware that legal compliance simply stipulates the minimum standards in terms of ethical behaviour towards employees. Some would argue that 'the rules of the ethics game' are set by legislators in the EU, Parliament and the courts – meaning that organisations and individuals do not have to ask themselves any further questions about the ethics of their actions if they are within the bounds of the law.

We would argue that this position could only really be sanctioned if the law were more robust – covering all issues and protecting all individuals. In the case of employment law, for example, there are several weak points, and employee protection from unfair treatment by their employers is only achieved in a patchy way – people can be disadvantaged due to their contract type, their length of service, their age (National Minimum Wage), the norms of their industry (Working Time Regulations exclusions), and so on.

Legal compliance is thus about meeting the minimum standards set by external bodies, whereas truly ethical business requires a proactive, internally-driven approach that seeks to continually work towards fairness for all.

HR AND ORGANISATIONAL PERFORMANCE

Over the last 15 years or so, there has been a lot of research interest in the HR–performance link – that is, the relationship between HR policies and practices and the overall performance of the organisation. Furthermore, the findings of much research have been positive – that organisations with certain combinations of HR policies and practices do indeed perform well.

It is important to be aware, however, that there are serious gaps in our understanding. For a start, the direction of causation is unclear – is it that a certain combination of HR practices are improving organisational performance, or is it simply that high-performing companies tend to invest in HR more and implement a range of policies?

Another issue to consider is the wide range of perspectives on which specific combinations of policies and practices are seen to constitute the 'magic HR formula' for organisational success. Dominant theories include 'best practice', 'best fit' or contingency theory, and the resource-based view.

The 'best practice' approach suggests that there is a set of HR practices that will create high performance in an organisation no matter what the context. The main underlying principle is that HR practices should be aimed at improving the commitment of workers – thus alternative names have been developed for this approach over time, including 'high-commitment' work systems or 'high-involvement' HRM. The idea is that a committed and involved employee is more likely to give 'discretionary effort' – going above and beyond the basic requirements of their role because they like their job and care about the success of the company.

Kew and Stredwick (2010, pp413–16) highlight the following ten 'best practices' as being linked to high levels of employee commitment:

- flexibility/teamworking: cultivating employees who are willing to undertake a range of tasks, irrespective of job title, in order to meet customer requirements. This is further emphasised through teamworking

- employee involvement

- employee voice

- performance-related reward: this includes other aspects of the total reward package and is not restricted to pay alone

- employee ownership: giving employees the chance to own shares in the company – so that employee and owner interests are aligned

- sophisticated selection

- internal promotion: showing employees that there are opportunities for advancement, provided they possess the ability and commitment

- employment security: showing that employees really are seen as the company's most important resource

- commitment to learning

- harmonisation: developing a culture that aims to remove unnecessary status differences.

Key research in the 'best practice HRM' field has been conducted by John Purcell and his colleagues at the Work and Employment Research Centre at the University of Bath. Central to the 'Bath Model of People and Performance' is ability, motivation and opportunity (AMO). The assertion is that for employees, individually and collectively, to engage in the sort of discretionary behaviour that is beneficial to the firm, the three conditions of AMO must apply:

- There must be enough employees with the necessary **ability** (skills, experience, knowledge) to do current, and perhaps future, jobs.

- There must be adequate **motivation** for them to apply their abilities. These motivation factors may be financial but will almost certainly include social rewards and recognition of employee contribution.

- There must be an **opportunity** for employees to engage in discretionary behaviour. This should be within the individual's specific job; as a member of a team or work area; and as 'citizen' of the whole organisation.

The **'best fit' approach**, also known as the contingency model, argues that there is no one model of HR strategy which will suit all circumstances and that organisations should seek the specific mix of HR practices that are appropriate to their specific context. This does not mean that there will not be common practices amongst companies – just as a company will tend to pursue one of a limited number of competitive strategies, they will tend to find that one of a limited number of HR policy configurations will be suitable.

The **resource-based view** turns traditional approaches on their head. Rather than seeking to identify an optimum set of HR practices and policies and use them to source and shape employees, the approach starts with the current 'human capital resources' (experience, skills, judgement and intelligence of managers and employees) of the company, and then develops policies and procedures around them – to make the most of what you already have. The belief here is that competitive advantage can be gained not only by acquiring resources, but also by developing, combining and effectively deploying existing resources in a way that adds unique value and is difficult for other companies to imitate.

CASE STUDY

👁 RESTRUCTURING HR

You are the newly appointed HR director for a national hotel chain that currently employs an HR team of 24 people – one stand-alone HR generalist in each of the chain's hotels. This HR structure has been in place for many years. The chain started in 1980 with only four properties in the north-west, and while each hotel had its own HR manager, they would contact each other frequently and write all policies and procedures together. In the last 30 years, the chain has expanded rapidly, via the acquisition of small independent hotels throughout the UK. Each time a hotel was taken over, the existing workforce were all offered continued employment, and where no HR provision was in place, a generalist HR manager was appointed from the local area. You have been appointed because the managing director is concerned that there is no consistency to the HR provision in the company: each hotel seems to operate different HR practices and procedures; the HR managers appear to have different levels of ability in different areas of the function; and there is virtually no lateral communication between members of the HR team. The managing director has informed you that the next board meeting will take place in three months, at which he would like you to make a presentation outlining suggestions for the function moving forward.

Questions

1 What would you need to do before writing the proposal?

2 You finally decide to suggest a model that includes a shared service centre and regional business partners with different specialisms (recruitment; development; reward; and employee relations). What would you need to include in the proposal to the board?

3 What are the advantages and disadvantages of such a transition?

FURTHER READING

CIPD (2012) Information pages [online]. Information pages are available on the website which provide factsheets, podcasts and survey reports on each of the following topics:

HR function: http://www.cipd.co.uk/hr-topics/hr-function.aspx

Change management: http://www.cipd.co.uk/hr-topics/change-management.aspx

Business partnering: http://www.cipd.co.uk/hr-topics/business-partnering.aspx

HR trends: http://www.cipd.co.uk/hr-topics/hr-trends.aspx

CIPD *HR Outlook* survey report series: quarterly reports based on the findings of large-scale surveys of UK HR practitioners – providing detailed commentary on the HR profession and emerging trends in HR activity.

REFERENCES

CIPD (2001) *Managing change: The role of the pyschological contract.* London: Chartered Institute of Personnel and Development.

CIPD (2007) *The changing HR function.* Survey report. London: Chartered Institute of Personnel and Development.

CIPD (2008) *CIPD code of professional conduct and disciplinary procedures.* London: Chartered Institute of Personnel and Development.

CIPD (2010) *Next generation HR.* London: Chartered Institute of Personnel and Development.

CIPD (2011) *Change management.* Factsheet. London: Chartered Institute of Personnel and Development.

CIPD *The HR profession [online].* Available at: http://www.cipd.co.uk/cipd-hr-profession/hr-profession/ [accessed March 2012]. London: Chartered Institute of Personnel and Development.

COPE, N. (2003) *The seven Cs of consulting.* 2nd edition. London: Prentice Hall.

GUEST, D. E. and CONWAY, N. (2001) *Public and Private Sector Perceptions on the Psychological Contract.* London: CIPD.

London: Department for Business, Innovation and Skills

HOFSTEDE, G. (1991) *Cultures and organisations: software of the mind.* London: McGraw-Hill.

KEW, J. and STREDWICK, J. (2010) *Human resource management in a business context.* London: Chartered Institute of Personnel and Development.

NAYAB, N. (2010) Evolution of human resource management. www.brighthub.com

SCHWARTZ, M. (2001) 'The nature of the relationship between corporate codes of ethics and behavior', *Journal of Business Ethics*, 32.

TAYLOR, S. (2011) *Contemporary issues in HRM*. London: Chartered Institute of Personnel and Development.

CHAPTER 3

Business issues and the contexts of human resources

Stephen Taylor and Krystal Wilkinson

CHAPTER CONTENTS

- HRM in the different sectors
- Developments in the external environment
- Forming organisational and HR strategies

KEY LEARNING OUTCOMES

By the end of this chapter, you should be able to:

- Understand key contemporary business issues affecting the HR function within private, public and third sector organisations.

- Understand the main external contextual factors impacting on organisations and the HR function.

- Understand the role of HR in the managing of contemporary business issues and external contexts.

- Understand how organisational and HR strategies are shaped and developed.

- Know how to identify and respond to short-term changes in the business and external contexts.

HRM IN THE DIFFERENT SECTORS

While there are some areas of HR practice that are carried out in a similar way across all types of organisation and plenty that HR managers operating in different sectors can learn from one another, it is important to recognise that there are also always going to be significant differences. Business objectives vary considerably, as do current business agendas and strategies. Different organisations also face a huge variety of diverse commercial and regulatory pressures. Some are in the position of being able to plan ten or twenty years ahead with considerable confidence that their plans will come to fruition. Others, due primarily to the volatility of their environments, cannot realistically plan in a detailed way more than a year or two ahead. There is an obvious knock-on effect for HRM, which has to take on a character that is appropriate for the particular context in which it is obliged to operate. Gaining an understanding of how organisations differ in terms of their objectives and the particular contexts in which they operate is therefore fundamental to the effective study of HRM.

A good place to start is by looking at the broad sectors that organisations form a part of. In fact, almost all belong to one of the three major economic sectors: the private sector, the public sector and the voluntary (or third) sector. There are, however, some organisations which cross the boundaries, being, for example, **private–public partnerships**.

THE PRIVATE SECTOR

The private sector is made up of businesses which are owned by private individuals or families, by other organisations or by large numbers of individual and institutional shareholders, including, sometimes, employee shareholders. Most are commercial in nature and aim to make profits for their owners. However, there are also not-for-profit organisations that operate as social enterprises.

Regulation

Legally, private sector organisations take one of three distinct forms: sole traders, partnerships or companies. In terms of their ownership, sole traders are one-man or one-woman organisations, but this does not mean that they can't employ people as well. They are not required to register with any authorities and are regulated fairly lightly. The downside of being a sole trader is that as an owner you are the business, so you are personally liable to an unlimited extent for all debts and can become bankrupt if your business gets into a great deal of debt. This means that a failure by a customer to pay you can have serious personal financial consequences – like the loss of your house.

Partnerships are firms owned and run by two or more people who have entered a joint partnership. As far as the law is concerned they are not companies, even though many call themselves companies or have '& Co.' in their titles. Legally they are 'unincorporated associations'. As with sole trading arrangements, regulation is light. There is no requirement to register and no requirement to produce audited accounts. Individual partners are agents of the firm and can enter into contracts on its behalf with other parties. When a partnership becomes insolvent, all partners are 'jointly and severally' liable to an unlimited level for the payment of debts. Professional services firms (accountants, solicitors, stockbrokers, and so on) are able to have as many partners as they like, but other types of business are generally restricted to a maximum of 20 partners. Since 2001 it has been possible for traditional partnerships to become limited-liability partnerships. In practice, this means that they take on the rights and responsibilities of limited companies and are governed by company law, even though technically they remain partnerships rather than companies.

Companies, like partnerships, must have at least two members (that is, shareholders), but there is no limit on how many they can have. They are subject to a great deal more regulation than partnerships and sole trading organisations, but they also have important privileges. Of these, by far the most important is 'limited liability'. Essentially this means that the company is itself a legal personality separate from the people who own and run it. They may leave or die or become personally bankrupt, but the company continues trading indefinitely.

This means that a company can borrow money and can be taken to court as an entity separate from those who control it. It also means that if the company becomes insolvent, it can be liquidated without its owners being legally responsible for any of the debts. Liability is limited to the value of the shares owned (that is, to the extent that any individual or institution has invested in the company). Importantly, this is true even if a company is essentially controlled by a single person (that is, if there are 1,000 shares and 999 are owned by the chairman/managing director).

UK companies must register as in 'England and Wales' or in Wales or in Scotland or in Northern Ireland. All formal records and documents of companies registered in 'England and Wales' or in Wales are handled at Companies House in Cardiff to which companies must complete an annual return. They must also present their annual reports and accounts to Companies House, where they are publicly available for inspection. They must hold annual general meetings at which directors present reports to members (that is, shareholders). The letters 'Ltd' in a company name indicate a privately-owned concern, 'PLC' indicates a company whose shares are traded on the open market. If it wishes, a private company can apply to be listed on the stock exchange, in which case it can issue shares and raise capital by selling them on the open market. It then becomes a publicly limited company (PLC). The larger PLCs are not controlled by any one individual or family, or even by a group of partners. Instead, their shares are traded and can be bought and sold by anyone. In practice, the big majority of the shares in such companies are owned by institutional shareholders such as pension funds, investment funds and insurance companies.

In Scotland, the equivalent of Companies House in Cardiff is located in Edinburgh. Registration and administration of companies in Scotland is under the jurisdiction of Scots law.

The Northern Ireland administrative equivalent is in Belfast but is effectively a satellite office of Companies House in Cardiff.

HRM in the private sector

PLCs almost always employ teams of HR specialists to carry out much of their people management work. A substantial HR division or department will exist, headed by a senior director who will often report directly to the chief executive.

Companies vary in terms of how powerful their HR directors and HR functions are, but the trend is towards the function's assuming a higher profile. In recent years HR in large PLCs has become increasingly strategic in its orientation, focused on longer-term decision-making and proactively supporting the achievement of key business objectives. Administrative HR work has tended to be delegated to line mangers, outsourced or centralised in shared-service arrangements. The same trends can be observed in larger partnerships, but here they tend to be less well advanced. The bigger law firms, for example, have started to set up discrete HR functions in recent years. But HR managers report to senior partners and often struggle to develop cutting-edge HR strategies of the kind we associate with publicly limited companies.

Smaller private companies, partnerships and sole trading organisations do not in the main have sizeable HR functions. They may employ an HR specialist or two to carry out basic HR tasks (recruitment, payroll, training, and so on), but they do not generally have sufficient numbers of employees to justify the presence of a sophisticated, strategically focused HR department. Such organisations invariably rely on outside help when managing HRM matters. Many nowadays pay for advice from employment law consultancies and outsource their payroll function. They often make extensive use of recruitment consultants and buy in required training as and when they need it. HR managers in smaller organisations thus tend to be generalists, taking responsibility for the full range of standard HR activities we described in Chapter 1 and, often, many other management tasks too.

In most smaller firms there remains a preference for informality in the way that managers deal with staff (Edwards and Ram 2010). Features of HR practice that are almost standard in larger companies – such as performance appraisal, clear disciplinary procedures, standardised induction programmes, pay spines, pension schemes and written policies on employment matters – are often absent or undeveloped in smaller firms. There are advantages and disadvantages arising from informality. On the positive side, it allows the retention of a family atmosphere which is conducive to effective teamworking and high levels of job satisfaction. Flexible working is also the norm in an informal employment setting, as is open communication between managers and employees. On the negative side, informality can easily lead to perceptions of unfairness and undue favouritism arising. The absence of clear policies which are generally applied means that 'one rule' does not apply to all. The result is demotivation and reduced job satisfaction.

Larger private sector companies, particularly those operating in the **knowledge economy**, have pioneered most of the new approaches to the management of people that have proved influential in recent years. These have tended to focus on delayering management hierarchies and empowering employees, the aim being to benefit from positive engagement, a willingness to share ideas and the extra effort that can result when a sustained and genuine attempt is made to involve and inspire people.

Another major recent trend in the private sector has been a reduced role for trade unions and for **collective bargaining** as the major means of determining pay and conditions. Trade unions remain a significant presence in road haulage, mining, energy production, construction and in car manufacturing, but across most of the private sector their role is nowadays, at best, marginal. The most recent **Workplace Employment Relations Survey** (WERS) reported that 49% of UK workplaces employing more than 25 people have no union members at all, which means a good majority of private sector organisations (Kersley et al 2006, p11). This trend has allowed the HR function to revolutionise itself in many organisations. Whereas 40 years ago most large companies participated in national-level collective bargaining exercises which set the same terms and conditions for all employees across an industry, it is now more common for pay determination to be individualised. Pay rises are conditional on effective personal performance, other conditions of employment being set by managers without the need for union negotiations. As a result, companies have been able to develop their own distinct HR strategies and to develop 'employee value propositions' (EVPs) which are deliberately distinct from those of their major competitors. The result is considerable competition between employers to attract and retain the best performers. Moreover, as unions have withered away, HR managers have had to find new ways of establishing what employees are really thinking about their employer. We have thus seen much more use of staff survey tools and of upward and downward communication exercises of various kinds.

THE PUBLIC SECTOR

The major types of public sector organisation are:

- central government departments
- local and regional government organisations
- public service providers
- QUANGOs (quasi-autonomous non-governmental organisations)
- publicly-owned corporations.

These are largely if not wholly funded by the taxpayer. They are also subject to a degree of public accountability, being managed either directly or indirectly by elected officials such as ministers, or the majority group on a local council. In the case of public corporations and some **QUANGOs**, ministers have no direct day-to-day responsibility for their management. Around 20% of the UK's workforce is employed in public sector organisations.

There used to be large numbers of public corporations in the UK, but they have almost all now been privatised and have thus become PLCs. However, public corporations remain a major feature of the commercial landscape in many countries. In the UK there are currently three major public corporations: the BBC, the Royal Mail and Network Rail. A fourth, the Bank of England, is technically a publicly-owned corporation. In practice, however, despite the extent of its independence, it has become an integral part of government.

In recent years governments have sought to encourage public service providers to organise themselves according to commercial principles, not only having to meet government targets, but also having to compete for business with other organisations in 'internal markets' and sometimes 'external markets' too.

Public sector organisations tend to have large HR functions which carry considerable managerial clout. HR directors are prominent and influential members of most senior executive boards, enabling them to insist that good HR practice is followed, particularly in respect of legal compliance. HR divisions carry out a wide range of tasks, specialists often being employed to work alongside generalists and to head up recruitment, employment relations, reward management and HRD departments. In recent years, as in larger private sector organisations, moves have been made to make HR more business-focused, more strategic in its activities and less cautious in its approach. But older styles still survive and thrive in many places. As a result, HR practice in the public sector is often criticised by other functions for being a touch old-fashioned, overly bureaucratic in its approach and limited in terms of the value that it adds.

In recent years the major pressures faced by HR managers working in the public sector have derived from the recession of 2007–09 and the subsequent need to reduce public spending in order to reduce the government's financial deficit. This has led to recruitment freezes, extensive reorganisations and to many thousands of redundancies. The HR function is not generally classed by ministers as providing any kind of 'front-line service' and so has been a major target for savings itself. In the process a lot of 'fat' has had to be cut, which has resulted in less bureaucracy, more use of outsourcing arrangements and slimmer HR departments.

There are a number of features which differentiate HRM in public sector organisations from that which prevails across most of the private sector. First, as Bach (2010, p563) points out, employment decisions are 'subject to levels of public accountability and transparency that arise from the government's role as a custodian of public funds'. This inevitably means that a reasonably high standard of management practice has to be observed. People have to be treated with respect and fairness. This tends to be achieved by having in place quite detailed written policies that have to be followed by everyone without exception. There is thus less room for spontaneity in people management than is the case in the private sector and much less opportunity for 'maverick' managers to develop innovative approaches that differ from the norm. HR managers in the public sector tend to be keener than their private sector counterparts to avoid employment tribunal proceedings and are not in a position simply to pay people off with lump sums in order to ensure that cases are not lodged. The result is a tendency towards bureaucracy and much less freedom of manoeuvre for line managers in terms of how they go about leading their teams.

Another distinguishing feature of HRM in the public sector is the continued presence of trade unions. Membership levels vary greatly, but there has not been anything like the decline that has characterised the experience of private companies and PLCs in recent years. Despite attempts by successive governments to introduce performance-related pay and **decentralised bargaining** arrangements, in the main national pay scales still survive across each of the major public services. The amount each person is paid owes much more to how their job is graded than it does to their performance in the job. This means that managers have fewer levers to use in order to motivate their staff and hence exercise less control. If someone is not suitable for promotion, little can be done to motivate them extrinsically. Pay scales are also transparent, everyone effectively knowing what all their colleagues at all levels are paid in relation to them. Trade unions also have the right to be consulted on employment-related matters and can be intransigent in their dealings with managers. Low-trust employment relations climates thus often prevail, which tends to make HR managers rather more cautious in their approach than is the case in the private sector.

REFLECTIVE ACTIVITY 3.1

The 2011 CIPD survey on absence management reported that the average number of days of absence in the UK is 7.7 per employee, a figure that has come down significantly in recent years. There remain, however, big differences between organisations. In smaller private sector companies, rates of 3 or 4 days a year are achieved, while in the bigger public sector organisations it is common for average absence figures to be in excess of 10 days per employee over the course of a year.

1 What factors do you think might explain why overall absence levels in the UK have fallen in the last four or five years?

2 Why do you think that absence rates in public sector organisations are typically so much higher than those in private sector companies?

THE THIRD SECTOR

This comprises organisations that do not fit either into the public sector or private sector categories. They are either:

- co-operatives
- campaigning organisations or pressure groups
- charities
- controlled by boards of trustees and are subject to the law of trust

    or

- are chartered bodies such as universities and professional bodies.

These organisations are run on a not-for-profit basis and are neither subject to direct government control nor to company law. In some countries the terms 'community sector' and 'civic sector' are more commonly used to describe the third sector.

HR varies vastly across the third sector organisations. In some it is well resourced and operates very much as it does in a large PLC or public sector organisation. Resources, however, are often a problem, particularly in charities and in smaller campaigning organisations. Here HR tends to have quite a peripheral role, is not represented on the senior management team and carries out what are essentially basic, administrative activities. HR practices therefore tend to lack sophistication and there is little opportunity for HR managers to add significant strategic value. Developing a more sophisticated, commercially minded approach to HR has thus tended to preoccupy senior HR people working in the third sector in recent years.

Kelliher and Parry (2011), drawing on analysis of the data on voluntary organisations collected for the 2004 Workplace Employment Relations Survey, conclude that there have been major attempts in recent years to professionalise HRM in the sector and that these have had considerable success. In particular they found evidence of increased use of formal performance management mechanisms, employee welfare programmes, written policies of various kinds and employee involvement initiatives. Interestingly they conclude that the model the voluntary bodies tend to imitate is closer to that of the public sector than to the private sector's commercially-oriented alternative. This, they think, is because government, and particularly local government, exercises a growing and profound influence over the third sector. Voluntary organisations are increasingly involved in contracting for services that are either wholly or partially publicly funded. They do not secure these contracts unless they are able to satisfy public bodies that they operate the same high standards of HRM practice. James (2011) agrees with this analysis, but argues that reductions in available resources in more recent years are forcing voluntary sector organisations to downgrade HRM standards again, reducing pay and conditions in order to secure public contracts.

DEVELOPMENTS IN THE EXTERNAL ENVIRONMENT

Just as HR practice tends to vary from sector to sector, it also necessarily has to change in response to major developments in the external business environment. As these affect some organisations more than others and in different ways, the impact on HR is also varied.

The external environment is huge in its scope and complex. It covers developments in the worlds of politics, economics and technology at national, international and local level. It also encompasses major trends in social attitudes and behaviour, population and in government regulation. In one short chapter it is not possible to deal with all of these issues. So we have to be selective and focus on those trends which are having, in combination, the biggest impact on contemporary HR practice. Two which stand out can loosely be defined as relating to 'developments in product markets' and 'developments in labour markets'.

KEY CONTEMPORARY DEVELOPMENTS IN PRODUCT MARKETS

In recent years we have seen very profound changes occurring in the operation of markets for goods and services. The net result has been a very substantial increase in the extent to which pretty well all organisations in countries such as the UK are obliged to compete with others. In some industries, such as financial services and technology, competition has become particularly intense. Some economists now describe the position in some industries as being 'hyper-competitive' in that no single organisation, however large, is able to hold on to a position of competitive advantage for long (McNamara et al 2003).

Measuring competitive intensity in any precise, objective way is impossible because the characteristics of each industry vary so much. But all the proxy indices which are typically used, such as reductions in the length of time leading firms are able to maintain dominance of a market, increases in the extent of churn in 'industry membership' and increases in the incidence of financial instability in an industry, have all been accelerating in recent years. Moreover, interview-based studies which draw on the reflections of people who have spent their careers in particular industries also suggest much increased competition and, more importantly, the likelihood of greater competitive intensity in the future. Some industries have been much more affected than others, but everywhere, including in the public services, competition between providers has been increasing and accelerating in terms of its intensity over the past three or four decades.

The major causes of increased competitive intensity have been widely studied. There are three that are particularly important, none of which shows any signs of moving in a different direction – globalisation, technology and government policy.

Globalisation

Since the end of World War II we have seen a steady growth in the extent to which goods and services are traded internationally and to which national economies have integrated across the world. Dicken (2011) explains that during the second half of the twentieth century, while total world output (that is, the value of goods and services produced and consumed) increased sixfold, the volume of world trade increased twentyfold. Moreover, the trend has accelerated considerably in the past two decades, with the rise of China as a major exporter, industrial development in agricultural economies throughout Asia, Africa and South America, and the reintegration of the Eastern European countries into the world economy.

The impact on competitive intensity has been huge and very rapid. Companies that previously dominated national markets have found themselves within a few short years simply to be small fry in much bigger international markets. Some UK-based companies have responded by cutting costs dramatically and by outsourcing much of their work to overseas countries where labour costs are lower. Others have abandoned low-cost, lower value-added activities altogether, focusing instead on hi-tech, cutting-edge industrial activities. A third group have either gone under altogether or have survived by merging, being taken over or forming strategic alliances with overseas competitors.

Every major sector has been affected, most profoundly. In the UK some formerly dominant industries are now mere shadows of their former selves, if they exist at all. Shipbuilding, textile manufacturing and mining are all good examples. Labour costs in the UK are simply too high to withstand competition from the developing world. Other traditional industries have survived, but only by embracing new technology and integrating themselves internationally. The car and steel industries are good examples, as is food production. These industries now employ far fewer people than they used to, but are much more productive. Moreover, those who remain employed in them work for overseas-based corporations such as Toyota, Tata and Kraft.

In the UK **globalisation** has brought with it massive industrial restructuring, which is still very much in the process of transforming the industrial landscape. No longer able to earn our living in the world as a manufacturing powerhouse (as was the case for most of our history), like other highly developed economies, we have had to develop our service sector very quickly in order to compete effectively. Despite its recent difficulties, the UK's financial services sector remains pre-eminent in Europe, London being one of the world's three great financial centres. It is three and a half times bigger than Frankfurt and four and a half times bigger than Paris in terms of the amount of business it transacts. In terms of international business (as opposed to domestic business), London is by far the major financial centre in the world. The UK financial services sector is thus a major exporter – earning the country about £20 billion a year in foreign currency. It accounts for between 5% and 10% of national GDP. Alongside financial services we have seen rapid growth in business services (consultancy, accountancy, and so on), cultural industries (film, TV, theatre, computer gaming), in higher education and tourism – all of which are major UK exporters operating very competitively in global markets. At the same time we have seen substantial growth in retailing, hotels and restaurants, leisure services of all kinds (gyms, hairdressers, and so on) and media-related industries of all kinds.

Technology

The advent of new technology is both a major cause of increased globalisation and a driver of increased competitive intensity in its own right. The rapid growth in international trade we discussed above was largely made possible by developments in transportation and in ICTs (information and communication technologies). Put crudely, these twin developments now mean that a consumer in the UK can purchase a product manufactured anywhere in the world with terrific ease and can have that product shipped to their home or office within a few weeks. The World Wide Web and broadband technology in particular (still only a dozen years old) have created a situation in which anyone with the resources to do so can buy any goods or services from anyone else across the planet. Modern container ships circumnavigate the world in eight weeks or so, connecting production lines in China with European and American shopping malls in less than a month. The volume of goods shipped across the world by air (in a few hours) has also grown hugely in the last 20 years as costs have plummeted. The competitive landscape thus continues to be utterly transformed by technology.

Technology drives competition in other ways too – mainly by increasing productivity levels all the time. Organisations which fail to adopt new technologies soon enough find that their cost bases are simply too high to allow them to compete effectively. So there is a big premium now placed on research and development (R&D), organisations being obliged to stay ahead of the technological game just in order to survive. Technologies rapidly become obsolete, rendering companies that rely too heavily on them unproductive and uncompetitive vis-à-vis others.

It is not just a question of productivity, though. Sudden breakthroughs in technology can destroy whole industries, transform them and create new ones very rapidly. At the present time we are witnessing the rapid development of industries in the **biotechnology** sector, for example, creating new medical procedures which are increasing average life expectancy across the world, developing new sources of energy (for example solar panels, biofuels) and increasing agricultural production through genetic modification of seeds and of livestock.

The impact on the competitive environment of all of these developments and of others in **nanotechnology** looks as if they will have as big an impact on our lives over the next 50 years as IT had in the last 50.

Government action

The third major driver of increased competitive intensity in recent decades has been government. As with technology, governments have acted in order to promote globalisation in order to boost international economic development. It has often been a rocky road, steps backwards occurring alongside steps forward. But the overall trend internationally over the past 20 or 30 years has unquestionably been towards the active promotion of global economic exchange.

This has been achieved by a mixture of regulation and deregulation. Of particular importance has been the relaxation and, in many countries, the total abolition of foreign exchange controls. It seems strange now to reflect that 40 years ago people were heavily restricted in the amount of currency they could legally take out of the UK to spend overseas (£60 in the 1960s). Overseas trade was vastly limited as a result, as was tourism. The position has now utterly changed. The USA abandoned restrictions altogether, followed by the UK in 1979. Since then the same has occurred in most countries: 150 now have no meaningful controls. They still remain in major economies such as China and India, but in both cases it is now a question of *when* it would be most prudent to remove them rather than *if.*

At the same time, through the auspices of the **World Trade Organization** (WTO), governments have negotiated major reductions in import tariffs, while customs unions such as the European Union have developed, allowing free movement of capital, goods, services and people across national boundaries. In each case the result has been to foster international competition.

Some industries that were until recently very heavily regulated are now subject to hardly any regulation, transforming their competitive environment. Nowhere is this more true than in the airline industry, which used to be subject to heavy government control. Until the 1990s government officials used to allocate routes to airlines across Europe, a practice that continued until 2008 as far as trans-Atlantic routes were concerned. National flag-carrying airlines (British Airways, Lufthansa, Air France, and so on) were owned and operated by governments and took all the most profitable routes, leaving only the less profitable 'pickings' for a small independent sector to mop up. Open skies policies are now proliferating across the world. Government has withdrawn, permitting airlines to compete with one another to fly routes that are agreed with the airports without ministerial interference. The volume of air traffic has increased massively as a result, the competitive structure of the industry being transformed with the rise of low-cost carriers such as easyJet and Ryanair, which are now as big as many of the national carriers.

Another major deregulatory step of great significance has been the move towards **privatisation** of state-run industries. The UK pioneered this approach in the 1980s when the Thatcher Government privatised most state-run corporations, including British Telecom, British Steel, British Airways, British Gas, the train and bus companies, the electricity and water generators, the mines, the car manufacturers, the airports and a host of smaller concerns. Wherever possible, privatisation was accompanied by the breaking up of corporations into separate parts that were thenceforth obliged to compete with one another in free markets. Subsequent governments continued to privatise where they could, also seeking to engineer commercial discipline in the public services. Internal markets were created in the health and education sectors, competitive tendering being introduced in many areas so that private concerns (companies and charities) competed with one another for contracts to provide public services. All over the world governments have been taking a similar approach in recent years, privatising state assets, creating markets and generally pursuing an agenda of 'competition and choice'.

It is important to remember, though, that regulation has played an important part in this process alongside deregulation. Globalisation has been promoted in large part by establishing standardised approaches through international conventions. Hence we now see the same standard size of containers shipped around the world and lifted onto the back of lorries and trains for distribution. Airline tickets, where they are still used, take the same form, and we have also seen the standardisation of accountancy conventions. Copyright is increasingly well protected by international law, as are patents and property rights. Within the European Union extensive regulation is seen as a necessary prerequisite for free trade between members states. It ensures 'a level playing field' (that is, fair competition) and means, for example, that extensive employment law has been passed and can be enforced at the European level.

COMPETITIVE INTENSITY AND HRM

Increased competitive intensity and, particularly, increased global competition have necessitated a transformation of management thinking in organisations – a revolution that we are still very much in the middle of. HRM has had to change in response and continues to do so. The impact has been greatest in industrial sectors, which have felt the full force of technological change and globalisation, but there are few parts of the public sector that have been untouched. Even the armed services, the prison service and the police are now obliged to contract out parts of their operations. In addition, of course, they like all the rest of the public sector have to become a great deal more productive in order to help meet the government's deficit reduction plans.

So what does all of this mean for HRM practice? A number of major points can be made. First, and most significantly, increased competitive intensity brings with it uncertainty and unpredictability. This means that organisations cannot plan ahead with any great certainty beyond three or four years, in some cases less. Whereas in the past it made sense to develop strategic plans that focused ten or twenty years ahead, this is less and less possible. The volatility of markets has rendered this sort of approach much less plausible.

The knock-on effect on HRM is profound because uncertainty in product markets has necessarily meant that organisations are less able than they once were to offer long-term, stable employment to anyone. Even where this is possible, contracts need to be written in such a way as to allow for considerable flexibility. We may still remain employed with the same organisations for many years, but increasingly our roles change regularly as a result of internal reorganisations and we are obliged to retrain and embrace new approaches regularly. In short, organisations have had to become a great deal more agile. They regularly have to morph as a result of exercises in downsizing, upsizing, outsourcing, offshoring and mergers and acquisitions. Companies become part of a big international group, then get reorganised and sold on. Management buyouts occur, while contracts are won and lost, resulting in parts of an organisation growing while others are shrinking.

As far as HRM is concerned, a key implication is a need to be actively and much more frequently involved in change management than used to be the case. All the research on the effective management of organisational change (cultural and structural) demonstrates clearly that success or failure depends in large extent on how effectively the 'people aspects' are managed. This requires active involvement by HR people, including at the most senior levels, in the planning and communication of change. This has required HR people to acquire more political skills, because change is very often a deeply political process. There are winners and there are losers, there are perceived winners and losers and there are people who, while not hugely affected personally, are allies of perceived winners and losers.

Change also therefore tends to breed conflict. Managing these matters is very difficult. It involves sensitivity in terms of management style, combined with a hard-headed appreciation of commercial realities. Moreover, there is a need to have in place policies and practices which allow an organisation to become increasingly agile and able to respond more rapidly than its competitors can to changed circumstances in the business environment. This tends to mean less bureaucracy and much more flexibility. Administrative convenience is less and less possible to use as a reason for not changing rapidly when it is necessary to do so. HR also needs actively to build a culture which embraces change and expects it. Central here is the development of a generation of leaders who are emotionally intelligent, politically savvy, flexible, good at communication of all kinds and very well informed about wider developments in the business environment.

Flexibility has also become central to HRM practice. People are increasingly employed on non-standard or atypical contracts. We employ many more people on a short-term basis, for example, to avoid a need to make people redundant during periods of change. We also employ more people on a part-time basis but without fixed hours, so that they can be deployed flexibly as required. There is more sub-contracting, more employment of self-employed professionals, much more employment of agency workers and more use of annual hours and zero hours (that is, casual contracts). This marks a very significant change in HRM, which has traditionally focused on employing people on traditional, permanent, full-time contracts with an intention of forging a long-term relationship with them. Atypical contracting makes people management much harder to achieve effectively simply because there is no expectation of a long-term, stable relationship. Promising pay rises and future promotions as a means of exercising management control becomes less plausible, as does securing employee commitment generally. How can we say to people 'We want you to work really hard and demonstrate great commitment to us' if at the same time we as managers are less and less able to show commitment to our staff?

Secondly, increased competitive intensity inevitably leads to greater work intensity. It is only possible to compete effectively internationally if we match and beat the levels of productivity that our competitors are able to achieve. This means that we are continually obliged to look for ways of 'achieving more with less' and, in short, extracting greater effort from our people at minimal cost. Technology plays a big part here, but it is also increasingly a matter simply of finding ways of encouraging people to work harder without paying them more. This can be done using harsh management techniques, such as threatening people with the sack if they do not increase their work rates.

HRM, however, is increasingly associated with the development of more sophisticated approaches to the management of performance which try to intensify work in a more positive manner, extracting greater effort from staff in ways which benefit them as well as the organisation. You will be reading about all of these later in this book as well as in other books in the series, so it is only necessary to summarise here. Major examples are the evolution of 'high commitment working practices', performance-related and profit-related pay, accelerated management development programmes, employer branding, employability initiatives, employee involvement exercises, strengths-based management thinking and, most important of all, HR practices which serve actively to engage staff in their work and with their organisations.

Thirdly, it is important to appreciate that increased competitive intensity is also having a profound effect on the way the HR function organises itself and approaches its objectives. Like all management functions, HR has to organise its own activities so as to be as efficient as possible. In recent years this has led to the adoption in many organisations of innovative approaches which involve HR professionals specialising rather than taking a traditional generalist role. Business partners work closely with line managers on day-to-day casework, while others manage HR administration out of shared-service centres. They are then supported by expert trainers, reward specialists, employment lawyers and recruiters, many of whom are employed as sub-contractors. Another major change that the HR function itself is having to get used to is the need continually and effectively to justify its own existence. This can no longer be taken for granted in a highly competitive business environment. The function is thus increasingly obliged not just to add value, but also to demonstrate that it does so – and in raw financial terms too.

REFLECTIVE ACTIVITY 3.2

Think about a major HR activity such as recruitment, management development or reward management.

In respect of one or all of these, how can HR managers go about evaluating their contribution to organisation success and then demonstrating this in financial terms?

KEY CONTEMPORARY DEVELOPMENTS IN LABOUR MARKETS

The term 'labour market' refers to the market for staff and their skills that employers compete in so as to ensure that they can employ the best people in the jobs they have available. Like all markets, labour markets operate according to the rules of supply and demand. Ultimately this means that employers who can offer the best terms and conditions, the best chance of long-term job security, the best career development opportunities – or all three – give themselves the best opportunity of recruiting and retaining the strongest performers. And it is not just employers that compete in labour markets; would-be employees do too, as do existing employees vying with one another for promotion.

There are many contemporary developments in labour markets which are having an impact on HR practice. We only have space here briefly to summarise some of the most striking and significant of these: increasing cultural diversity, increasing regulation and increasing inequality in UK labour markets.

Cultural diversity

In recent years we have seen a substantial increase in the level of international migration. According to the United Nations, in 2010 there were 214 million people living long term in a country other than the one they were born in. Of these, the vast majority are part of a group labelled 'economic migrants', meaning that their major motivation in moving across an international border was the wish to earn more money or to develop their careers. Numbers of international migrants have been growing for most of the past 50 years, but there has been a substantial acceleration in the past decade. Back in 1970 the UN estimated that just 81.5 million people fell into this category.

Large numbers of people both leave the UK and enter it each year, but since the early 1990s we have seen rising net inward migration. In the year to June 2011, government statistics record that an estimated 593,000 people entered the UK to stay for a period of a year or more.

This compares with 343,000 people leaving. These figures are very similar to those that have been recorded in most recent years, allowing us to conclude that net inward immigration into the UK is currently running at around 250,000 a year.

The result has been a fast period of growth in the UK's overall population (now well over 62 million) and far greater levels of cultural diversity. Moreover, because people entering the UK tend on average to be rather younger than those who leave, the impact on the diversity of our labour markets is greater still, particularly in the major urban areas, where immigrants from overseas tend to prefer to settle.

The implications of this trend for HRM have been profound and are likely to become more prominent in the future. Put simply, we are now obliged to manage and make effective teams of staff from all over the world who have a variety of different cultural backgrounds. Furthermore, the globalisation of business activity means that UK-born employees are far more likely than they were in the past to be working in international corporations and reporting to senior management teams that are themselves culturally diverse.

Over many years extensive research has been carried out into cultural variations between workplaces across the world (for example, Hofstede 1980, 1991, Trompenaars 1993, House et al 2004). While there are disagreements between the authors about the detailed conclusions, all find evidence of substantial differences between countries across a range of measures. In other words, it makes complete sense and is entirely accurate to talk about a defined 'UK business culture'. This is similar to those found in other 'Anglo-Saxon' countries such as the USA, Canada and Australia, and also quite similar to the workplace culture in the Netherlands, but is nonetheless quite distinct in key respects. Moreover, it is much more different from the prevailing cultures found in Southern Europe, in the Scandinavian countries, in Eastern Europe and across Asia and Africa.

International migrants, and particularly those who work as **expatriates** on behalf of their companies in relatively senior roles overseas, often find it difficult to acclimatise to their new workplace cultures and to work effectively in them. Multicultural teams therefore need careful and sensitive management if they are to operate successfully. As Richard Sennett (2012) rightly argues, effective co-operation with people who are different from ourselves is a skill that has to be learned. Goodwill alone is not enough. We cannot simply assume that everyone will fit in naturally and work well with one another. There is a major training and development role here, the significance of induction and socialisation programmes being particularly important. Everyone's expectations need to be managed and people have to become a great deal more culturally aware in order to help ensure that international diversity becomes the very real strength that it can become rather than a cause of sub-optimal performance.

Regulation

A second labour market trend of great significance has been the considerable increase we have seen over recent years in the amount of regulation that employers are obliged to take account of when employing people.

A generation ago the UK was highly unusual internationally in having very little employment law. The long-held consensus here was that the state was best staying out of the way as far as the employment relationship was concerned. Strong trade unions and national/industry-level collective agreements helped to protect social justice at work, ensuring that people were not overworked, underpaid or dismissed for no good reason. The situation has now wholly changed, giving the UK one of the most regulated labour markets in the world. Change started to occur in the 1960s with the introduction of regulations that required employers to make severance payments to their staff when making them redundant. The 1970s then saw the introduction of equal pay law, sex and race discrimination law, unfair dismissal law, comprehensive health and safety legislation and the right to take paid maternity leave. More recently we have seen the extension of many of these rights as well as many additions to them in the form (to name just a few) of disability discrimination law, age discrimination law, the National Minimum Wage, working time rights, a variety of trade union legislation and new rights for agency workers, fixed-term employees and part-timers.

There are now more than 80 separate types of claim that can be heard in the employment tribunal and many others that are employment-related but which remain the preserve of the county court and the High Court. More than 200,000 tribunal cases are lodged each year, these cases tending to become more complex over time as the body of case law that the courts are obliged to follow grows over time. Governments periodically assure the business community that they intend to 'reduce the burden' of employment regulation, but in practice this rarely happens – if at all – to any significant degree.

Here too the impact on the practice of HRM has been profound. As long ago as 2002, before much recent legislation was passed, a CIPD survey found that two-thirds of HR specialists were spending in excess of 20% of their time 'dealing with employment law issues', while a further quarter reported apparently spending 40% of their working time on such matters (CIPD 2002). In a further CIPD survey carried out five years later, 'securing compliance with employment regulations' was one of the top five objectives for 40% of HR professionals, while 90% saw employment regulation as likely to become more important for their organisations in the future (CIPD 2007).

Many organisations nowadays have simply decided, as a matter of policy, not to fight employment tribunal claims. They do this not because they don't think they can win them, but simply because the costs and sheer hassle that are involved with mounting a defence nearly always outweigh the costs of settling cases out of court by a substantial margin. But there are still costs, so even in such organisations HR people need to be continually aware of how their actions and those of line managers may have potential legal consequences, even if there is no intention whatever of acting outside the law. This is particularly true when hiring and firing staff, but as the increasing case load in areas such as working time, unlawful deduction from wages and whistleblowing testifies, the need for legal vigilance extends across almost all HR activities. Risks continually have to be assessed, and in order that this can be done in a timely and effective manner, HR officers now need as a matter of necessity to possess a good working knowledge of employment legislation. They also need to have access to advice in the form of lawyers, consultants and/or reference materials.

Labour market inequality

A third key development is one that shows every sign of growing in importance in the future. This is the tendency for the UK labour market to take on 'an hourglass' character over time (see Nolan 2001, Goos and Manning 2003). That is to say that we are seeing the emergence of a divergence between conditions in markets for higher-level skills (that is, professional, managerial, graduate jobs) and markets for lower-skilled jobs that are suited to people who do not have higher-level qualifications.

Mainly as a result of globalisation and the industrial restructuring that has had to follow in its wake, the vast majority of new jobs and of new job vacancies that are now being created in the UK economy are higher-skilled, higher-paid roles that require people who can bring with them considerable experience as well as specific skills. The problem is that the stock of skills in the UK labour market is rather lower. As was pointed out in the government-sponsored **Leitch Report** (2006), the UK's performance in educating its people to meet the needs of our evolving knowledge economy is 'mediocre' by international standards. In short, over time we are building an economy that has too many opportunities for highly skilled people, and far too few for lower-skilled people – hence the hourglass effect. There are more jobs than there are jobseekers in the top half of the hourglass, even during the recent recession. This means that these labour markets are relatively tight and that employers struggle to recruit and retain strong performers. Wages are pushed up as a result and job-holders are treated well. By contrast, the opposite is the case in the lower half of the hourglass. Here there are many more people with limited skills and experience chasing relatively few jobs. As a result there is downward pressure on wages and little reason for employers to increase the quality of jobs. They know that when someone leaves they will have no problem filling the vacancy quickly.

From a practical HR perspective it is developments in the top half of the hourglass that pose the greatest challenges. Severe skills shortages emerged in these labour markets in the early years of the twenty-first century, resulting in the evolution of 'a war for talent' as employers fought harder to recruit and retain appropriately qualified people. The heat was taken out of this battle during the recession years, although even then CIPD surveys reported that a good majority of employers struggled to recruit some groups of higher-skilled staff.

As the economy recovers in future years, there is every reason to anticipate that skills shortages will return, pushing effective and smart recruitment and retention back up to the top of the HR management agenda. Importantly, other factors are likely to make these high-skill labour markets even tighter in the future. The retirement of the large Baby Boom generation (born in the 20 years following World War II) is now progressing, there being some 3 million fewer people in Generation Y (born 1985–2004) coming into the labour market to replace them. In addition, we are now seeing quite serious efforts being made by government ministers to reduce net inward migration into the UK. In the future employers are going to be much less able than was the case to rely on overseas immigrants as a supply of skills that are in short supply. In addition, the considerable rise in female participation that occurred during the past 40 years can now be judged largely to have run its course. As many women are now in paid work in the UK as in pretty much anywhere else in the world (75% or so). This is a huge change from the position in the 1950s and 1960s, when the majority of women did not work outside the home. So here we have three reasons – Baby Boomers, overseas migrants and women – that can explain how supply of labour kept up with demand for labour in the past, which are going to have much less impact in the future. In short, there are going to be fewer people looking for work in the future vis-à-vis demand and, more importantly, far too few who are qualified to do the jobs that the economy is creating fastest.

REFLECTIVE ACTIVITY 3.3

You attend a conference for HRM professionals at which a speaker argues that 'the credit crunch is temporary, but the talent crunch is permanent'. She goes on to argue that employers should not lose sight of this reality when managing people in the tough economic times.

Explain what exactly the speaker means in making this statement.

Comment on its relevance for your organisation or one that you are familiar with.

FORMING ORGANISATIONAL AND HR STRATEGIES

In the first parts of this chapter we have tried to explain why HR practice in organisations varies so much, and indeed why it should vary. The business context is different across the private, public and voluntary sectors, resulting in necessarily different approaches to HR. At the same time some organisations are much more affected by increasing competitive intensity than others are, while some have seen their labour markets become much more culturally diverse than others. There is also much variation in the extent to which organisations are affected by skills shortages. In this final section we focus on organisational responses to developments in the business environment. How do business strategies get formed? And what kinds of alternatives are available when shaping HR strategies to support them?

A focus of much academic debate in the field of business strategy has been on the issue of how, in practice, strategy is formulated by organisations. Here it is possible to distinguish three basic alternative approaches:

1 rational/classical

2 emergent/logical incrementalism

3 symbolic/radical.

First there is what is known as the rational approach, which is often characterised as being the 'classical' or 'mainstream' approach. Here the task of strategy-making is entrusted to senior managers. Their job is to undertake a continual appraisal of both the external and internal environments (using tools such as **SWOT analysis**) and to use this information to formulate goals, aims or objectives for the organisation.

Having chosen the strategic direction, the next task is to put it into effect by organising appropriately, and particularly by gathering together the necessary resources (raw materials, technologies, capital, people). Central to the rational model is the idea that organisations should appraise different possible strategic courses of action, evaluate them all and then make a choice. This might involve an organisation which consists of several separate businesses, shedding some in order to focus investment on another. Alternatively, it might involve a business competing in one defined market seeking to increase its share by developing new products, moving existing products up-market or cutting its costs so as to reduce prices.

The idea of emergent strategies originates in the work of analysts such as James Quinn (1980), who studied, in depth, what actually happened in organisations. He found that in practice the rational strategy formulated at senior levels influenced the actual strategic direction an organisation took, but that other factors also intervened, so that the organisation ended up pursuing a rather different strategy. In practice what happens is that a strategy emerges incrementally over time as an organisation responds to the realities of its environmental position opportunistically. Trial and error determines what happens as much as any rationally planned top-down strategy.

The approach is sometimes labelled 'logical incrementalism' in that each step taken is logical and consistent, but is not planned many years or months in advance. Senior managers set general goals, but responsibility in formulating a strategy for getting there lies in the hands of people throughout the organisation, responding to situations as they arise.

The third approach (symbolic) turns the whole process on its head. In practice, it argues, most organisations get on with the business of competing, evolving tactics as they go, trying different things and sticking with things that work well. In other words, they muddle through opportunistically, often succeeding because of luck rather than judgement. They then formulate a written strategy in response. In other words, in reality the tail wags the dog. Implementation precedes the formulation of a strategy. We try things, find which work best and then retrospectively articulate this as our strategy. According to this view, strategy formulation is merely a symbolic action designed to give an organisation gravitas and credibility. In practice, little strategic leadership occurs; what we say is our strategy is actually just a post-hoc rationalisation of what we actually do.

Henry Mintzberg is the most influential thinker in this field of study. He is also well known for having formulated a contingency model which sets out the circumstances when the above types of strategy-formation process are appropriate. He suggests that the key variables are the complexity of the organisation and its environment and the rate of change in that environment. These, he states, can be different for different organisations at different times, so the type of approach used for strategy-making which is most appropriate will itself vary over time.

Figure 3.1 Change and complexity

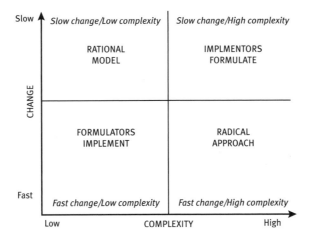

The top left-hand box indicates organisations which operate in relatively stable circumstances and which are themselves either small or relatively uncomplicated. Examples would include most small businesses as well as larger organisations which carry out one or two relatively unsophisticated activities – such as a pizza factory, a retail chain which consists of small stores (bakeries, hairdressers, and so on) or a bus company.

Here a rational strategy is possible because the environment is both stable and very readily fully understood. A small team of managers can thus practically develop a business strategy in the classical fashion and implement it. There is little uncertainty and low risk.

The top right-hand box is where organisations that are complex but operate in stable conditions are placed. They are thus faced with moderate uncertainty which derives from the many different environmental trends that impact on them. Examples are major government departments, hospitals and universities. Here an emergent strategy is appropriate and it should be one involving all levels in the organisational hierarchy. Senior managers cannot fully understand all the facets of these organisations and cannot impose a single strategy on the whole organisation.

'Moderate uncertainty' is also a feature of organisations in the bottom left-hand box, but here it derives from the speed of environmental change rather than the complexity of the environment. A small hi-tech company such as an independent software house is a good example. The uncertainty in terms of strategy-formation is there because of continual technological developments. Speed of response is what determines survival. There is no time to formulate a rational strategy and it would be out of date quickly. So an emergent strategy is appropriate, but it has to be one which is formulated and implemented by the same people. The manager decides what to do and does it, but the strategy itself develops in response to changes in the environment.

Finally, the bottom right-hand box contains organisations that are both complex and also faced with a fast-changing environment. A large hi-tech organisation is an example, or an international bank – or any large international organisation. Here the level of uncertainty is high, both because of the organisation's complexity and the speed of change. Rational strategic planning serves no purpose, so an opportunistic, decentralised approach to decision-making is needed. This is then rationalised, post hoc, by senior managers in the form of a strategy document. It impresses investors, but it does not really drive decision-making on a day-to-day basis.

Mintzberg's two big ideas then come together in his argument that organisations are becoming increasingly complex and environments increasingly fast-changing – hence greater uncertainty and 'discontinuity'; hence the 'fall' of traditional, rational approaches to strategy-formation.

CONTINGENCY THINKING

As far as HRM is concerned, it is having a defined strategy to respond to that matters more than how that strategy is arrived at. Where an organisation opts for a classical, rational approach to strategy-making, it is not difficult for HR managers to see clearly what are the organisation's key strategic objectives. This is sometimes a lot less straightforward in the case of emergent or symbolic strategy-making because it is not always clear precisely what the strategic priorities are at any one time and how they are likely to evolve in the future. Nonetheless, it is self-evident that some clarity needs to be established if a meaningful HR strategy is to be developed which supports the wider organisational strategy and enhances the likelihood that it will be successfully achieved.

For many years managers have made use of contingency thinking and contingency models in order to help them align HR strategies with business strategies. Numerous such models have been published over the years, all of which can be very useful tools in helping to clarify the sort of approach to follow. These are best understood by looking at examples such as Michael Porter's (1985) highly influential model, which focused on the major alternative ways that organisations gain competitive advantage. Here Porter identified three core alternative strategies that firms follow:

- cost leadership (that is, value for money)
- differentiation (via quality enhancement or innovation)
- focus.

The third approach involves using either the cost leadership or the differentiation approaches, but in a niche market, or a specific market segment – one sex, one income group, one geographical area, one age group, one definable type of lifestyle, and so on. So in practice Porter argues that an organisation has a choice of three major strategies to use in order to compete effectively: it can produce goods and services that are cheaper than those of its competitors, it can produce goods and services that are of higher quality (and hence more expensive) or, finally, it can produce goods and services that are more innovative than those of its competitors.

Porter's generic strategy model has been attacked not because it isn't true and useful, but because of his claim that organisations will not gain competitive advantage if they pursue a hybrid strategy. According to Porter, your chances of success are highest when you plump for one of the three and pursue it strongly. Later critics (notably Johnson et al 2010) have argued not only that hybrid strategies can succeed just as well, but that in the modern business environment it is necessary to achieve all three simultaneously – high quality, low price, innovative and able to appeal to niche markets as well as mass markets. But it is accepted that this is difficult to achieve in practice.

From an HR point of view, the kind of policies and practices that need to be in place in order effectively to support each of Porter's three sources of competitive advantage are different (Schuler and Jackson 1987). For example, where an organisation pursues a strategy of cost leadership, the HR strategy will inevitably be focused on keeping the overall wage bill at as low a level as possible. That may mean paying at below-market rates and managing the consequences in terms of recruitment, retention and morale. Or it may mean paying well but requiring staff to be a great deal more productive than those of competitors who pursue different strategies. Cost leadership tends to be associated with bureaucracy, low levels of employee involvement and a lack of sophisticated, cutting-edge approaches to HR that set out to engage staff positively by developing them. By contrast, a strategy that is focused on innovation requires a heavy focus first on recruiting and retaining people with specialised skills and then encouraging them to take risks, share ideas and act creatively. Finally, a strategy that is concerned with quality enhancement is likely to lead to HR policies which enable employees to meet the highest customer expectations. This requires relatively high pay, genuine employee involvement, good training and development opportunities and a consultative management style.

There are numerous other contingency models that take a similar approach. Among the best known and most influential are those derived from the Boston Consulting Model (Purcell 1989), which suggests how HR practices should vary depending on an organisation's relative market share and whether or not its markets are growing or in decline. Miles and Snow (1978), by contrast, focus in their model on identifying the appropriate HR practices for different types of competitive strategy – defensive, prospecting or analysing.

All of these, and several others, have the same strengths and weaknesses. They are effective guides that help the HR function in organisations to think strategically about their activities and about how they can best add value. However, they are also rather one-dimensional and prescriptive, failing to take account of all manner of variables that might actually make a different strategic approach appropriate in a particular case. For example, they take no account of an organisation's competitive position vis-à-vis its labour markets. A company facing severe skills shortages, for example, has no choice often but to push up its wages simply in order to attract and retain the workforce it needs in order to operate – whatever business strategy it is pursuing.

Contingency thinking in HRM has also been widely criticised by the 'best practice school', a group of highly influential thinkers who argue that whatever strategy an organisation adopts, from an HR point of view the same basic bundle of practices needs to be followed in order to enhance its chances of success (Pfeffer 1994, Huselid 1995, Purcell et al 2003). There is no need to differentiate according to wider organisational policy. If you take a sophisticated approach to the management of people, selecting the best staff, paying them according to their individual performance, involving them in decision-making and providing them with job security and career development opportunities, the result is likely to be an effective workforce that is motivated to put in the effort required to deliver wider organisational objectives, whatever they are.

RESOURCE-BASED THINKING

Another widely discussed approach to the formation of HR strategy takes a rather different perspective. Theories developed from 'the **resource-based view of the firm** (RBV)' are sometimes described as using 'inside-out' thinking rather than the 'outside-in' thinking that characterises contingency theories. Here the analysis starts with an audit of an organisation's existing resources in terms of their key competitive strengths. This extends well beyond people management concerns to take account of all potential strengths (goodwill, brands, physical resources, and so on), but there is also a very important potential role for HRM to play.

The key to understanding RBV is to appreciate that organisations typically enjoy attributes that are both strengths competitively and that also differentiate them in key respects from their competitors. Having established what these are, resource-based thinking requires that ways are found of protecting, enhancing and reinforcing them so as to build towards sustained competitive advantage over time. Barney (1991) argues that the focus needs to be on understanding which resources (including human resources) are most:

- valuable

- rare

- inimitable (that is, hard for competitors to replicate)
- non-substitutable.

As far as the HRM contribution is concerned, this kind of analysis may lead to the identification of particular individuals whose significance is so great that the organisation simply cannot afford to lose them to a competitor. However, more often there are factors which are not readily defined, such as a type of organisational culture, a body of knowledge that is collectively held, a positive reputation as an employer or simply a stock of skills. Whatever they are, the prime aim of a resource-based HR strategy is to protect, enhance and reinforce these key strengths.

CASE STUDY

THE NEW COLLEGE OF THE HUMANITIES

In the summer of 2010 the philosopher A. C. Grayling announced that he and a group of other high-profile academics were to found a new university in London. The New College of the Humanities (NCH) would operate as a private institution, wholly independent of government and funded privately. Each year its students would register, along with 50,000 others from across the world, as members of the University of London International Programmes, sitting existing exams and following existing syllabuses. However, rather than studying overseas using distance learning materials, NCH students would be based in Bloomsbury, central London, where they would receive outstanding teaching from the world's leading academics.

Despite the project being highly controversial and being much criticised in the press, the college opens in October 2012 offering five degree programmes – economics, English, history, law and philosophy. It has had no difficulty attracting applicants and appears likely to be able to survive and thrive from a financial point of view. 200 students will enroll each year to start, with numbers steadily expanding to 400 over time.

NCH charges annual fees of £18,000, twice the maximum that universities accepting government funding are able to charge. However, 25% of its places are awarded on a scholarship basis, reducing the fees to £7,200. In return its students are guaranteed a staff-student ratio of 1:10, 13 contact hours each week, one-to-one tutorials and teaching by leading figures in their fields, including major international names such as Richard Dawkins, Niall Ferguson, Steven Pinker and Ronald Dworkin.

Unlike most universities in the UK, the college will be run on a for-profit basis. £10 million of initial finance was raised from private equity, it being intended that NCH will break even and start making a profit for its investors by its third year. Interestingly, a third of the enterprise is owned by A. C. Grayling himself and 13 academic colleagues, who stand to make a considerable amount of money if it is successful and develops a first-rate international reputation.

Questions

1 How would you expect HR policies and practices at the New College of the Humanities to be similar to those in most UK universities? How would you expect them to differ, and why?

2 What trends in the business environment make 2012 a favourable time to be launching an institution of this kind?

3 To what extent could contingency thinking and resource-based thinking about HRM be relevant to NCH, and how?

FURTHER READING

Most of the issues covered in this chapter are discussed at greater length and in more detail in some other books published by the CIPD. *Contemporary Issues in HRM* by Stephen Taylor and *Human Resource Management in Context: Strategy, insights and solutions* by David Farnham are examples.

Texts that focus on the business environment generally, including labour market issues, include *The Business Environment: Themes and issues* edited by Paul Wetherly and Dorron Otter and *The International Business Environment: Challenges and changes* by Ian Brooks and his colleagues.

Global Shift: Mapping the changing contours of the world economy by Peter Dicken, now in its sixth edition, is an excellent introduction to globalisation and its impact on business in recent decades.

REFERENCES

BACH, S. (2010) HRM in the public sector. In: WILKINSON, A., BACON, N. and SNELL, S. (eds) *The Sage handbook of human resource management*. London: Sage.

BARNEY, J. (1991) Firm resources and sustained competitive advantage. *Journal of Management*. Vol 17, No 1. pp99–120.

BROOKS, I., WEATHERSTON, J. and WILKINSON, G. (2010) *The international business environment: challenges and changes*. 2nd edition. London: FT/Prentice Hall.

CIPD (2002) *Employment law: survey report*. London: Chartered Institute of Personnel and Development.

CIPD (2007) *The changing HR function: a survey report*. London: Chartered Institute of Personnel and Development.

DICKEN, P. (2011) *Global shift: mapping the changing contours of the world economy*. 6th edition. London: Sage.

EDWARDS, P. and RAM, M. (2010) HRM in small firms: respecting and regulating informality. In: WILKINSON, A., BACON, N. and SNELL, S. (eds) *The Sage handbook of human resource management*. London: Sage.

FARNHAM, D. (2010) *Human resource management in context: strategy, insights and solutions*. London: Chartered Institute of Personnel and Development.

GOOS, M. and MANNING, A. (2003) McJobs and Macjobs: the growing polarisation of jobs in the UK. In: DICKENS, R., GREGG, P. and WADSWORTH, J. (eds) *The labour market under New Labour*. Basingstoke: Palgrave.

HOFSTEDE, G. (1980) *Culture's consequences: international differences in work-related values*. Beverly Hills, CA: Sage Publications.

HOFSTEDE, G. (1991) *Cultures and organizations: software of the mind*. London: McGraw-Hill.

HOUSE, R., HANGES, P., JAVIDAN, M., DORFMAN, P. and GUPTA, V. (2004) *Culture, leadership and organisations: the GLOBE study of 62 societies*. Thousand Oaks, CA: Sage.

HUSELID, M. (1995) The impact of human resource practices on turnover, productivity and corporate financial performance. *Academy of Management Journal*. Vol 38, No 3. pp635–72.

JAMES, P. (2011) Voluntary sector outsourcing: a reflection on employment-related rationales, developments and outcomes. *International Journal of Public Sector Management*. Vol 24, No 7. pp684–93.

JOHNSON, G., WHITTINGTON, R. and SCHOLES, K. (2010) Exploring strategy: text and cases. 9th edition. New York: FT/ Prentice Hall.

KELLIHER, C. and PARRY, E. (2011) Voluntary sector HRM: examining the influence of government. *International Journal of Public Sector Management*. Vol 24, No 7. pp650–61.

KERSLEY, B., ALPIN, C., FORTH, J., BRYSON, A., BEWLEY, H., DIX, G. and OXENBRIDGE, S. (2006) *Inside the workplace: findings from the 2004 Workplace Employment Relations Survey*. Abingdon: Routledge.

MCNAMARA, G., VAALER, P. and DEVERS, C. (2003) Same as it ever was: the search for evidence of increasing hypercompetition. *Strategic Management Journal*. Vol 24, No 1. pp261–78.

MILES, R. E. and SNOW, C. C. (1978) *Organization strategy, structure and process*. New York: McGraw-Hill.

MINTZBERG, H. (1994) *The rise and fall of strategic planning*. New York: Prentice Hall.

NOLAN, P. (2001) Shaping things to come. *People Management*. 27 December.

PFEFFER, J. (1994) *Competitive advantage through people*. Boston: Harvard University Press.

PORTER, M. E. (1985) Competitive advantage. New York: Free Press.

PURCELL, J. (1989) The impact of corporate strategy on human resource management. In: STOREY, J. (ed.) *New perspectives on human resource management*. London: Routledge.

PURCELL, J., KINNIE, N., HUTCHINSON, S., RAYTON, B. and SWART, J. (2003) *Understanding the people and performance link: unlocking the black box*. London: Chartered Institute of Personnel and Development.

QUINN, B. (1980) *Strategies for change: logical incrementalism*. Homewood, IL: Irwin.

SCHULER, R. and JACKSON, S. (1987) Linking competitive strategies with human resource management. *Academy of Management Executive*. Vol 1, No 3. pp207–19.

SENNETT, R. (2012) *Together: the rituals, pleasures and politics of co-operation*. London: Allen Lane.

TAYLOR, S. (2011) *Contemporary issues in HRM*. London: Chartered Institute of Personnel and Development.

TROMPENAARS, F. (1993) *Riding the waves of culture: understanding cultural diversity in global business*. London: McGraw-Hill.

WETHERLY, P. and OTTER, D. (2011) *The business environment: themes and issues*. 2nd edition. Oxford: Oxford University Press.

CHAPTER 4

Developing professional practice

Ted Johns and Graham Perkins

CHAPTER CONTENTS

- The HR contribution
- The 'thinking performer'
- HR professionalism
- Self-management at work
- Teamworking

KEY LEARNING OUTCOMES

By the end of this chapter, you should be able to:

- Understand what is required to be an effective and efficient HR professional.

- Add value for your organisation through your personal contribution to efficient and effective HRM.

- Perform efficiently and effectively as a self-managing HR professional.

- Perform efficiently and effectively as a collaborative member of working groups and teams.

THE HR CONTRIBUTION

Historically, what is now generally known as 'the HR function' played a role that was largely administrative in nature. Its principal purpose was to carry out a range of quite basic tasks that are necessary whenever an organisation employs people, such as issuing contracts, placing job advertisements in newspapers, maintaining absence and training records, running the payroll, setting up selection interviews, designing appraisal documentation and, more generally, drawing up policy statements for line managers to follow when managing their staff. In unionised organisations, the role also used to encompass the maintenance of reasonably strong, trusting relationships with employee representatives. In recent years the role has both changed and developed so that these traditional activities have tended to form a much less significant part of the typical HR manager's activities.

Much more time and energy nowadays is focused on getting the best out of people as corporate contributors. In this context the term 'people' means both individual employees and staff as a collective group. The HR function contributes to organisational success by enabling and encouraging each member of staff to maximise their personal contribution, and more generally by ensuring that people across the organisation are led well. This requires the creative application of a mix of two ingredients, both essential:

Infrastructure factors: These are the 'hygiene' factors which have to be present if employees are to perform at all, but which don't by themselves generate high levels of commitment and enthusiasm. While the presence of hygiene factors plays no major role in positively motivating people, their absence can demotivate. Making sure that people are paid what they are owed for their contribution, and paid on time, is a good example of an HR hygiene factor. Few are likely to be induced to perform superbly simply because they have received a regular monthly pay cheque, but the absence of payment is very likely indeed to have a seriously negative effect on performance levels.

Differentiators ('motivators'): These are the elements which turn satisfactory or average performers into good and excellent performers. They include factors such as the opportunity to carry out interesting and stimulating work, the ability to exercise discretion over how that work is carried out, the potential for career development, positive feedback about progress and more generally a sense of feeling valued by the organisation.

Hygiene factors are not difficult to achieve in practice. However, because there are costs associated with getting them right, managers are sometimes tempted to cut back, often leading to negative HR outcomes, such as poor staff morale, active disengagement on the part of employees, high levels of absence, low levels of staff retention, an increased volume of employment tribunal claims and low-trust employment relations.

By contrast, the differentiators are much harder to achieve consistently and to continue achieving over the long term. Some are very specific to an organisation, emanating for example from a particular management culture or approach to doing things which is both difficult to define and even harder for rival organisations to imitate. However, many decades of research into human motivation and effective people management have also demonstrated that no magic ingredient is necessary. We know what the 'secret' of differentiation is, and we also know that it is not at all easy to achieve in practice. This is why some organisations perform much more effectively than others on the people management front. Those that strongly differentiate themselves are able to attract, retain, motivate and engage people much more effectively than those that do not.

The key difference is between those organisations that don't do more than manage their people legalistically, systematically and efficiently, in accordance with the dictates of 'best practice', and those organisations that lead their people positively, inspirationally and imaginatively, in line with their vision of 'next practice'. This is what effective HRM is about – creating an efficient infrastructure and also mobilising an effective set of differentiators that together make an impressive difference to the quality of the organisation and its resulting performance.

A good starting point is to manage people in accordance with some clear and strong core principles:

- Employees are human beings who deserve to be treated with dignity, consideration and sensitivity from the moment they first apply for a job to the moment they finally leave the organisation.

- They are actual or potential sources of 'added value' for the organisation.

- They are all individuals with capabilities that can be developed and utilised for the benefit of the business.

- As employees, they have a right to derive satisfaction from their work and rewards commensurate with their contributions.

REFLECTIVE ACTIVITY 4.1

On its recruitment website Tesco lists the attitudes and competencies that it wants its employees to have – they should be:

- **passionate** about retail
- **focusing** on the customer and striving to understand them better than anyone
- **driven** to achieve results through determination and commitment
- **committed** to treating people in a fair and consistent way
- **willing** to roll their sleeves up to get things done
- **determined** to respond energetically to customer feedback
- **motivated** to work in partnership with others to achieve individual and team objectives
- **adaptable** and **flexible** to thrive in a 24/7 business
- **devoted** to seeking feedback on their performance and investing time in their own development.

Questions

1 How might this list be adapted in order to put together a generic statement of the kinds of attributes needed by an effective HR manager?

2 Can you think of any other attributes which would also be appropriate for today's HR professional?

ADDING VALUE

A key difference between traditional personnel management of the kind
we described above and what is required of a successful, contemporary HR
function can be summed up by the phrase 'adding value'. In the vast majority
of organisations it is no longer sufficient for HR managers simply to carry out
administrative tasks; they need to add commercial value – and, as importantly, be
seen to do so. But how do we go about ensuring that we maximise the value that
we add?

One way of thinking about the question of adding value is to divide our activities
at work into the following four categories:

1 Maintenance activities

Maintenance is about keeping the show on the road. Maintenance activities are
necessary, but they don't add a great deal of value simply because they ensure that
everything continues to function as it did before.

2 Crisis prevention activities

Crisis prevention is about making sure that things don't go wrong or, if they
do, that the resultant damage can be contained. This is where procedures and
processes fit. Here, too, value added is relatively limited.

3 Continuous improvement activities

Continuous improvement is where added value really begins, because it focuses
on performing current tasks better, faster or more cheaply in ways which are
customer-relevant and preferably noticed by the customer. You can introduce and
implement continuous improvement in many ways.

4 Change management activities

Change management is about proposing, contributing, energising, persuading
and/or implementing change. Making change happen is a key added-value
performance indicator.

A final requirement, underpinning all four of these active roles, deserves special
emphasis. Recent high-profile instances of corporate wrongdoing and managerial
misbehaviour have emphasised once again the importance of ethical conduct –
for organisations, for directors, for executives, for managers, (especially) for those
in the HR function, and for employees in general.

Both maintenance and crisis prevention are essential, but their capacity to add
value is limited. A contribution to the achievement of competitive advantage is
made when an organisation achieves these things more efficiently and effectively
than their competitors can, but that is the extent of any real added value. An
HR function can be good at maintenance and crisis prevention activities and
be respected for this. But it is insufficient as far as adding real long-term value

is concerned. For that to be achieved, HR people need to switch their energies, as far as is possible, to continuous improvement and change management activities.

In fact, it can be persuasively argued that spending less time on maintenance and crisis prevention is a prerequisite for achieving greater added value. This is because it releases time and resources which can be used for more productive and authentic added-value purposes.

BEING 'BUSINESS SAVVY'

Being what the CIPD refers to as 'business savvy' is increasingly being recognised as one of most important attributes of effective HR practitioners. No longer – as once tended to be the case in some organisations – can HR people expect to function in 'professionally detached ivory towers', issuing edicts and prohibitions for others to follow which have no clear business justification (that is, being based largely on notions of 'good practice' or a highly risk-averse interpretation of employment law). If an HR function is to be successful, the way people are managed needs to enhance rather than restrict an organisation in achieving its objectives. Being 'business savvy' is also important for HR people because it helps hugely to enhance our credibility among other managers in our organisations and therefore our ability to influence events rather than simply react to them.

According to recent CIPD research (CIPD 2012), there are four elements to being 'business savvy':

- **understanding the business model in depth** – knowing where value is created and destroyed within the organisation, and identifying people-related improvement points which can drive value and enhance organisational performance

- **generating insight through evidence and data** – having the courage to ask questions and look for explanations even when the knowledge required seems masked in technical or professional jargon

- **connecting with curiosity, purpose and impact** – demonstrating curiosity about why and how the business operates, with the purpose of identifying opportunities for improvement; not waiting to be asked, but taking a proactive approach to making connections across the business and collaborating at all levels

- **leading with integrity, consideration and challenge** – serving stakeholders, not power structures, by retaining a strong stewardship role centred on the courage to challenge the pursuit of short-term business goals that are detrimental to an organisation's people and longer-term success.

> ### ❓ REFLECTIVE ACTIVITY 4.2
>
> To what extent do you agree with the following point of view, and why?
>
> In some HR circles a legal and compliance orientation predominates, especially in organisations which regularly face the threat of employment tribunal claims. HR people may then suggest that they have added value because the number of such claims and hearings has fallen, or because the business has 'won' more cases. In truth, nobody ever truly 'wins' such cases and no well-managed business should be dismissing people unfairly or discriminating against people unlawfully in the first place. If employees believe they have been treated unlawfully and go to tribunal, it is an indication that an organisation is being managed ineffectively.
>
> It is far preferable, surely, to add value by introducing an effective people-management and people-leadership culture characterised by genuine engagement. Certainly that is much better than trying to claim that we are adding value because we have created a scenario in which the number of costly, reputationally damaging and energy-sapping events has been reduced.

THE 'THINKING PERFORMER'

The **'thinking performer'** concept is something that sits at the very heart of professional practice and has been promoted by the CIPD through its professional qualifications framework for many years. In the personnel and development arena, the 'thinking performer' is the person who not only performs operationally but the person who also thinks about what they are doing. These are two competencies which don't always go together, but when they do, the combination is very impressive – and very valuable both for the individual and the organisation, provided always that there is some resonance between the individual's desire to think and the organisation's wish to perform.

Authentic thinking performers tend to display the following behaviours and attitudes:

- Consciously seeking to contribute to underlying organisational purposes – and therefore taking the trouble to find out what these underlying (strategic) purposes are. Thinking performers are more concerned with ends than with means.

- Reinforcing the legalistic and compliance role of the HR function when it is necessary, yet fully appreciating that to do so is not a sufficient condition for the HR function's genuine added-value effectiveness.

- Diplomatically challenging the way things are done to find solutions that are:
  - better (higher standards of cost-effective quality)
  - cheaper (lower costs, measured financially or via some other means of resource utilisation, including time)
  - faster (improved response times and personal/team productivity).

- Having continuous contact with 'customers' through networking in order to better understand the business, reacting to feedback appropriately and proactively developing their performance.

- Looking not just inside but also outside the organisation to learn about new thinking, new ideas, new practices or new evidence which their organisation might be able to exploit by copying or adapting for its own purposes.

Conversely, it is relatively easy to spot individuals who are not thinking performers because their behaviour and attitudes will display the following features:

- They do their job but pay minimal attention to what is going on around them.

- They are much more concerned with means than with ends.

- They think that the organisation's strategy is nothing to do with them – and may even believe that the organisation doesn't have a strategy, not because they genuinely know it doesn't have one but rather because they've never taken the trouble to seek it out.

- They see their role, especially within HR, as ensuring that 'the law' is obeyed at all times.

- They believe that the overriding goal of the HR function is to ensure that everyone (whether inside or outside the organisation, employees or job applicants) is treated 'fairly', which for them will mean that everyone is treated the same.

- They pay little or no attention to the opinions of their 'customers' about their performance – indeed, they may even reject the notion that they have 'customers'.

- They never constructively challenge the way things are done.

Why is it important to become a thinking performer? Essentially the thinking performer concept has grown in importance because professionals have recognised that it can move both them and their organisations forward intellectually, professionally and ethically. In today's organisations, a thinking performer culture is the optimal mechanism for attaining competitive supremacy and mobilising the talents of the workforce as a whole. Whatever the organisation – manufacturer or service provider, private or public, large or small, profit-making or not-for-profit – all its employees need to understand and be able to implement its strategy. They need to know how their jobs push the strategy forward and, if nobody can show them any link between the strategy and what they do, in all probability their jobs don't need to exist at all.

One way of bringing the concept of the thinking performer to life is illustrated in Figure 4.1. Here the vertical axis represents 'effectiveness' and 'doing the right things' (that is, adding value, making a difference, focusing on outputs, outcomes and results) – in a word, **thinking.**

The horizontal axis represents 'efficiency' or 'doing things right', concentrating on process conformity, legal and ethical compliance, putting things right when they've gone wrong – in a word, **performing.**

Figure 4.1 The thinking performer

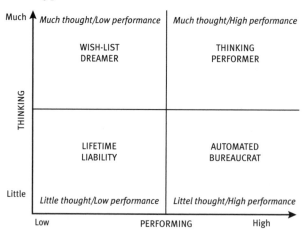

The **automated bureaucrat** is the non-thinking performer, the person who carries out instructions blindly, without necessarily knowing (or caring) about their purpose. These individuals believe it to be acceptable to be told that a procedure is justified because 'it has always been done that way' and will take refuge in plausible arguments about, say, the legal justification for certain HR actions without bothering to check whether indeed the law does actually specify what is being done in its name.

The **wish-list dreamer** – the thinking non-performer – will privately regard many of the things they are required to do as absurd, indefensible, inefficient, even maybe immoral or corrupt, but will say nothing about these concerns even when invited to do so. The wish-list dreamer often knows a better way yet does not share it with others (apart, perhaps, from those outside the organisation) and therefore loses some valuable opportunities to 'add value' to the business. Wish-list dreamers tend to keep quiet either for fear of 'rocking the boat' or because, rightly or wrongly, they perceive that their views will not be listened to if they express them.

The **lifetime liability**, as the title suggests, is a non-thinking non-performer. Such people rarely deliver task performance, results or improvements, yet often devote a good deal of time and energy to the development of 'reasons' for why agreed outputs have not been attained and specified tasks have not been performed. The lifetime liability can be a poisonous influence on others, subverting an organisation's goals and values, interpreting its vision cynically, and infecting others with similar attitudes.

Thinking performers, occupying the fourth quadrant, deliver both everyday performance and added-value improvement, both for and through themselves and for and through their wider accountabilities for the HR function and the business as a whole.

It is important to recognise that thinking performers do not challenge everything that goes on in their organisations, even strategies and practices which are supported by no evidence whatsoever as to their effectiveness. They understand the need to act in a politically adept fashion and to select battlegrounds carefully. They challenge on fertile ground, when the time is right, preparing a strong case, securing some respected allies and proceeding with caution.

REFLECTIVE ACTIVITY 4.3

The thinking performer concept owes a great deal to the ideas of the American consultant and academic Gary Hamel (1996), as set out in his seminal article entitled 'Strategy as revolution'. In this Hamel expressed the view that all employees of an organisation carry the potential to become what he calls 'strategy activists' – a concept very similar to that of the thinking performer.

A key part of Hamel's thesis is that 'the capacity to think creatively about strategy is distributed widely in an enterprise' and that the common assumption among senior managers is that strategic creativity is possessed by only a few (that is, them). The article goes on to describe how an idea for a multi-million-dollar opportunity came from a 'twenty-something secretary', and how some of the best ideas about a company's core competencies originated with a forklift operator.

In Hamel's view, genuinely strategic innovation can happen where 'senior managers ... supplement the hierarchy of experience with a hierarchy of imagination'. In his view this can be done by 'dramatically extending the strategy franchise' into three constituencies which are conventionally under-represented in the 'innovative thinking' stakes:

- **young people** – 'or, more accurately, people with a youthful perspective', who do not necessarily have to be young

- **people at an organisation's periphery** – who are often forced to be more creative because they have fewer resources and also because they are more exposed to ideas and developments that do not conform to the organisation's traditional shibboleths

- **newcomers** – 'people who have not yet been co-opted by an industry's dogma'.

Questions

1 Why do you think senior managers are often reluctant to take on board ideas such as Hamel's on strategy?

2 What roles could the HR function play in helping to make Hamel's ideas a reality in organisations?

HR PROFESSIONALISM

How should we define the word 'professional', and do HR managers have a legitimate right to call themselves 'professionals'? These are not straightforward questions to answer because people have a variety of different opinions about how to define a 'profession'.

Lester (2009, p2) sums up a commonly held point of view when he argues that a professional is someone who:

> makes proficient use of expert and specialist knowledge, exercises autonomous thought and judgement, and makes voluntaristic commitment

to a set of principles. Such a person need not be a member of an easily-defined profession or of a professional association; it is possible to work as a professional from a set of expertise and skills that is relatively unique to the individual.

According to this rather broad definition a 'profession' can be distinguished from an occupation due to its having the following characteristics:

- It is based on a body of knowledge (usually comprising theory, knowledge and practice) which can be taught and learned.

- Its practitioners possess appropriate expertise to which they apply their knowledge and judgement.

- It is underpinned by a code of conduct or ethics.

Another definition is narrower and more restrictive, only conferring the label 'professional' to occupations that are controlled to a considerable extent by a governing body which has a formal membership structure with admission barriers and performance criteria that must be met. Professional bodies of this kind not only promote high ethical standards, but reinforce them with a disciplinary procedure. You become a member of the profession when you join the professional body, and can cease to be a member if you fail to meet its standards and are required to leave.

Under either of these definitions there is a case for arguing that HR managers, at least in the UK, can legitimately regard themselves as being professionals. However, there also remain some grounds for arguing against this point of view.

On the one hand there is a definite body of knowledge that has to be learned (such as how to handle disciplinary events or set down reward strategies) and individuals certainly have to apply their judgement in their own organisations. It is also the case that the CIPD acts as a governing body for the profession in the UK and Ireland, and that it has a code of conduct that members are expected to adhere to. On the other hand, unlike some other professions, notably law and medicine, membership of the professional body is not compulsory and so CIPD membership does not constitute a formal 'licence to practise' (as is the case with law and medicine).

A factor that tilts the balance in favour of 'professionalism' is the fact that a good majority of HR practitioners in the UK are members of the CIPD, and that the CIPD is the only professional body currently operating in the HR arena. Its credibility level is very high, not just as the guardian of HR standards but also, even more importantly, as a forward-looking organisation which consistently sets forth its vision for the future HR profession as well as its standards for the conduct of the HR profession today.

Another way of looking at professionalism and defining it is more concerned with the general approach that people take to their work, the key point being that it is characterised by a high level of quality. Here we are thinking about individuals, the way they carry out their jobs and the approach they take to building relationships with others.

According to this definition, whether you are a member of a professional body or possess some special expertise is irrelevant. A professional is someone who carries out their job – whatever it is – to a high standard. There are professional and unprofessional postmen, professional and unprofessional lawyers and, so it follows, HR managers who act professionally and HR managers who do not.

According to this definition professionalism in HR is not one-dimensional. There are in fact many elements that can be nicely summarised as the following 'four concentric circles of HR professionalism':

● managing self

● managing in groups/teams

● managing upwards

● managing across the organisation.

At the core of professionalism is the ability to manage one's own skills, knowledge and behaviours. Without this ability it is not possible to effectively manage relationships or other individuals. At the second level HR professionals must be able to manage in groups and teams. This might involve working with other HR practitioners to solve problems in an organisational setting or working with other relevant stakeholder groups. The next level is termed 'managing upwards'. HR professionals will be required to work closely with their managers and senior professionals in organisations. Without the ability to manage upwards in an organisation, HR professionals will not be able to integrate their specific strategies and plans with wider organisational strategies.

The final circle of professionalism is given the title 'managing across the organisation'. Once strategies and plans have been agreed and set in place, HR professionals must then be able to set these plans in motion across their organisations. Managing horizontally across the organisation means having the professional knowledge and skills to communicate and influence line managers, highlighting the benefits that can arise from successful and integrated HR activity.

CODES OF CONDUCT AND ETHICS

Ethics and the need to observe high standards of conduct are common to all of these different definitions of professionalism, and we can thus conclude with confidence that a failure to act ethically means that someone cannot claim to be professional and should not be considered to be a member of a profession. This is as true of HRM as any other profession.

For a long time the CIPD has had a code of professional conduct to which its members are expected to adhere. A number of different versions have been published over the years, the current version having become effective from 1 July 2012. The code is designed around the CIPD's core aims, namely 'to drive sustained organisation performance through HR, shaping thinking, leading practice and building HR capability'. Moreover, it is written 'to be applicable at all stages of an HR professional's career, working in organisations of every size and type; and in all work roles, for example generalist and specialist, in house and consultancy, in line management, or as an individual contributor'. It has four major parts:

- professional competence and behaviour
- ethical standards and integrity
- representative of the profession
- stewardship.

The following extract highlights key points that appear under these four headings, but HR professionals must ensure that they become familiar with all of the code's detailed stipulations. The full code can be found by following this web link (www. cipd.co.uk/code-of-conduct).

Professional competence and behaviour

Members of the CIPD shall:

- maintain professional knowledge and competence
- ensure that they provide a professional, up-to-date and insightful service
- accept responsibility for their own professional actions and decisions.

Ethical standards and integrity

Members of the CIPD shall:

- establish, maintain and develop business relationships based on confidence, trust and respect
- exhibit and defend professional and personal integrity and honesty at all times
- demonstrate sensitivity for the customers, practices, culture and personal beliefs of others
- advance employment and business practices that promote equality of opportunity, diversity and inclusion and support human rights and dignity
- safeguard all confidential, commercially sensitive and personal data acquired as a result of business relationships.

Representative of the profession

Members of the CIPD shall:

- always act in a way which supports and upholds the reputation of the profession
- comply with prevailing laws and not encourage, assist or collude with others who may be engaged in unlawful conduct
- exhibit personal leadership as a role model for maintaining the highest standards of ethical conduct.

Stewardship

Members of the CIPD shall:

- demonstrate and promote fair and reasonable standards in the treatment of people who are operating within their sphere of influence
- challenge others if they suspect unlawful or unethical conduct or behaviour
- promote appropriate people management and development practices to influence and enable the achievement of business objectives.

As with many other professional codes of conduct, the document developed by the CIPD highlights the ethical and professional responsibilities of members. There is a focus on confidentiality, sensitivity and professional knowledge as well as a need for HR professionals to act as role models in organisations. Broadly speaking, the CIPD's code of professional conduct is a mechanism to prevent the exploitation of HR practitioners and is also intended to preserve the integrity of the profession.

CUSTOMERS AND STAKEHOLDERS

For many people, being 'professional' involves taking a stakeholder perspective on the activities of an organisation. This means accepting that a variety of different groups of people have a legitimate stake in an organisation and that their interests must be taken into account by managers when making decisions. This does not mean that a commercial organisation should not seek to maximise its profits or make money for its shareholders, nor does it mean that a public sector organisation should be run to suit the interests of its staff. It means that a reasonable balance has to be struck and that broad principles of fairness must be observed by managers. The major groups of stakeholders are as follows:

- customers
- shareholders/owners
- managers and their staff
- suppliers
- the community.

The adoption of a stakeholder perspective places a particular requirement on HR managers to act as champions for effective and fair people management. It is not our job to take the side of employees against that of management, but it is our job to ensure that genuine employee concerns are communicated to senior managers and that legitimate employee interests are looked after.

It has become fashionable for HR managers to use the term 'customer' when referring to those they supply some kind of internal service to, such as professional colleagues, line managers and senior executives. The word 'customer' is also used sometimes to describe people outside the organisation with whom HR managers form professional relationships, such as job applicants. People have different views about the desirability of this trend. Some see it as something of a fad that will pass in time while others argue that it is a misuse of the term 'customer' to apply it to colleagues and would-be colleagues. Many also argue that it is wrong to equate real (external) customers, on whom an organisation relies for its survival, with its staff, who are major beneficiaries. The major argument in favour of using the term 'customer' in this internal context is that it serves to remind us of the need to treat our employees and colleagues with due respect, to provide them with a service that is of the highest possible quality and to deliver it with skill and integrity. In other words, it helps to make us act professionally in our dealings with others.

SELF-MANAGEMENT AT WORK

A key set of skills and habits that underpin effective and professional HRM practice, as well as becoming a 'thinking performer', can be grouped together under the heading 'self-management'. These encompass effective time management, a capacity to manage projects well, analytical and critical thinking, and a range of communication skills. In one short chapter we cannot cover these in any detail, but it is possible to summarise some of the key principles in each case.

TIME MANAGEMENT

Time management essentially revolves around exercising conscious control over the time that is spent completing certain activities. In day-to-day working life HR professionals are faced with competing priorities and there are several methods through which these tasks can be prioritised. One relatively straightforward method is called 'ABC analysis'. Here, tasks are written down into some form of list, perhaps in a notebook or on a computer program, and the professional assigns each task either an 'A', a 'B' or a 'C' depending on its relative level of importance. 'A' tasks are perceived to be urgent and important, 'B' tasks are important but not urgent, and 'C' tasks are neither urgent nor important.

HR professionals must find a time management method that works for them. It is important to understand that every individual is different and will therefore optimise his or her productivity in a different way. Having said this, professionals who do not think carefully about time management often become overwhelmed with competing tasks and their productivity drops as their stress levels rise.

PROJECT MANAGEMENT

Alongside time management, HR professionals must also possess the ability to manage specific projects. The number of projects that HR professionals might need to manage will vary between organisational settings. There may be occasions when individuals are involved with projects for extended periods of time or, alternatively, individual projects may be relatively short in duration. A project can be split into five basic steps or phases that must be completed:

- initiation
- planning and design
- execution
- monitoring and controlling
- completion.

At the initiation stage the nature of the project is determined and a broad plan developed. For instance, an HR manager might want to investigate the effectiveness of an organisation's induction process. The second stage of the process takes this broad plan and plans the project to an appropriate level of detail. Keeping with the example above, here the HR manager might state that CIPD guidance is to be reviewed, employees are to be interviewed and retention statistics analysed. The next stage, execution, is all about putting this plan into practice. Our HR manager would now set the plan in motion, collecting the data and drawing conclusions from it.

Monitoring and controlling occurs while the execution phase is going – in other words, the HR manager must monitor the project, identifying any issues and correcting for them. In this example, the HR manager might find that interviews are not providing enough data and he or she might therefore set up some form of organisation-wide survey to ensure the success of the project. At the final stage of the process, completion, the project is evaluated, files are archived and lessons learned.

There are many tools and techniques that professionals can use to manage projects successfully. A key technique that is useful in this regard is milestone monitoring. Successful projects will have milestone or review points built in so that professionals can monitor their progress, making small corrections as and

Figure 4.2 A sample Gantt chart

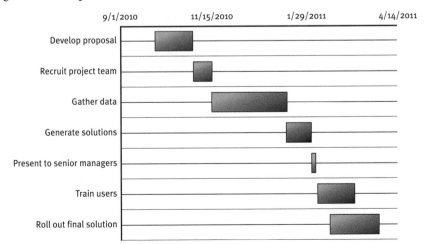

where necessary. In many cases professionals might make use of something known as a 'Gantt chart'. This sort of chart shows the start and end points of a project and highlights the location of different tasks or activities. Gantt charts are useful as they show links between the different elements of projects and highlight where more than one task might be completed at the same time. An example of a Gantt chart is shown in Figure 4.2.

By using a Gantt chart, professionals can see exactly where issues in their project plan might occur. In the example in Figure 4.2, it can be seen that if the presentation to senior managers is delayed, this will impact on the training of users and the rolling-out of the final solution. The chart also shows that the training of users and the rolling-out of the final solution can occur at roughly the same time. This information will allow professionals to plan workloads and direct resources to potential problem areas.

ANALYTICAL AND CRITICAL THINKING

The ability to think analytically and critically is fundamental to all professional practitioners, including those who work in the HR field. It is important to understand that the ability to think analytically and critically does not always occur naturally and is something that often develops over time. When thinking analytically, professionals must:

- evaluate how far materials, processes or systems are appropriate
- evaluate whether evidence or examples really prove the points that are being made
- weigh up opinions, arguments or solutions against appropriate criteria
- follow lines of reasoning through to logical conclusions
- check whether evidence and arguments really support conclusions.

Thinking which follows the points above is particularly useful when professionals encounter situations where they need to make decisions based on evidence or ensure that their choices really are suitable or likely to solve specific problems. An example of this might be taking the time to evaluate whether an element of HR strategy really aligns properly with corporate strategy. HR professionals might, for instance, be developing a new reward or pay strategy, and without analytical thinking it might well be difficult to ensure that this strategy links with wider organisational goals.

Let's now turn our attention to the concept of critical thinking.

The words 'criticise' and 'critical' are often used in the context that something or someone must be wrong. Being 'critical' in this context means making statements suggesting that theory X is right and theory Y is incorrect. It is very important to understand that this is not what critical thinking is about. Thinking critically involves using 'methods of disciplined, systematic analysis of written or oral discourses'. In other words, a critique is impersonal; professionals are not focusing on an individual. Instead the focus is on analysing the structure of a particular thought, process or system. In order to critique something, HR professionals need to arrive at an informed opinion based on technical knowledge, specific training or their personal or professional experience. HR professionals must recognise that they cannot exercise critical thinking without first having requisite professional knowledge, skills and experience.

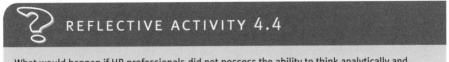

REFLECTIVE ACTIVITY 4.4

What would happen if HR professionals did not possess the ability to think analytically and critically in organisations?

EFFECTIVE COMMUNICATION

HR managers are required to communicate clearly, effectively and professionally all the time. It is thus a key component of the role and a set of skills that we all have to learn and continually seek to improve. In most cases we become more effective communicators as we gain in confidence and become more practised across the range of communication situations. The major examples are:

Presentations

HR professionals make formal presentations very regularly to a variety of audiences. Whether we are briefing senior managers about our activities, leading training sessions for staff, welcoming new starters at induction sessions, opening negotiations with trade unions or summing up after presenting evidence at a disciplinary or tribunal hearing, the same broad principles apply.

Key is the need to tailor the message to the audience. When preparing a presentation it is vital to put yourself in the position of your audience and to speak appropriately. Do not assume that people have knowledge that they may not have, and particularly avoid the use of obscure terminology and acronyms that will mean nothing to them.

Secondly, it is important to get the tone of a presentation right. Sometimes, for example, using humour is appropriate and helpful as a means of conveying a key message. On other occasions it is wholly inappropriate due to the seriousness of a situation.

Thirdly, it is advisable to make as much use as you can of communication aids. PowerPoint slides, provided they are not overcrowded and rushed through at inappropriate speeds, can greatly enhance your ability to get points over in presentations. Handouts written to accompany a presentation are very helpful in many situations, not least because they release the audience from the need to take notes, thus permitting them to concentrate on what you are saying.

Finally, it is necessary to judge the appropriate time to speak. Keeping it short and sweet is often the best advice here. Only say what you have to say and do this concisely and with as much clarity as you are able to. Avoid repeating yourself and saying things that are largely irrelevant to the key message.

Report writing

Many of the skills that underpin effective presentations also apply when it comes to writing effective reports, particularly the general one about tailoring your approach and language to the particular audience. Being concise is also as important, as is clarity of expression. Here, though, there tends to be a need for rather more formality in the language that is used than is the case with a presentation.

A good report, unlike a written narrative, starts with an 'executive summary', which is, in effect, a brief statement of the contents and its conclusions/recommendations. The reader knows what is coming and should therefore not get any surprises when reading on beyond the summary to the main body of the report. Another key feature of an effective report is the way that evidence is always provided to back up the key points. It should also be possible for someone to speed-read profitably, focusing on the summary at the front and the conclusions at the end, while reading the central sections more haphazardly. Signposting helps a lot here. The text should be divided up with subheadings, a full contents list being provided at the start. It also helps if detailed information is placed in appendices at the end of the report so that they can be referred to easily as and when necessary.

Networking

HR professionals, like many groups of people, benefit greatly from building up a network of contacts, both inside and outside the organisation they work for. Being plugged into a wide network of fellow HR professionals means that you have plenty of people to turn to for advice and information. It is also crucial to the development of a career in the profession because it helps you to 'get known' and to be seen as someone who exercises a degree of professional influence. Effective HR managers also understand that it is vital for them to build up effective networks inside their organisations, the purpose being to develop high-trust relationships with colleagues through whom influence can then be exercised. Only if you are respected and trusted by your fellow managers can you expect to have any say over how they manage the people in their teams.

We plug into networks and build them naturally in the course of our working lives. The skill is to maintain them over time as people who we once worked with closely drift away from us. Maintaining networks requires, above all, effort. It is a question of taking steps to ensure that we do not lose touch with people and that a positive relationship is retained. Social networking websites are hugely helpful in enabling us to achieve these objectives, but they can be impersonal sometimes. So there is a need for regular, direct communication and face-to-face meetings in order to supplement web-based tools. The more relaxed and sociable such meetings can be, the more effective they will be as the basis for maintaining and building networks.

Difficult relationships

In any organisation and in many teams that we work in, relationships become strained. We are often required to work with colleagues we personally dislike or whose values and ways of working we disapprove of. Difficult relationships frequently span organisational hierarchies, resulting in our working for people we perceive as difficult and, very commonly, having to supervise such colleagues.

The first point to make about this is that it is the normal state of affairs. A team of people that operates entirely functionally without clashes of personality and disagreements is very unusual. Relationships in organisations are very often difficult and frequently strain to the point (almost) of breaking, particularly when stress is applied in the form, for example, of change which is perceived as threatening. We may wish that organisational life was not like this, but it is. Complaining about it is no more fruitful than complaining about the weather. We need to get on and cope.

The second key point is to appreciate that relationships can be made to work if the people concerned put a concerted effort into doing so. It is important to try to build good working relationships with all colleagues, even those with whom any relationship is always going to be strained or rocky. As with other forms of communication, building these relationships is something that we learn from experience. Over time, for example, we learn that it is often best to 'bite our tongues' in order to prevent tension from rising unnecessarily. We also learn how important it is to separate disagreements about what needs to happen in an organisation from personal relationships. It should be possible to disagree fundamentally with a colleague and to argue the case passionately without falling out personally at all. Finally, we learn that the best policy always is to treat our colleagues with respect, even when in truth we may not have huge respect for them. This means being as supportive as possible, trying always to understand their point of view and refraining from taking any action which they may see as undermining their position. In short, we need to communicate with others in as mature and emotionally intelligent a manner as we are able to. This often requires us to suppress our natural urges, but that is part and parcel of acting professionally at work.

TEAMWORKING

The dynamics of organisational life means that all professionals must be able to work with one another. HR professionals are no exception to this and must work with colleagues within their function as well as individuals and groups from other backgrounds. There are many academic texts that discuss teamworking and these typically focus on issues such as group dynamics and conflict resolution. It is very important to state that poor teamworking can lead to serious losses in both organisational productivity and individual motivation. This is why it is crucial to understand the various dynamics of group situations.

Huczynski and Buchanan (2010) tell us that teams can take many forms in our organisations, including:

- advice teams (for example review committees or quality control circles)
- action teams (for example negotiating teams)
- project teams (for example planning or research teams)
- production teams (for example assembly teams or manufacturing cells).

Teams vary significantly in their size and structure depending on the specific reasons behind their formation. It is important to understand that HR professionals can be members of different teams at the same time. It is also crucial to remember that HR professionals do not just work with others in formal teams or groups; they may work with a variety of stakeholders while simply going about their day-to-day tasks.

GROUP DYNAMICS

HR professionals must be aware that the dynamics of group environments are affected by a number of different factors. These factors include:

- the nature of the individuals in the group
- leadership
- the structure of the group or team
- power and status issues
- communication structures or processes.

In order to operate effectively when working with others, HR professionals must understand that the presence of different individuals with different agendas and needs will affect the balance of group environments. Alongside this important issue, groups are very significantly affected by those in leadership positions. Power and status issues likewise cannot be ignored, and Huczynski and Buchanan (2010) highlight that power-plays and the negative use of political activity can hamper a group's effectiveness.

In order to operate successfully in environments where working with others is the norm, HR professionals must understand the skills associated with collaborative working and conflict resolution. There will, of course, be times where individuals have competing agendas or requirements, and this is when conflict often can arise (Forsyth 2009). In order successfully to resolve conflicts, HR professionals must be clear about the scene and gather relevant information about the other party's needs and wants. The problem situation must then be clearly highlighted (for example, that both parties need financial resources to implement their plans) before both parties brainstorm possible solutions. After coming up with a variety of options, individuals then need to negotiate an effective solution which may involve compromise on both sides in order to arrive at a satisfactory outcome.

INFLUENCING

There are many academic textbooks and articles that discuss the concepts of influence and negotiation. Yemm (2008) argues that in order to successfully influence others, HR professionals must spend time thinking about their broad message and how they wish to convey it. It is important to understand that HR professionals often need to influence others in order to bring about some sort of change or to gain buy-in to a new process or way of thinking. An example of this might occur when an HR professional has developed a new employee reward strategy and needs to gain the buy-in of line managers before rolling it out across an organisation.

Yemm (2008) argues that effective influencers possess the following attributes:

- friendliness
- empowerment
- vision
- the ability to build alliances
- expertise and knowledge
- bargaining skill.

In order to influence others, HR professionals must also have requisite knowledge and expertise. Keeping with the reward strategy example discussed above, it is important to understand that without appropriate knowledge and expertise line managers would no doubt be able to undermine the HR professional's position by asking 'difficult' questions. Alongside knowledge, HR professionals also need to be friendly but assertive. By being open and creating an atmosphere of trust, HR professionals will be better able to communicate their thoughts and listen to the genuine concerns that other stakeholders might have. Another key skill which influencers possess is the ability to strike a bargain. There will be times where compromises have to be made and HR professionals must have the skills to reach agreements in difficult situations.

NEGOTIATING

The purpose of negotiation is to reach a common understanding or viewpoint or produce an agreement upon a common course of action. Effective negotiation skills help all professionals to resolve situations where what one person or group wants conflicts with what another individual or group wants. The best outcome of negotiation is what is known as a 'win-win' situation, where both parties gain or feel that they have achieved a satisfactory outcome.

In order to successfully prepare for negotiation, HR professionals must understand:

- **goals:** what is the aim of the negotiation?
- **trades:** what can be traded between the parties?
- **alternatives:** are there any alternatives if an agreement cannot be reached?

- **relationships:** what history do the parties have? Will this impact on the negotiation?

- **expected outcomes:** what is expected to occur from the negotiation?

- **consequences:** what are the consequences (for both parties) of winning or losing the negotiation?

- **power:** who has power in the relationship?

All of the factors above will impact on negotiation. If HR professionals fail to consider the points above, it is likely that they will be unprepared for negotiation and other individuals or groups may well be able to undermine their position as a result. Style is also an important consideration when negotiating with others. If discussions can be positive and constructive rather than negative and adversarial, there is a greater chance of the parties' coming to a mutually beneficial outcome.

Negotiations often involve a degree of compromise on both sides. Professionals who approach these discussions with the mind-set that they will not move from their starting position in any way often cause tension and aggression, extremely negative states from which it is difficult to arrive at positive outcomes. HR professionals must seek to achieve 'win-win' outcomes as often as possible, especially where there is to be an ongoing relationship with the other party.

CASE STUDY

👁 FIRST DIRECT

Banking is an industry which has never been noted for its innovative flair, but in 1994 the Midland Bank set up First Direct, initially as a telephone bank and later as an Internet bank, using approaches which were then revolutionary. For example, it had the courage to ask its customers what they wanted from a bank – which, incredibly, no conventional bank had ever done before. They said they wanted five things:

1 Make it easy for me.

2 Leave me in control.

3 Know me as an individual.

4 Treat me as an equal.

5 Give me confidence.

In response, First Direct established a business model arranged around these principles:

- **processes designed around the customer** – not around the bank's preferences (and certainly not around the preferences of the IT specialists)

- **staff empowered to 'manage' interactions with customers** – without any reliance on 'scripting' or any form of interactive voice response (IVR) system

- **staff treated as respected contributors** – with 'people people' as team leaders and managers

- **ideas for change and innovation regularly solicited from employees** – with their active involvement in continuous-improvement programmes

- **staff self-confidence maximised** – through extensive training and coaching.

First Direct's initial breakthrough was to find out what its customers wanted from a bank and then give it to them. The second breakthrough was the realisation that if the five fundamental customer needs were to be satisfied, those same needs had to be met so far as the bank's employees were concerned:

1 **Make it easy for me:** ensure that the

bank's systems are as simple and straightforward as possible.

2 **Leave me in control:** empower me to act discretionally with our customers and don't expect me to function mechanically through a repertoire of repetitive scripts.

3 **Know me as an individual:** respect me for who I am, call me by my name, go some way to respect my need for a reasonable work–life balance.

4 **Treat me as an equal:** allow me to influence decisions on matters that directly concern me, and also to make my own choices.

5 **Give me confidence:** train me, develop me, support me.

First Direct set out to create an organisational culture that deliberately offered a positive contrast to the relatively poor reputations of the traditional and established players in banking circles. Candidates with appropriate personal qualities and attitudes are accepted, irrespective of their level of banking knowledge. Indeed, in most cases the company rejects applicants who have worked for a significant period of time in a conventional bank, because they believe that any capacity for original thinking and imaginative insight will have been destroyed by exposure to an atmosphere of relentless conformity and dogmatic systems.

Questions

What evidence is provided in the case study for:

1 effective HR management which genuinely adds value?

2 the development of 'thinking performers'?

3 HR policies and practices which are 'business savvy'?

4 professionalism in the approach taken to managing people?

5 the promotion of effective teamworking and communication skills?

FURTHER READING

HARVARD BUSINESS ESSENTIALS (2005) *Time management: increase your personal productivity and effectiveness*. This text discusses time management in detail and shows how professionals can prioritise tasks, deal with workplace stress and find an effective work–life balance.

SPELLMAN, R. (2011) Don't shoot the boss just yet. *People Management*. 5 July. This article discusses the issues faced by professional managers, including the need for effective time and project management.

THE CRITICAL THINKING COMMUNITY (2011) *Defining critical thinking [online]*. Available at: http://www.criticalthinking.org/pages/defining-critical-thinking/766. This website provides in-depth information about the concept of critical thinking, highlighting why it is of crucial importance to professionals. The website also provides links to other relevant material.

YEMM, G. (2008) Influencing others – a key skill for all. *Management Services*. Vol 52, No 2. pp21–4. Influencing skills are discussed in detail in this article. Specific tactics for influencing others are highlighted and the development of rapport is also considered.

REFERENCES

CIPD (2012) *Business savvy: giving HR the edge [online]*. London: Chartered Institute of Personnel and Development. Available [for members] at: http://www.cipd.co.uk/hr-resources/research/business-savvy-giving-hr-edge.aspx [Accessed 23 May 2012].

FORSYTH, D. R. (2009) *Group dynamics*. 5th edition. Pacific Grove, CA: Brooks/Cole.

HAMEL, G. (1996) Strategy as revolution. *Harvard Business Review*. July–August. pp69–82.

HUCZYNSKI, A. A. and BUCHANAN, D. A. (2010) *Organizational behaviour*. 7th edition. London: FT/Prentice Hall.

LESTER, S. (2009) *On professions and being professional [online]*. London: Institute for Learning. Available at: http://www.ifl.ac.uk/_data/assets/pdf_file/0017/6803/dr-lester-professional-article-may09.pdf [Accessed 23 May 2012].

YEMM, G. (2008) Influencing others – a key skill for all. *Management Services*. Summer. Vol 52, No 2. pp21–4.

CHAPTER 5

Using information in human resources

Graham Perkins and Carol Woodhams

CHAPTER CONTENTS

KEY LEARNING OUTCOMES

By the end of this chapter, you should be able to:

- Effectively identify a relevant area of research within an organisation.

- Analyse the differences between 'primary' and 'secondary' and 'qualitative' and 'quantitative' data.

- Critically evaluate various different research approaches and designs.

- Critically discuss the different ways in which data might be collected in organisations.

- Evaluate the broad ways in which data might be analysed.

- Highlight the various components of **business cases** and critically discuss why these documents must be tailored to the needs of different stakeholders.

INTRODUCTION

This chapter concentrates on the use of information in human resources. It has a primary focus on how HR professionals can undertake small-scale research projects and present their findings in clear, concise, business-focused reports. To begin, the chapter highlights how professionals might identify an area of research, exploring the 'roadmap' of a typical project before the various types of data are investigated. It is important to understand that data exists in a variety of forms and that HR professionals must use different techniques to gather and analyse it.

After examining the various types of data, the chapter then moves on to consider sources of data. There are many different places in which we might find information relevant to research projects, including academic journals, online databases, industry reports and the Internet. After thinking about the forms and sources of data, our attention then turns to research methodologies and specific methods of data collection. Please do not be put off by the term 'methodology'; during the chapter we examine the various ways in which we can design our research in simple, straightforward language.

Towards the end of the chapter we reflect on the various ways in which we can analyse data. It is important to understand that without effective data analysis techniques, we are unable to draw firm conclusions and this can hinder the effectiveness of our research projects. These discussions then flow into how we might present information in a business case format, before we close the chapter by considering the needs of different stakeholders.

IDENTIFYING AN AREA OF RESEARCH

There are many different ways in which HR professionals might identify a potential area of research. Horn (2009) asserts that these methods are:

- the 'burning desire' strategy
- the replication strategy
- the practical problem strategy
- the convenient access strategy.

Horn (2009) suggests that the 'burning desire' strategy is borne out of a personal interest in a particular area; for some practitioners this might be investigating the causes of workplace stress, while for others it might revolve around assessing the effectiveness of an appraisal process. By contrast, the replication strategy seeks to apply some sort of previous research in a new context. Here the HR professional is seeking to replicate a previous research project in their own organisation, adjusting the scope of the project to fit effectively with the context of their organisation.

The 'practical problem' strategy may be the most common method of identifying an area of research. Perhaps senior managers have highlighted a key area of concern in their organisation or perhaps a staff survey has thrown up an issue which the workforce is concerned about. Either way, there is a practical problem that needs to be addressed through some kind of focused research project. In many ways the practical problem strategy feeds into the convenient access strategy. Within this approach, HR practitioners select a particular area of research because of the access that they have. An example of this might be a pensions administrator's conducting some kind of research into the consequences of altering an organisation's pension scheme. The key issue to remember here is that the professional has access to specific data or individuals which will enable the research project to go ahead.

From a practical perspective, Horn (2009) notes that there are several issues which HR professionals need to consider when identifying an area of research. The first of these is searching for similar studies. When embarking on a research project HR professionals need to assess the current knowledge that surrounds their particular topic, whether this is from the academic literature or practical understandings that already exist in their organisations. The second is that HR professionals also need to think about the research process itself and assess whether they have the time, resources and skills to complete their chosen project successfully. It is very important to understand that without necessary time, resources, skills and access, research projects are likely to fail to meet their initial objectives.

Anderson (2009) also advises on the selection of research projects and highlights that HR professionals need to consider the opinions of various stakeholders before settling on a final area of research. From an organisational perspective, Anderson (2009, p36) suggests that key questions worth asking are:

- What is currently bothering me/my boss/my department/my organisation?
- What changes may be occurring in the near future?
- What HR developments may impact on the organisation in the next few weeks and months?

By answering these questions, HR professionals will have a clearer understanding of the specific issues facing their organisations and will therefore be better able to target their research projects. Once an initial area of research interest has been identified, Anderson (2009) then suggests that HR professionals must take time to think carefully about their subject area. It is very important to narrow the scope of research projects so that they can purposefully contribute to organisational performance. While the broad area of a given research project might be 'employee engagement', a more specific aim might be to 'investigate the impact of changing communication strategies on employee engagement'. It is important to understand that by focusing research in this way, HR professionals will be able to target specific issues and gather meaningful information which can then be used to inform strategic decisions.

This initial part of the chapter has considered the various ways in which HR professionals might identify potential areas of research. The paragraph above has also highlighted the importance of focusing research carefully to ensure that it provides meaningful information. To build on this introduction to the subject area, the next section highlights the broad roadmap that research projects generally follow. Before sources of data and analysis techniques are discussed in greater detail, it is important to understand how the various steps in research projects interlink and the basic skills that HR professionals need in order to conduct meaningful research.

THE RESEARCH PROJECT: A ROADMAP

Anderson (2009) notes that unlike in other areas of study or work, research projects and the resulting production of managerial information are often conducted independently. For this reason HR professionals need to ensure that they have the skills to complete these tasks, collecting data and submitting clear reports within given timescales.

The main skills that HR professionals need in order to successfully undertake research projects are those associated with project management. While this chapter does not cover project management methodologies and theories in detail, HR professionals must be able to break large projects down into smaller tasks and then link these effectively in order to produce useful management information. After identifying an area of research, HR professionals must note down the key steps in the research process, including data collection and analysis, and work out which of these can be conducted at the same time and which must follow in a sequential manner. Different research projects require different amounts of time to be assigned to the various stages of the research process – for example, one project may require a detailed look at the current literature while another may require more time to be allocated to data analysis.

Helpfully, Anderson (2009) has produced a roadmap which lists the various stages of the research process. This diagram has been reproduced in Figure 5.1. It is important to state here that not all research projects will include all of the steps shown. Figure 5.1 should be seen as a guide rather than a prescriptive 'how to'.

Figure 5.1 The research project journey

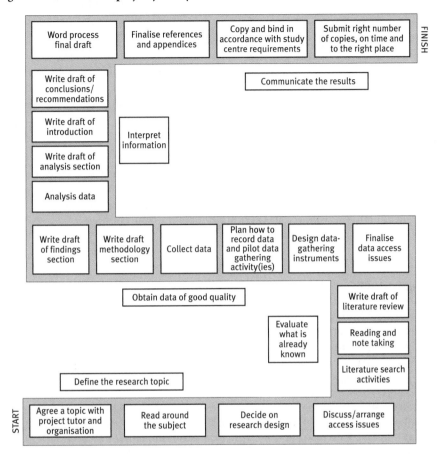

Source: Anderson, V. (2009) *Research Methods in Human Resource Management.* 2nd edition. CIPD. Page 66

A final key point that is worth mentioning in this section revolves around monitoring. One key benefit of setting out a research roadmap is that it allows for progress to be monitored against initial expectations. Certain aspects of research projects occasionally take longer than expected – for example, one-to-one interviews. HR professionals can use project plans and roadmaps to highlight where these issues may occur. By thinking about these issues in advance HR professionals will be able to plan for contingencies and it will be easier to meet final deadlines as a result.

Having thought about how an area of research might be identified and the importance of setting out a roadmap for this sort of project, attention now turns to the various types of data that may be gathered within research studies.

TYPES OF DATA

When conducting research projects of any size, HR professionals need to collect and review data which is relevant to their area of research. Figure 5.1 shows that at the very start of research projects, HR professionals must spend time reading around their subject area, evaluating what is already known, before collecting any new data. It is important to understand that there are different types of data that are used in research projects; essentially they fall into the following categories:

- primary or secondary
- qualitative or quantitative.

The bullet points above should not be seen as mutually exclusive; in other words, we can have **primary data** which is qualitative or quantitative, or **secondary data** which is qualitative or quantitative. Before the latter terms are explored, the differences between primary and secondary data must be clarified.

PRIMARY AND SECONDARY DATA

Horn (2009) points out that primary data refers to information that has been collected for the study in which it is used. In this sense primary data is 'new' in that it has not been captured by previous research projects. In contrast to this, secondary data refers to information that has been included in or discovered through previous research projects or academic writing. In essence, secondary data is data that already exists and it is often found in books, webpages or professional reports.

Anderson (2009) suggests that effective research projects begin by reviewing secondary data sources before HR professionals start collecting new primary information. Despite making the distinction between primary and secondary data sources, it is crucial to understand that neither is 'right' or 'wrong'; they are simply different sources of information that are relevant in different situations.

REFLECTIVE ACTIVITY 5.2

Can you think of any examples of primary or secondary data?

QUALITATIVE AND QUANTITATIVE DATA

While the terms 'qualitative' and 'quantitative' may appear offputting at first, they are used to represent a fairly basic distinction between different types of data.

Bryman and Bell (2007) point out that **qualitative data** is usually based around words and meanings, rather than the collection and analysis of numbers. In contrast to this, **quantitative data** usually contains numbers and can be analysed through statistical analysis software. Anderson (2009) goes a little further than these definitions by suggesting that qualitative data can help HR professionals to understand why certain things are happening in organisations. Anderson (2009) points out that while quantitative data can identify the extent to which things are or are not occurring in organisations, it is much less helpful in terms of working out *why* things are the way that they are.

Later in this chapter it is shown that qualitative and quantitative data are collected through different methods and are analysed in different ways, but the key point for the moment is that qualitative data is based around words and meanings, while quantitative data is based around numbers and statistics.

So far this chapter has thought about how HR professionals might identify an area of research and highlighted the broad steps in research projects. This section has clarified the distinctions between both primary and secondary data and qualitative and quantitative data. To move on, the following section builds on the territory covered so far by exploring the various sources of data that HR professionals may choose to make use of in their research projects.

SOURCES OF DATA

Once an area of research has been identified and a research project has been mapped out, HR professionals must gather information which already exists about their area of study. In some 'desk-based' research projects this is as far as data collection goes, but in more involved research projects this data-gathering phase is a precursor to a period of study in one's own organisation. In essence this review of the literature provides the basis of further inquiry and data collection. So, what are the main sources of data?

Anderson (2009) and Horn (2009) suggest that the most important source of data is often likely to be the academic literature on a given subject. If an HR professional is researching an element of employee reward in their organisation, for example, they may wish to consult textbooks or journal articles written about their topic. By doing this they will find out what is currently known in a particular field. Academic literature can be accessed through a variety of sources, including university or public libraries, academic journals which can be purchased online, or electronic databases which can be searched for key words or phrases. Examples of academic journals relevant to the HR field include the *British Journal of Industrial Relations*, *Employee Relations* and the *Human Resource Management Journal*.

In addition to the sources of data listed above, many professional associations, including the CIPD, the Chartered Institute of Management, or the Institute of Leadership and Management, also provide access to libraries of material and these can be very useful sources of data. Aside from physical libraries, some useful online databases for HR research include (Anderson 2009):

- Business Source Premier
- Emerald
- XpertHR

- Google Scholar
- Science Direct.

Electronic databases such as those listed above can enable HR professionals to quickly assess what is currently known about a particular topic and can be very powerful sources of data. The Internet itself can also be a very useful source of data, although it is important to remember that just because something has been written on a website, it does not mean that it is correct. When searching the Internet for information, it is perhaps best to prioritise well-known organisations and sites such as those listed below:

- the CIPD (www.cipd.co.uk)
- *People Management* (www.peoplemanagement.co.uk)
- the Office for National Statistics (www.statistics.gov.uk)
- Companies House (www.companieshouse.gov.uk).

While this is just a brief selection of websites, the key point to keep in mind is that there can be a large amount of sometimes conflicting data on the Internet. Bryman and Bell (2007) suggest that some sources can be too commercially oriented or very opinionated, and point out that these issues can impact on the quality of final research. They note that key words must be chosen carefully and that HR professionals must take time to think critically about what they are reading. By taking time to assess the relevance of data sources and the quality of information contained within them, HR professionals will produce reports and reviews that stand up to scrutiny.

Finally, in terms of data sources, HR professionals may wish to review media sources such as newspapers, magazines or general periodicals such as *The Economist*. These sources of data often include up-to-date, practical examples and case studies and can be used alongside more 'academic' material. In addition to media sources, there are various other commercial and company sources such as labour market reports and commercially published industry reports that may provide useful information which can be used in research tasks.

So how does this process of reviewing various sources of data operate in practice? How can HR professionals ensure that they focus their efforts towards a particular goal rather than adopting a scattergun approach? While Horn (2009) points out that it is very important to assess data from a variety of sources at the beginning of a research project, it is also important to focus this search. In other words, HR professionals investigating the concept of 'total reward', for example, would not review every journal article that mentions the wider field of 'employee benefits'. Instead, HR professionals would concentrate on searching for data sources that mention the impacts of 'total reward' or articles that highlight practical examples of it. The key point to take from this discussion is that HR professionals must focus their search for data by defining their overall aim relatively tightly.

Having now considered the various sources of data that might be used within research projects, the next section of this chapter concentrates on the various ways in which research tasks can be designed. It is important to recognise that different designs are applicable in different situations and the following section considers these 'methodological' issues in detail.

RESEARCH APPROACHES AND DESIGNS

Having settled on an area of research and thought about the various types and sources of data, HR practitioners then need to think about how their projects might be impacted by methodological issues. Although this term may appear complex at first glance, it has a very basic meaning. Essentially, methodological issues are issues connected with how research projects are constructed and carried out. It is important to recognise that there are many different frameworks that HR professionals can use to collect data and these are explored in this part of the chapter.

Before thinking about specific ways in which research projects can be designed, Bryman and Bell (2007) point out that final research designs must meet three basic criteria. They must be:

- reliable
- replicable
- valid.

Reliability relates to whether the results of a particular research project are repeatable and whether data-collection methods are consistent. Research methods must be replicable: in other words, another researcher must be able to come along and replicate a given study, and its outcomes will be the same, even though it has been conducted, perhaps, in a different setting. Finally, research designs must be valid, meaning that conclusions that are drawn must be consistent with the data that has been collected. Or, in other words, the data-collection instrument needs to measure the item it believes it is measuring to be valid.

Keeping the three basic criteria in mind, Anderson (2009) points out that there are four basic research strategies or 'designs' that HR professionals can choose from. It is important to understand that each of these designs is appropriate in different situations, and so we cannot say that one specific design is 'better' or 'worse' than any other design. The research designs that Anderson (2009) has discussed include:

- cross-sectional
- case study
- action research
- comparative.

CROSS-SECTIONAL DESIGN

The cross-sectional design simply involves the collection of data in a relatively standardised form from groups or individuals at a single point in time. Data might be gathered through surveys or interviews. Cross-sectional research is useful when researchers are attempting to uncover patterns or make comparisons between groups or scenarios. The advantages of this research design include the fact that it is relatively cheap to organise and administer and can achieve a broad coverage. This research design can also lead to the production of a large amount of information.

Thinking more critically, the cross-sectional design can be inappropriate at times because depth is sacrificed for breadth and poor survey or interview questions can lead to poor-quality data being collected. It is also important to recognise that there is a lack of control over how individuals respond to questions, and that different individuals may interpret questions in different ways.

CASE STUDY DESIGN

The second design in Anderson's (2009) list is known as the case study design. Whereas the cross-sectional design looks to gather data from individuals or groups at a single point in time, this method involves a detailed investigation into a situation which might be a single case or small number of related cases. The case study design is useful where the issue being examined is very difficult to separate from its wider context. Within the case study design, interviews and periods of observation are often used to collect data.

The advantage to this design is its focus on one specific issue and the fact that it can focus on only one department or group if necessary. From a critical perspective, we can argue that case study designs often produce a large amount of qualitative data which can be difficult to analyse. And it is also important to note that it is often difficult, if not impossible, to cross-check information. Our ability to generalise – that is, draw recommendations and learning from one context to another – is also limited when there is only a single research setting.

ACTION RESEARCH DESIGNS

Anderson (2009) points out that action research designs are firmly grounded in problem-solving. The overall aim of this research design is to understand and promote change. Within action research, researchers are involved in a continual cycle of planning, taking action and then observing the effects of that action. While this design is useful if the researcher is attempting to solve a specific problem inside an organisation, there are drawbacks to keep in mind.

A significant drawback to action research is that it can often be descriptive rather than explaining why things are the way that they are. Researchers can state the effects of certain actions but may not be able to tell precisely why these actions have occurred or what has motivated them. It is also important to state that action research involves a significant time commitment and that it can be difficult to justify any value in terms of knowledge and understanding outside of the specific research setting.

COMPARATIVE DESIGNS

The final design described by Anderson (2009) is termed 'comparative'. As suggested by the title, comparative research designs allow for comparisons to be made between different groups or situations, usually internationally. Comparative research often uses standardised surveys or interviews to collect data in different settings, allowing researchers to compare and contrast findings. We could perhaps use comparative research to compare levels of staff engagement at different company sites or within different departments in one particular organisation.

The main drawback to comparative research designs is that they can be difficult to administer and organise. Another difficulty lies in making valid and accurate comparisons. It is important to recognise that not all environments have a sufficient amount in common to enable comparative research to be successful. Despite these challenges, Anderson (2009) points out that comparative designs can tell researchers a great deal about how HR practices and frameworks operate in different situations.

REFLECTIVE ACTIVITY 5.3

Which research design do you think would be most useful if you were attempting to investigate a single issue in detail within an organisation?

Moving on from research approaches and designs, the next part of the chapter explores the various ways in which HR professionals can collect data. You will remember that surveys, interviews and observation were all mentioned in this section, and these (along with other methods) are now discussed in detail.

COLLECTING DATA

Before thinking about specific data-collection methods, this part of the chapter needs to address the concept of **sampling**. What is sampling, and why do researchers use it?

Broadly speaking, sampling is useful where there are large groups and researchers cannot collect data from every individual. Suppose an organisation has 1,000 employees and a researcher wants to collect data through interviews. It is important to recognise that interviewing all 1,000 staff would involve a considerable amount of time and produce an inordinate amount of material. For these reasons, interviewing all employees would be ineffective and inefficient. In this instance, authors including Creswell (2007) and Horn (2009) point out that HR professionals would normally choose to interview a proportion of the employees to speed up data collection and save costs.

Bee and Bee (2005) and Creswell (2007) describe several different sampling strategies that HR professionals might choose from. The primary concern when choosing a sample is that it reflects the wider characteristics of the group. If, for instance, an organisation employs 500 individuals in a production department and 500 individuals in a marketing department, it would be inappropriate to interview 250 production employees and only 50 marketing employees. This approach to sampling would not be representative of the real situation. This is a key point that is worth keeping in mind. Sampling strategies, however they are chosen, must be representative of the wider groups from which the samples are drawn.

Having thought about issues relating to sampling, this part of the chapter can now move on to examine specific methods of data collection. Anderson (2009) and Bryman and Bell (2007) point out that research projects typically make use of one (or more) of the following data-collection methods:

- surveys/questionnaires
- interviews
- focus groups
- participant observation.

SURVEYS

Many research projects involve the use of some form of survey or questionnaire. Bryman and Bell (2007) state that surveys involve researchers producing documents which detail specific questions that respondents then provide answers for. Surveys are generally cheaper and faster to administer than interviews and are typically more convenient for respondents as they can complete them when they have a period of free time. Thinking more critically, it is important to understand that surveys do not allow for researchers to prompt individuals to provide more information about particular topics and it is also difficult to ask complex questions. There is in addition the risk that respondents might not answer specific questions and that response rates in general might be low.

In order to improve response rates, it is important that surveys are clear and concise so that they do not appear bulky and offputting. Questions may be either 'open' or 'closed' – in other words, they may require a yes/no answer or a tick to be placed in a box (closed) or they may require a few words or a sentence of explanation (open). The format of questions and the content of the survey will be driven by the topic that the researcher is investigating.

INTERVIEWS

Horn (2009) points out that interviews are normally classified as a qualitative method for gathering data and that the skills required for interviewing are different from the skills required for preparing a survey. While researchers may use similar questions in interviews as they do in surveys, it is important to understand that interviews are predominantly about listening and understanding what the respondent is saying.

Broadly speaking, interviews are useful where researchers need to investigate a small number of issues in a significant amount of detail. While surveys may be useful in capturing broad perspectives and understandings of specific topics, interviews allow researchers to dig into specific details, opinions and views. Both Horn (2009) and Bryman and Bell (2007) note that interviews can be either 'structured' or 'unstructured' – in other words, they can follow strict question sets or they can flow in a more discursive way. It is important to recognise that different topics and question sets lend themselves to either structured or unstructured formats.

Interviews can allow researchers to gather a wealth of information about specific topics, although it can be time-consuming to analyse the output and the interviews themselves take a significant amount of time to organise and administer. Researchers need to decide whether the time commitments involved in interviewing are offset by the potential benefits of gathering more detailed data.

FOCUS GROUPS

Some researchers assume that focus groups are just interviews that are conducted with a group rather than with individuals on their own. Walker (1985) points out that this is not the case and that focus groups should be used where researchers are interested in how groups of individuals make sense of specific concepts or ideas.

Building from the points above, it is important to understand that focus groups are relevant where researchers are investigating tightly defined issues or concepts. Focus groups themselves promote dialogue and discussion and allow researchers to find out about a range of attitudes and opinions on a given topic. A practical example of the use of focus groups might be where an organisation is attempting to gauge reactions to a new product or to a new internal reward package. The participants in the focus group can be questioned about specific issues and researchers will be able to see how the group forms its opinions.

It is important to understand that while there are benefits to the use of focus groups, there are also drawbacks. It can sometimes be difficult to get participants together and there is always the risk that one or two individuals might dominate the discussion. It is also important to remember that the focus group participants need to be representative of the group which is the focus of the study.

PARTICIPANT OBSERVATION

The final data collection method to be examined in this part of the chapter is participant observation. Bryman and Bell (2007) indicate that participant observation occurs where the researcher immerses himself or herself in a social setting for an extended period of time. During this time the researcher observes behaviour and listens to what is said in conversation and might ask questions to find out more detailed information about specific events or issues.

From a positive perspective, participant observation can allow researchers to observe the realities of the workplace and it can also be an efficient way of gathering data about practical problems. Thinking more critically, it is important to understand that researchers may not actually view the 'realities of the workplace' because observed individuals may modify their behaviour or conduct simply because of the presence of the observer. It is also important to think through the ethical considerations of observing others. Nevertheless, this data-collection method can provide a useful insight into the inner workings of organisations.

In this part of the chapter, the concept of sampling has been discussed and several methods through which HR professionals might collect data to use within their research projects have been explored. Having now collected this data, the next step in the research process is to analyse this data to search for key themes and issues. The following section considers these issues in detail.

ANALYSING DATA AND DRAWING CONCLUSIONS

Methods of data analysis vary depending on the type of data that has been collected within research projects. Quantitative data (that is, data which is numerical in nature) is often best analysed through spreadsheets or bespoke statistical software such as SPSS. Qualitative data (that is, data which contains words and meanings) is most often analysed through visual comparison and computer database programs or specialist software, such as NVivo. The choice of analysis method will very much depend on the nature of research projects. If an HR practitioner has gathered only a small amount of quantitative data, a spreadsheet package such as Microsoft Excel might be the best analysis tool, whereas a large amount of qualitative data must be analysed through a bespoke piece of software such as NVivo.

Once a broad analysis tool has been selected, HR practitioners must then examine the collected data looking for patterns, correlations and underlying meanings. Within quantitative research projects it is often easy to produce detailed analyses demonstrating the strength of various factors. For example, if an HR practitioner was conducting a staff survey, they might find that everyone answered a question concerning their work environment very positively. This finding would be made clear through statistical analysis and the HR practitioner would be able to draw reasonably firm conclusions.

Analysing qualitative data is often more complicated. Once data has been collected, sorted and perhaps input into a computer system or database, HR practitioners must then search for key words or phrases that repeat themselves throughout the data. If patterns are found, HR practitioners will be able to draw conclusions about particular issues. For instance, everyone might use specific words or phrases to describe the work environment or their relationship with their line manager. HR practitioners will be able to ascertain how 'strong' particular findings are depending on the number of references to specific issues.

REFLECTIVE ACTIVITY 5.4

Assume for a moment that an HR practitioner has undertaken a research project investigating the effects that an induction programme has had on overall levels of staff retention in an organisation. The data has been collected through semi-structured interviews and retention statistics.

What type (or types) of data will this HR practitioner have collected, and how might it best be analysed?

Once patterns and underlying meanings have been found, HR practitioners must then think about how best to present their data. Anderson (2009) suggests that charts and tables can be useful methods of displaying key findings, while Bryman and Bell (2007) indicate that practitioners might also want to produce bullet lists of more general points. For instance, was one particular phrase repeated on several occasions in a qualitative study? If so, practitioners might want to include this in their findings. Computer software such as Microsoft Excel and SPSS can be used to produce graphs and tables, and in some cases HR practitioners might want to produce more detailed analyses using pictograms, histograms or frequency tables. The purpose of this section is simply to provide an overview of the potential data analysis methods rather than full descriptions of techniques, so these particular issues are not explored in more detail here. Follow-up references are provided in the *Further Reading* section for HR practitioners who wish to investigate data analysis in greater detail.

Now that the basic issues surrounding data analysis and drawing conclusions have been discussed, the next stage in the research process is to present findings back to key stakeholders.

PRESENTING INFORMATION IN A BUSINESS CASE

Clarity is perhaps the most fundamental point to keep in mind when presenting research findings in a business case. Many sources, including Marchington and Wilkinson (2008) and Anderson (2009), indicate that business cases must be structured effectively so that they communicate findings and put forward recommendations clearly. Anderson (2009) suggests that reports and business cases generally contain the following elements:

- title page

- summary or abstract (short overview of project and its findings)
- introduction (why the topic is of significance and what the aims of the research are)
- literature review (setting out the wider context of the subject)
- methodology (how the issue was investigated, and how data was gathered)
- findings and analysis (the key findings from the data and what these mean)
- conclusions (the broad implications of the analysis and what it means for the organisation)
- recommendations (these should be action-oriented and describe costs, timescales and accountabilities).

It is important to understand that different projects will follow different formats, so methods of presentation will vary. In some cases, HR practitioners will not be required to construct a written report; instead they may be asked to present their findings verbally at some sort of meeting. Irrespective of whether the final business case is presented verbally or in a written report, it is important to follow the relevant elements of structure highlighted in the bullet list above. If this structure is not followed, key points may be underplayed and, as a result, the overall business case will not be clear.

Horn (2009) notes that HR practitioners may want to use graphs, diagrams and other visual aids to demonstrate key points within their business cases. If, for example, a research project was exploring the causes of absence in an organisation, an HR practitioner may be able to produce some sort of chart indicating the absence levels in different departments or divisions. An example of this sort of chart is contained in Figure 5.2.

Figure 5.2 Using charts in business cases

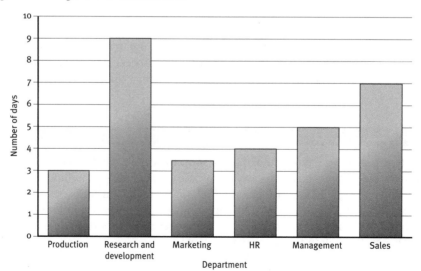

You will agree, I am sure, that Figure 5.2 demonstrates key findings more effectively than paragraphs of text and is likely to add clarity to a business case. Horn (2009) goes on to point out that effective HR practitioners will use their business cases to highlight key trends and present diagrams and charts to support their conclusions and recommendations.

A final topic to consider in this chapter is the needs of various stakeholders. When compiling business cases and reports, it is vital to recognise that different stakeholders have different needs. These issues are now explored in detail.

UNDERSTANDING THE NEEDS OF STAKEHOLDERS

Anderson (2009) suggests that a key part of writing effective business cases and research reports is understanding who the readers are going to be and what they are going to be looking for. HR practitioners must understand that senior managers have different needs from employees, who equally have different needs from professional bodies or educational institutions. Before compiling a research report or business case, HR practitioners must ask themselves who will be reading or listening to the information and think about what the stakeholders are going to want to know.

Senior managers as a stakeholder group are likely to be concerned with how research projects will enable them to operate more efficiently and effectively. As a consequence of this, business cases must highlight key findings and how they will feed into the wider strategy of the organisation. Contrastingly, employees are likely to want to know how the research project will improve their working conditions or processes. It should be clear that understanding the needs of stakeholders when writing business cases and reports is of paramount importance.

Once a business case (either written or verbal) has been drafted, HR practitioners must take time to review their work and evaluate its likely effectiveness. While going about this analysis, HR practitioners must think very carefully about the needs of stakeholder groups and whether their final report will meet these requirements. By thinking carefully about the needs of stakeholder groups, HR practitioners will inevitably produce more effective business cases and research reports.

RESEARCHING ABSENCE AT WORK

CASE STUDY

Tamara is a student in a hurry. She is a distance-learning student fulfilling a demanding role in an important government department in a fairly small overseas location. Tamara's organisation must change rapidly to meet new government modernisation requirements in her country. Absence from work is a big problem in Tamara's organisation and the government has set challenging targets in this area, so it is in this area that Tamara has decided to focus her research project.

Tamara and her manager have met to discuss her project and have decided that investigating the specific causes of absence would be useful for the organisation. In broad terms, Tamara and her manager agree that she needs to collect data from the 1,000-strong workforce, focusing in particular on the differences in absence rates between managers and front-line employees. The plan is that Tamara will be able to evaluate the effectiveness of current absence management practices and recommend improvements.

An issue that Tamara is attempting to deal with at the moment is how she will frame the research project as a whole and target specific questions to gather relevant data. Tamara's manager has pointed out that there are many different sources of data which discuss absence management, although Tamara has indicated that she is unsure as to the benefits of reviewing what has gone before.

A final question that needs to be addressed is how data will be presented back to various stakeholder groups. Tamara is aware that senior managers will be interested in hearing about the results of her research; however, they do not have much time to read through lengthy reports. The senior management team do meet every Monday to discuss strategic issues, although Tamara is still not sure about how to present information in this situation. Line managers will also want to see the results and Tamara has been told that this group would prefer to receive a report that they can keep for future reference.

Source: adapted from Anderson (2009, p11).

Questions

1 What methods might Tamara use to collect new data about absence management inside her organisation?

2 Why should Tamara take time to assess the current body of knowledge surrounding absence management before she embarks on her own data collection?

3 Critically discuss how Tamara might effectively present her findings back to the various stakeholder groups mentioned in the case study.

FURTHER READING

ANDERSON, V. (2009) *Research methods in human resource management*. 2nd edition. London: Chartered Institute of Personnel and Development. This detailed text provides HR practitioners with information about how research projects can be structured alongside various data collection and analysis techniques.

BRYMAN, A. and BELL, E. (2007) *Business research methods*. 2nd edition. Oxford: Oxford University Press. This more advanced text considers many of the theories that underpin management research and also discusses practical issues, including various research techniques and sources of data.

FREE MANAGEMENT LIBRARY (2012) *Basic business research methods [online]*. Minneapolis, MN: Free Management Library. Available at: http://managementhelp. org/businessresearch/index.htm. This website provides detailed information about various methods of data collection and considers how results can be analysed, interpreted and reported.

HORN, R. (2009) *Researching and writing dissertations*. London: Chartered Institute of Personnel and Development. This textbook provides a useful overview of important topics such as finding a research area, constructing an appropriate methodology and analysing data.

IBM (2012) *IBM SPSS statistics [online]*. Available at: http://www-01.ibm.com/ software/analytics/spss/products/statistics/. This website provides information about the statistical analysis tool SPSS.

LESSER, E. (2010) HR analytics: go figure. *People Management*. 20 May. This *People Management* article highlights the importance of collecting data in the HR field so that organisations can make effective strategic decisions.

QSR INTERNATIONAL (2012) *NVivo 9 [online]*. Available at: http://www. qsrinternational.com/products_nvivo.aspx. This website provides product information about the NVivo 9 software package.

TAYLOR, N. (2010) How to... write a business case. *People Management*. 2 September. This *People Management* article explores the practical issues around the construction of business cases in human resources.

REFERENCES

ANDERSON, V. (2009) *Research methods in human resource management*. 2nd edition. London: Chartered Institute of Personnel and Development.

BEE, F. and BEE, R. (2005) *Managing information and statistics*. 2nd edition. London: Chartered Institute of Personnel and Development.

BRYMAN, A. and BELL, E. (2007) *Business research methods*. 2nd edition. Oxford: Oxford University Press.

CIPD (2012) *CIPD [online]*. Available at: http://www.cipd.co.uk/ [Accessed 11 March 2012].

COMPANIES HOUSE (2012) *Companies House [online]*. Available at: http:// www.companieshouse.gov.uk/ [Accessed 11 March 2012].

CRESWELL, J. W. (2007) *Qualitative inquiry and research design.* 2nd edition. London: Sage.

HORN, R. (2009) *Researching and writing dissertations.* London: Chartered Institute of Personnel and Development.

MARCHINGTON, M and WILKINSON, A. (2008) *Human resource management at work.* 4th edition. London: Chartered Institute of Personnel and Development.

People Management (2012) *People Management [online].* Available at: http://www.peoplemanagement.co.uk/pm/ [Accessed 11 March 2012].

UK NATIONAL STATISTICS (2012) *UK National Statistics [online].* Available at: http://www.statistics.gov.uk/hub/index.html [Accessed 11 March 2012].

WALKER, R. (1985) *Applied qualitative research.* Aldershot: Gower.

CHAPTER 6

Developing the knowledge and skill of the HR professional

Carol Woodhams, Graham Perkins and Krystal Wilkinson

CHAPTER CONTENTS

- Introduction
- The CIPD's HR Profession Map
- The principles of continuous professional development
- The theory of CPD: reflective practice
- Managing your CPD
- CIPD membership and career progression
- Further resources to support your learning

KEY LEARNING OUTCOMES

By the end of this chapter, you should be able to:

- Feel familiar with the range of tools from the CIPD that guide the development of the HR profession.

- Evaluate the significance of continuing professional development (CPD) to HR and other professionals.

- Understand how to effectively manage your own CPD.

- Feel familiar with the content contained in the other textbooks in this series and understand the various sources of information that are available to HR professionals.

INTRODUCTION

It is noted in the introduction of Watson and Reissner (2010) that 'knowledge, skills and continuing professional development (CPD) are at the top of the twenty-first century human resources agenda'. Returning to themes established in Chapter 5, this final chapter explores the knowledge, skills and behaviours that are central to the work of an HR professional and their development. Important here are the linked concepts of the CIPD's HR Profession Map, to diagnose areas of developmental need and continuing professional development (CPD) as a means of meeting those needs. During the course of this chapter we analyse both. We also include a number of suggestions of resources that support learning. Initially, we prioritise areas for development by exploring the CIPD's 'map' of HR expertise. Then we analyse the principles of CPD, explain its importance in the modern business world and review the theory that underpins it. We then turn to more practical issues and explore the various tools and techniques that can be applied to maximise the potential of CPD in an HR role before we examine the connection between CPD and the CIPD's professional framework. Finally, to support your learning, this chapter summarises material from other titles in this series and provides an indication of the sources of information that you can access to further develop your skills and knowledge.

THE CIPD'S HR PROFESSION MAP

The CIPD's **HR Profession Map** sets out in detail the competencies which HR professionals will need in the foreseeable future. The map itself can be thought of as a competency framework and is the product of significant research into what it means to be an HR 'professional'. This section shows how it is useful in guiding development.

The map reflects a fundamental shift in the purpose of the HR profession: 'a move from a primary focus on supporting line managers in managing their people well, to a primary focus on driving sustainable organisational performance' (CIPD 2012a). What this means is that HR is becoming an 'applied business discipline with a people and organisation specialism'. The map also emphasises the role of HR professionals as contributors to sustainable organisation performance. This means that HR professionals must work 'from a deep business, contextual and organisational understanding' to develop actionable insights and change programmes, and to 'deliver meaningful, impactful solutions that work and stick' (CIPD 2012a).

The fact that HR professionals must work from a comprehensive understanding of business, contextual and organisational issues is a point which requires special emphasis. It is important to understand that the ten elements in the 'capability framework' of the HR Profession Map are intended to 'emphasise the contributions that everyone in the profession needs to make, regardless of role, level or specialism'. In other words, these 'professional areas' are not purely aimed at HR managers, HR consultants or HR directors – they are equally applicable to HR practitioners who are just embarking on their professional careers. People just like you.

The CIPD's HR Profession Map is shown in Figure 6.1. It contains ten different areas, which will now be explored in greater detail.

Figure 6.1 The CIPD's HR Profession Map

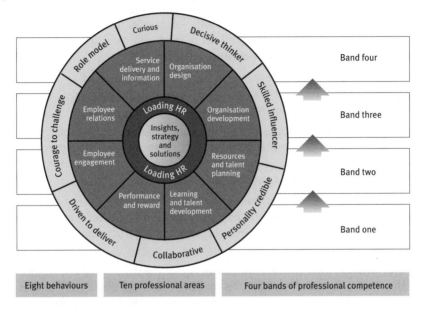

There are two areas at the heart of the Profession Map:

- insights, strategy and solutions
- leading HR.

The first area details the knowledge, skills and behaviours that are needed in order to develop actionable insights and solutions, structured around 'deep understanding' of the business, its context and the way it is organised (including its political and cultural character). Leading HR is built around the need for individuals to develop insight-led leadership, owning, shaping and driving themselves and others.

Alongside these two core professional areas there are eight additional functional professional areas in which HR professionals implement HR as an applied business discipline. The relevance of these areas will depend on the specific role that practitioners have in organisations. For instance, while performance and reward may be a key area for an employee reward specialist, the learning and talent development area is far more relevant to someone responsible for learning and development in their organisation. The basic content of each functional area is highlighted in the bullet list below:

- **Organisation design:** ensures that the organisation is appropriately designed to deliver its objectives and that structural change is effectively managed.

- **Organisation development:** ensures that the organisation has a committed, 'fit for the future' workforce. It plays a vital role in ensuring that organisational cultures, values and environments support and enhance performance.

- **Resourcing and talent planning:** ensures that the organisation is able to identify and attract key people with the capability to create competitive advantage.

- **Learning and talent development:** ensures that people at all levels of the organisation possess and develop the skills, knowledge and experience to fulfil the short- and long-term ambitions of the business, and that they are motivated to learn, grow and continue to perform.

- **Performance and reward:** revolves around the construction of a high-performance culture by delivering programmes that recognise and reward critical skills, capabilities, experience and performance.

- **Employee engagement:** against the background of the organisation's objectives, looks to ensure that all aspects of the employment experience are positive and understood, and that employees deliver greater discretionary effort in their work and for the organisation.

- **Employee relations:** ensures that the relationship between the organisation and its staff is managed appropriately, within a clear and transparent framework underpinned by coherent organisational policies and practices, and also by relevant employment law.

- **Service delivery and information:** ensures that the delivery of HR service and information to leaders, managers, fellow employees and other stakeholders (for example, job applicants) is accurate, efficient, timely and cost-effective.

The key point to take from this list concerns the diversity of the HR profession as a whole. On the one hand professionals can be tasked with sorting out reward management issues, while on the other they may need to advise on elements of contract law. And, in line with themes that were embedded in Chapter 4, there is a need for HR professionals to be both business- and change-focused. This is an important point, which should be fed into development plans – but more about them later in the chapter.

THE BANDS OF PROFESSIONAL COMPETENCE

Accompanying the ten professional areas, the CIPD's HR Profession Map also includes four 'bands' of professional competence. Alongside each activity that HR professionals engage with, such as 'identifying key organisation processes' in the 'Organisation Design' professional area, there are four distinct levels of competence.

Band 1 revolves around 'delivering the fundamentals', with a focus on supporting the immediate needs of clients. Professionals working at this level focus on providing information, managing data and delivering process support. Individuals at Band 2 operate at an 'adviser' level, where they are responsible for dealing with current or near-term priorities. Professionals operating at this level must be able to evaluate HR issues and parameters, providing effective and efficient solutions for stakeholders. Moving into Band 3, professionals become 'co-operative partners'. They will be expected to lead the professional area and deal with medium- to long-term challenges. Professionals must understand functional and business realities, provide ideas and insights, and challenge decisions as and where appropriate. Finally, Band 4 professionals operate as 'leadership colleagues'. They lead the function as a whole and develop strategy. They must understand industry and organisational dynamics and be able to partner strategically with key stakeholders and/or clients of the function.

Early career professionals will normally operate at one of the first two bands. The CIPD's HR Profession Map provides very useful information about how professionals can develop their skills so that they can prepare themselves for roles at either Band 3 or 4. To illustrate, Table 6.1 provides a brief extract from the CIPD's HR Profession Map. This extract has been taken from the 'Organisation Design' area of the map. In the first column of the table, the activity that HR professionals need to engage with can be seen – that is, 'identifying key organisation processes' – while the four columns to the right show what professionals are expected to be able to do at each of the four bands described above.

Table 6.1 An extract from the CIPD's HR profession map

Area of competence	Band one	Band two	Band three	Band four
3.4 Identify key organisation processes	3.4.1 Document process mapping as discussed with managers.	3.4.1 Prepare and facilitate process mapping discussions with managers and identify what will need to be in place to ensure implementation.	3.4.1 Lead the definition of end-to-end processes and how they will operate to ensure co-ordination of activities across departments.	3.4.1 Lead discussion on the core processes the organisation will follow and the structuring of resources that will best deliver those processes.

The content of Table 6.1 is not the most important point to be made here. The key learning point to keep in mind is that the CIPD's HR Profession Map not only defines activities in ten different functional areas, but it also highlights the progression from junior to senior roles.

REFLECTIVE ACTIVITY 6.1

In what ways do you think the CIPD's HR Profession Map will help you to guide your professional development?

THE PRINCIPLES OF CONTINUOUS PROFESSIONAL DEVELOPMENT

There are many varying definitions of **continuous professional development** (CPD), but they all contain similar points and themes. In many ways, CPD is a very basic concept – it is all about ongoing learning and improvement in the specific professional requirements of an individual's role. CPD is concerned with improving specialist knowledge, ensuring adherence to legislative and regulatory process and a general awareness of developments within a field. One of the early definitions of CPD was offered by Madden and Mitchell (1993, p12). Here's how they defined the term:

> the maintenance and enhancement of the knowledge, expertise and competence of professionals throughout their careers according to a plan formulated with regard to the need of the professional, the employer, the profession and society.

Madden and Mitchell (1993) make specific reference to the 'maintenance and enhancement of knowledge, expertise and competence'. This resonates clearly with the initial description of CPD presented above. An important point is that Madden and Mitchell suggest that CPD must relate to the needs of the professional, the employer, the profession and wider society. It is very important to remember that CPD is not something which solely benefits HR professionals; there are wider benefits which can be realised from effective practice.

CPD is not a one-off activity; it is a lifelong commitment to continually improving your knowledge and skills. It is a very personal business, and no one else can do it for you. When it comes to CPD, you will be your own objective-setter, implementer, funder (perhaps in money, certainly in time) and evaluator. The fact that you are currently completing a CIPD qualification suggests that you probably understand the value of CPD and may well have already made a commitment to it.

THE IMPORTANCE OF CPD

There are a number of important reasons for you to undertake CPD. The main reason is that it is a means of developing yourself continually in terms of your professional competence, and keeping track of your progress. In addition, many professional bodies view the activity as a prerequisite of continued membership. The Law Society, for example, stipulates a set amount of CPD hours per member per year – which must be logged ready for inspection if required. Also, a CPD record can prove to potential and current employers your skills, competence and suitability/readiness for new roles and challenges.

As an HR professional, the CPD of the organisation's workforce will also be of importance to you. An organisation in which everyone is actively engaged in continual personal and professional improvement constitutes a 'learning organisation' – one which is innovative and responsive to change. You will have a duty to support the CPD of the whole workforce via appropriate training and development policies, job design, and so on.

The reason that CPD is becoming ever more important to organisations and professional practitioners is that the business world is continuously changing. Due to this continuous and often rapid change, professionals in all fields who don't engage with continual learning and improvement will quickly find that their skills and knowledge fall out of date. CPD focuses on the development of transferable skills that not only help you to achieve the objectives of your current employer, but also help you obtain work elsewhere if you need to. CPD is a necessity, not a luxury.

WHAT IS THE FOCUS OF CPD?

There are a number of different levels on which CPD can, and should, be targeted:

- Personal, which means asking yourself how you, as an individual, can improve your effectiveness. This entails improving your self-awareness, your understanding of your values and personality, working on your time- and stress-management, and so on, as well as keeping up to date with key developments in your organisation, sector and profession.

- The external context (organisation, sector and profession) is always developing, and in order to make effective decisions, you will need to be aware of these changes and how they affect your role. To be an effective HR professional, you will need to keep abreast of political and legislative developments; demographic and labour market trends; technology developments; environmental concerns; and social trends.

REFLECTIVE ACTIVITY 6.2

Given what you know, what risks might there be for individual HR practitioners who do not engage in CPD?

SOURCES OF CPD

CPD can be found in any event, activity or encounter from which you have learned something . But the most obvious sources include:

- formal study (such as your CIPD programme)
- vocational training courses – internal and external
- seminars (employment law updates, and so on)
- CIPD local branch events (and the Annual Conference, if possible)
- sector/industry events
- literature (*People Management*, reputable newspapers, and so on)

- CD-ROMs, e-learning courses, Learn Direct courses
- networking events
- company committees and projects, especially where cross-departmental
- shadowing and role-modelling
- coaching and mentoring at work – from both sides of the relationship.

CPD can also be generated from reflection and learning within your day-to-day work and, of course, informal opportunities. At the heart of CPD is 'reflective practice'. While this term may seem a little daunting at first, the underlying concept is relatively straightforward. Essentially, reflective practice is the capacity to reflect on action so as to engage in a process of continuous learning. The key phrase here is 'reflect on action'. CPD revolves around thinking carefully about what has been done or experienced in order that we can facilitate further learning. Without reflective practice, development activities will be poorly targeted and will therefore be of little use to professional practitioners.

REFLECTIVE ACTIVITY 6.3

Recall a few events in your career, and specifically within training events, that you have been involved in that have either caused you considerable satisfaction or considerable anxiety, or both. Answer the questions below, or as many of them as are relevant:

- With regard to the balance between satisfaction and anxiety, how satisfied are you with your current levels of performance, and why?
- Do the tasks that you perform well have anything in common with each other? What about the tasks that cause you anxiety?
- What actions have worked for you when undertaking these activities?
- Where and when could you try out using these practices again?
- What didn't work in these situations, and why didn't it work?
- How could you have changed what you did to make it more successful?

THE THEORY OF CPD: REFLECTIVE PRACTICE

One of the earliest writers on the usefulness of **reflective learning** was Schön (1983). Schön expresses the view that many professionals seem to stop learning as soon as they leave graduate school, but those who become lifetime learners practise what he called 'reflection in action'. This is the ability to reflect on one's thinking while in the process of carrying out the activity. Schön believed that 'reflection in action distinguishes the truly outstanding professional'.

The following quote is taken from Schön so it cannot be changed, but please note that the masculine context is misleading and the quote applies equally to women. Schön states of reflective practitioners (Schön 1983, p69):

In each instance, the practitioner allows himself to experience surprise, puzzlement, or confusion in a situation which he finds uncertain or unique.

He reflects on the phenomena before him, and on the prior understandings which have been implicit in his behaviour. He carries out an experiment which serves to generate both a new understanding of the phenomena and a change in the situation ... When someone reflects-in-action, he becomes a researcher in the practice context. He is not dependent on the categories of established theory and technique, but constructs a new theory of the unique case.

His inquiry is not limited to a deliberation about means which depends on a prior agreement about ends. He does not keep means and ends separate, but defines them interactively as he frames a problematic situation. He does not separate thinking from doing .... Because his experimenting is a kind of action, implementation is built into his inquiry.

What does all this mean? Schön is identifying the limits to the use of prescribed best practice 'theories', suggesting instead that we all create our own best practice rules and theory in action through trial, error and reflective learning. It is common sense really, and it forms the theoretical basis of CPD.

Reflecting on your learning enables you to link your professional development to practical outcomes and widens the definition of what counts as useful activity. Quite simply, you need to keep asking 'What did I get out of this?' As a reflective learner, you'll think about how you'll use new knowledge and skills in your future activities – so learning is always linked to action, and theory to practice. It is also useful to reflect on how you learn best. This may be through private study, networking with peers, formal courses, mentoring or a combination of techniques.

MANAGING YOUR CPD

Now we have defined continuous professional development, considered its importance in the modern business world and examined what it covers and its potential sources, turn your attention to your own CPD and the strategies you can employ to manage the process effectively. We address each of the following in turn: identifying your learning needs; making **personal development plans**; embedding reflective practice (learning logs); identifying support; and overcoming barriers

IDENTIFYING YOUR LEARNING NEEDS

There are a number of approaches and techniques that you can use to identify areas for development. These include:

- **Situational approach** – consider where you have been, where you are now, where you want to be in the future, how you can get there, and how you will know when you have arrived. This is especially useful if you are considering a significant change.

- **Benchmarking** – against national professional standards or role-models.

Observe the behaviours of people you consider to be very successful, or who are doing what you would like to be doing in the future. Identify the behaviours that you think make them successful and measure yourself against them. You could talk to the individual about the values, beliefs, emotions and attitudes that inform their behaviour. You could also ask how they developed themselves and what advice they would give. They may even consider acting as a mentor through your development.

- **Request feedback** from as many different sources as possible. Try to ensure that feedback relates to areas of your job, that it is precise and that it uses measurements (time, quantity and cost wherever possible). Your formal appraisal with your manager especially should provide useful information on areas for development.

MAKING PERSONAL DEVELOPMENT PLANS

It is important to take a structured and formalised approach to personal development planning. This is so that all needs are covered, objectives are set, learning activities are focused and take place in a logical order, and outcomes can be measured (against objectives). It also enables you to build up a portfolio of evidence, which could lead to exemptions towards a qualification or contribute to a CIPD membership upgrade (which we address later).

There are six steps to successful personal development planning:

Step 1:   Personal skills audit and identifying learning needs (as detailed above).

Step 2:   Setting objectives. Once you know what you want to improve, you can set a clear objective for each area. You will surely have come across the acronym SMART – indicating that every objective should be specific, measurable, achievable, realistic and timebound. By keeping these key points in mind HR professionals will be able to set clear objectives within their CPD plans. If these points are not considered, objectives are likely to be ill-defined, meaning that HR professionals will not be able to track their progress or guide their CPD activities effectively. An example of a poorly defined objective might be:

'To stop leaving important pieces of work until their deadline'.

This objective is not very specific and there is no measurable outcome. There is no time component to the objective and its achievability is debatable. Here is a much better way of phrasing a CPD goal or objective:

'To increase the time I have for planning and managing (as opposed to fire-fighting) by 10% within three months'.

This objective specifies a clear goal and there is a measurable output. We can see that the objective has a relevant timescale and that it should be achievable and realistic depending on the individual's access to relevant development experiences.

Step 3:   Selecting opportunities. Once your objectives are set, you need to identify opportunities for development in each area, both inside and outside the workplace. For the objective above, opportunities may include:

- understanding my use of time, and where I waste time
- delegation
- learning from others
- practising outside the workplace.

Step 4:   Actions. You should now develop an action plan of precise activities to be undertaken over time. This should include details of WHAT activities, HOW they will be carried out, WHERE (workplace, classroom, and so on) and WHEN. For the example above, activities might include:

- attending a time management workshop (venue and timing as dictated by course availability)
- observing/shadowing colleague X, who seems to manage his time more effectively (timing according to mutual availability)
- keeping a time log for a week, and assessing where you waste time, and so on.

Step 5:   Implementation and progress. During the implementation phase, it is important to have someone that can give you support and guidance. A mentor who can provide input and help to monitor your progress is a valuable asset.

Step 6:   Assessment. It is important that there is a formal assessment of your development by an objective party – such as your manager, tutor or a colleague. Assessment can come from numerical measurement (time saved, money saved, database accuracy, number of customer complaints, and so on); observation of your performance/ behaviour (interviewing, delivering training, and so on); a review of documentation you have prepared; and so on.

EMBEDDING REFLECTIVE PRACTICE AND THE LEARNING LOG

As mentioned above, one of the key skills required for successful continuous professional development is reflective practice, which is closely linked to the notion of experiential learning. You will have been carrying out reflective practice as you have worked through this chapter – especially when responding to the Activity sections, which encourage you to reframe past experiences; consider what skills you possess, and at what level; assess your strengths and weaknesses; and identify specific areas for development. The trick now is to get into the habit of taking moments to reflect in your everyday job – turning every experience into a formal learning opportunity on which you can draw in the future. You can do this by asking yourself a simple question: 'What did I get out of this event or experience?'

One of the key tools used in reflective practice is a learning log. Some professional study courses require the submission of a formal learning log, and many people use them to demonstrate learning and competence to current or potential employers.

Keeping a learning log does more than just provide a record of development activities undertaken; it forces you to adopt a more structured approach to learning and to reflect on each experience – reducing the usually haphazard nature of learning experiences in everyday life.

There are a variety of different formats that you can use, but each entry should include the following: the date; details of the learning experience (something significant that happened that you learned from); a brief conclusion – what you learned; actions that you will now take; and a deadline for actions.

The principles are that entries should be brief (a log should not be seen as a burden), timely (as soon as possible after a learning event) and honest, and that further actions should be realistic.

REFLECTIVE ACTIVITY 6.4

Reflect on something that you have done recently that resulted in your learning something. Write a learning log entry, structured as follows:

Learning experience:

Conclusion:

Actions:

Deadline:

You may wish to keep a portfolio of evidence (of your development). This can supplement your reflections (your learning log) with documentary evidence and third-party testimonials of your competence. Documentary evidence can include things such as letters, emails, reports, PowerPoint presentation slides, meeting minutes, surveys, budgets, and so on. Third-party testimonials should come from someone who is able to comment critically and directly on your skill or behaviour. This may be your line manager, other managers, colleagues, suppliers/customers, college tutors, and so on. Testimonies need to be written and explicit: 'I have always found Carla Conrad to be a very efficient manager' may be gratifying to hear but does not provide much in the way of evidence; 'I can confirm that Carla Conrad led the successful negotiation with ABZ Direct' does.

IDENTIFYING SUPPORT

Support can be very useful in helping you identify appropriate development opportunities, sustaining you through the development, and providing you with opportunities to put your learning into action after completion. Personal and professional support can be drawn from a number of sources, including your line manager, a workplace mentor, colleagues, subordinates, college tutors, your training and development department, professional or sector networks, family and friends.

Gaining support will be easier in a company that values and invests in CPD. The Rolls-Royce case study (adapted from Simms 2005) illustrates the difference such an approach can make.

CASE STUDY

ROLLS-ROYCE

HR is often too busy looking after other people's development needs to attend to its own. But thanks to a pioneering professional development scheme, that's no longer the case at Rolls-Royce ...

Back in 1999, it had become apparent to John Rivers, Company Director, Human Resources, that managers in other functions such as engineering, procurement and finance were looking to HR to help them support a growing focus on continuous professional development (CPD). This prompted Rivers to accelerate the drive towards greater professionalism within HR too – a case of 'Physician, heal thyself'.

Although HR professionals already participated in regular training programmes and many of them sat CIPD exams, Rivers felt the function needed a company-specific framework of standards and competencies and a more structured approach to CPD ...

Rolls-Royce involved the CIPD from the outset in designing its professional development framework for HR. In a stroke of good timing, it came as the Institute was looking for companies to pilot the internal professional upgrading of practitioners to membership or fellowship.

'We saw a real opportunity to make an explicit link between individual personal development, business development and development of the Institute itself,' says Ken Boyle, who is Vice-President, Membership and Education at the CIPD.

'Many people don't upgrade, partly because

of the paperwork involved in compiling portfolios of experience and qualifications, and partly because they feel it wouldn't make much difference to their career prospects. But we were keen to encourage upgrading activities as part of our drive for professionalism,' says Boyle.

He argues that if you use CPD as a learning opportunity rather than a box-ticking exercise and put it into an organisational context, both the company and individuals take it more seriously ...

The scheme involved setting up an in-house upgrading panel ... and training internal mentors covering eight company sites to help people eligible for upgrading to put their portfolios together. 'They coach people through the process and act as sponsors,' explains Martin Shipley, CIPD Education and Development Adviser ...

Within Rolls-Royce itself, one reason for the success of the scheme is the development diaries that members of the HR team now keep. These record evidence of their training and professional development in a format that is consistent with the Institute's upgrading process.

To support the upgrading scheme, Rivers, Boyle and their colleagues created an internal competency framework that categorised all HR jobs into four groups: HR director, HR manager, HR adviser and HR administration. For each, the framework set out a series of required competencies, the appropriate professional grade (CIPD or its overseas equivalent) and a series of education and development programmes, including CIPD courses and qualifications as well as internal seminars and master classes.

'You quickly get to the stage where there is an expectation that people will be operating at these specified professional levels, which helps to make the link between the value of CPD and internal career progression more obvious,' says Boyle ...

Question

1 You have been asked by your local CIPD branch to give an input to an annual event for new CIPD students in your area on the benefits of CPD. As you are aware, students need to provide evidence of CPD in order to progress their career. It is advisable that they start this at the beginning of their studies and see it as a lifetime journey.

2 Based on the material in the case study and in this chapter, what personal and professional benefits of CPD would you include?

OVERCOMING BARRIERS TO CPD

Despite an upsurge in interest in continuous professional development for all professional groups in academic and practitioner literature, and for the HR profession in particular, evidence of CPD in practice is somewhat patchy. The following extract (Rothwell and Arnold 2005) reports on research that has been done with CIPD members on engagement with CPD:

We found that the value attached to CPD was high, but this did not necessarily translate into levels of participation .... The most popular updating strategies were informal, related to job role, emphasising organisational–procedural aspects rather than professional knowledge. Some widely promoted strategies, such as reflective diaries or online media, were hardly used, and there was little emphasis on courses and qualifications. Respondents were more positive about targets and recording than previous research had indicated, but some highlighted challenges in identifying CPD opportunities, especially if self-employed.

Twenty per cent of respondents identified 'strategic HRM' as a CPD priority. Only two variables had an impact on the perceived value of CPD: professional commitment and gender. The more professionally committed the respondents – especially women – are, the more likely they will value CPD. Other variables, such as past career success, perceptions of future employability, position in the company, graduate status, and professional membership, hardly had any influence.

So what factors might hinder your CPD? Table 6.2 contains a list of common barriers and suggested strategies for overcoming them:

Table 6.2 Factors acting as barriers to CPD

Barriers	Strategies
Lack of time	Put a little time aside on a regular basis for learning. Consider alternative types of learning that can fit around commitments.
Lack of support	Be assertive with your managers about the importance of CPD. Be prepared to ask others for support and offer to support others in return.
Lack of opportunities	Look for these yourself; don't wait for others to offer them. Be prepared to undertake voluntary work or duties to get experience, and to attend events in your own time.
Lack of resources	Try to link personal learning needs to organisational needs and then argue a case for resources.
Low expectations	Don't just think about short-term extrinsic rewards; identify the long-term and intrinsic rewards that can be gained via learning CPD activities.
Previous bad experience	This is usually associated with a learning activity, rather than with learning as a whole. Treat this experience as a learning point in itself – what did it tell you about how you learn? See if you can find alternative activities.
Lack of enthusiasm	CPD puts you in the driving seat; make sure you are working to your own agenda and that there is something in it for you.
Personality factors	Certain activities may be incongruent with your personality. An introvert, for example, may not relish the idea of a networking event. Consider alternative learning activities where possible, but do try to experiment with moving out of your comfort zone.

CIPD MEMBERSHIP AND CAREER PROGRESSION

CIPD membership is a key indicator of professional competence, and CPD is a key requirement for CIPD membership. There are a number of different levels of membership and your aim should be to work up the levels throughout your professional career. The three main professional levels are:

- **Associate:** working in a support role to key HR areas
- **Chartered Member:** able to demonstrate the expertise needed to plan and manage generalist or specialist HR operations
- **Chartered Fellow:** holding a strategic position and able to demonstrate the expertise to lead the key areas of HR.

To apply for an upgrade to a professional level of membership (Associate, Chartered Member or Chartered Fellow), you will need to apply using the CIPD's online Membership Assessment process. This will assess your knowledge (based on qualifications), activities (based on a self-assessment Impact Report) and behaviour (based on workplace questionnaires) against the membership criteria you are applying for.

It is in the Impact Report, workplace questionnaire and other associated correspondence that you will have the opportunity to provide evidence of your CPD. The CIPD advice for compiling CPD records is to consider the following questions based around past and planned learning, as shown in Table 6.3:

Table 6.3 CIPD's recommended approach to recording CPD

Last year	Next year
What were the three most important things you learned last year? How did you learn them?	How do you identify your learning and development needs?
What value did you add (to your organisation, clients or colleagues) through professional development?	What are your three main development objectives, and how will you achieve them?
What were the tangible outcomes of your professional development over the last 12 months?	What differences do you plan to make (to your role, organisation, clients and colleagues)?
Has anyone else gained from your professional development? How?	When will you next review your professional development needs?

There is a section of the CIPD website dedicated to CPD. A guidance and support page is available, which includes examples, templates and case studies. This can be accessed at: www.cipd.co.uk/cpd/guidance/ (CIPD 2012b). There is also a CPD online page, where you can enter and edit your own CPD plans and records, and can submit them to the CIPD as required. This can be accessed at: www.cipd.co.uk/cpdonline/ (CIPD 2012c).

FURTHER RESOURCES TO SUPPORT YOUR LEARNING

As you read in Chapter 1, this textbook covers the core elements of the CIPD's level 5 programme. In addition to this textbook, two further texts have been produced which are relevant to the human resource development (HRD) and human resource management (HRM) streams. These books are *Developing People and Organisations*, edited by Jim Stewart and Patricia Rogers, and *Managing People and Organisations*, edited by Stephen Taylor and Carol Woodhams. Each contains chapters by a number of expert writers. This part of the chapter provides you with an overview of the content included in each of these textbooks and also highlights further key resources that can be used to support professional development in the HR field.

DEVELOPING PEOPLE AND ORGANISATIONS

The first chapter of *Developing People and Organisations* discusses the concept of 'organisation design'. This chapter, by Ian McLean, Michael Mcfadden and Gary Connor, highlights how HR professionals can make sure that organisations are appropriately designed to ensure that they deliver on both their short- and long-term objectives. Driven by organisation business strategy and operating context, organisation design is a conscious process of shaping and aligning the various organisational components: structure, size, systems, processes, people, performance measures, culture and communication. The chapter explores, through a review of theories and models, the elements that contribute to organisation design and the development of organisation insight crucial to building agile and adaptable organisations, with healthy cultures that are essential to meet current and future challenges.

Building on the concept of organisation design, the second chapter is written by Sophie Mills, Amanda Lee and Kirsten Stevens and focuses on organisation development. This chapter provides a good foundation of underpinning organisation development theory and knowledge, including its relationship to organisation design and change management, and how effective organisation development interventions can increase business performance and productivity. Organisation development focuses on making interventions and driving improvements to organisational success by facilitating the ways in which employees – individuals, groups and teams – are motivated to perform and are rewarded for performance; are involved in the business decision-making processes; interact with, and relate to, each other; acquire and develop knowledge, experience and skills in the context of rapidly changing organisational environments.

Chapter 3 by Jim Stewart and Dalbir Sidhu aims to provide the learner with a broad understanding of the factors to be considered when implementing and evaluating inclusive learning and development (L&D) activities within varying organisational contexts. It covers what is required to support the learning of individuals, groups and organisations to drive sustained business performance. It also considers the role and impact of learning facilitation as it is used in a range of delivery methods and types of activities, for example through one-to-one coaching, formal courses, action learning, and the in use of e-learning or blended learning.

Continuing the learning and development theme, the purpose of Chapter 4 by Rosalind Maxwell-Harrison, Jill Ashley-Jones and Terry Brathwaite is to enable the learner to contribute to the development of coaching and mentoring activities within organisations. As an HR professional, the learner is encouraged to analyse the extent to which coaching and mentoring exist within an organisational context, the efficiency and effectiveness of coaching and mentoring interventions and the role of line managers as coach and mentor. The chapter invites learners to consider how they can make a personal contribution to coaching and mentoring activities within an organisational context

Chapter 5, 'Contemporary Developments in Human Resource Development', by Jim Stewart and Sharon McGuire, explores key developments in the theory and practice of human resource development (HRD) both within and beyond the immediate organisation context. It specifically covers recent debates and discussions in the HRD field and highlights how external trends and data have implications for HRD practice. The chapter also evaluates a range of theories and models that can be applied to professional, management and leadership development and assess the implications of emerging technologies for HRD practice.

Chapter 6, by Graham Perkins and Carol Woodhams, explores the concept of knowledge management. It is crucial to recognise that effective knowledge management is a vital enabler of organisation performance, and the chapter pinpoints what knowledge is, the forms it can take and how knowledge is created in organisations. The concept of the 'learning organisation' is explored in this chapter, and a range of approaches to knowledge management is discussed and evaluated.

The final chapter in this textbook, by Patricia Rogers, Michelle McLardy, Raymond Rogers and Susan Barnes, focuses on improving organisational performance. A specific focus of this chapter is on how organisations can drive sustained performance by creating high-performance work organisations and involving line managers in the performance management process. The concept of 'high-performance working' is explored in detail and learners will understand how they can develop a business case for creating a high-performance work organisation. Alongside this the chapter discusses the role of line managers in the performance management process and considers how collaborative working practices can help to build high-performance cultures.

MANAGING PEOPLE AND ORGANISATIONS

The third textbook in this series is *Managing People and Organisations*. Chapter 1 by Gail Swift explores how contemporary organisations are using a variety of different models of HR service delivery, highlighting how they have evolved and changed to suit the needs of different organisations. This chapter asks why organisations might want to change the structure and/or location of HR service provision and discusses the challenges involved in maintaining and managing HR services.

One of the areas of HR practice that is a CPD priority is employment law. Chapter 2 provides an overview of employment law written by Stephen Taylor and Krystal Wilkinson. It is important to understand that this chapter only provides a brief synopsis of the main issues and developments in employment law, for the territory is vast. The chapter will nonetheless enable learners to understand the purpose of employment regulation and the various ways that it is enforced in practice. After examining the purpose of employment regulation, attention switches to how HR professionals can manage a range of issues lawfully. These issues include recruitment and selection, change and reorganisation, pay and working time, and performance and disciplinary matters. The chapter also discusses the principles of discrimination law and highlights how HR professionals can ensure that employees are treated fairly at work.

Another key area of practice is resourcing and talent planning. This is covered by Krystal Wilkinson and Stephen Taylor in Chapter 3. The purpose of this chapter is to provide an overview of the way different organisations effectively manage resourcing and talent planning activities within the context of diverse and distributed locations. A fundamental part of HR management is the mobilisation of workforces, ensuring that organisations can access relevant skills at the time and in the places that they need them to drive sustained performance. This chapter explores key labour market trends, highlighting their significance for different types of organisations, and demonstrates how HR professionals can forecast demand and supply of skills. One of the major aims of this unit is thus to introduce learners to the strategic approaches that organisations take to position themselves as employers in the labour market and to plan effectively so that they are able to meet their current and anticipated organisational skills needs. To this end, the chapter highlights how HR professionals can contribute to the development of effective resourcing strategies, including recruitment, selection, retention and dismissal issues.

Chapter 4, by Ted Johns, explores the concept of employee engagement. This chapter covers the components of employee engagement and highlights how it can be linked to and yet be distinguished from other related concepts. Specific attention is focused on how employee engagement links with relevant HR policies, strategies and practices and learners will see how employee engagement can be a contributor to positive corporate outcomes. The chapter shows how HR professionals can evaluate the findings of employee engagement surveys and demonstrates how strategies and practices intended to raise levels of employee engagement can be implemented. Learners will also understand the future for employee engagement, both in the UK and the wider world.

Chapter 5, by Cecilia Ellis, is called 'Contemporary Developments in Employment Relations'. The chapter is designed to encourage learners to assess and understand broader developments that influence the effective management of the employment relationship in organisations. It outlines key developments in the theory and practice of employment relations, the main sources of employment relations legislation, and the approaches that organisations can adopt, such as unitarism and pluralism. It also highlights the effect of management style and trade unions on employment relations and explores the concepts of employee involvement and participation. Conflict resolution is discussed in this chapter and learners are given guidance to understanding different forms of conflict behaviour and different methods of dispute resolution.

The final chapter in this textbook explores the concept of reward management. The purpose of this chapter, by Graham Perkins and Carol Woodhams, is to provide the reader with a wide understanding of how the business context influences reward strategies and policies. It locates reward management in the wider business context and highlights key issues that drive reward strategies and policies. Learners are introduced to the main theories that underpin reward strategies, and the concept of 'total reward' is discussed in some detail. Specific reward initiatives and practices such as job evaluation are briefly discussed, as is the role of line managers in reward management. The chapter ends with an outline of how HR professionals can evaluate the impact of reward management.

SOURCES OF INFORMATION

Each of the chapters outlined above has a section of additional resources to support learning that is specific to the topic. There are a number of other generic sources of information that early-career HR professionals can access and that will be useful.

Academic journals can be very useful sources of information and research data because, in order to get published, any article is first subjected to 'peer review'. That means that it must first be scrutinised anonymously by reviewers who are specialists in the field. They typically suggest that amendments must be made before publication is possible. As a result, before you read an account of any research findings, the article concerned will have been rewritten, resubmitted to the journal and re-reviewed, often extensively and on a number of occasions.

In the UK the most respected peer-reviewed journals in the field of HRM include:

- *Human Resource Management Journal* (endorsed by the CIPD)
- *British Journal of Industrial Relations*
- *Work, Employment and Society*
- *Employee Relations*
- *Personnel Review*
- *Gender, Work and Organisation*
- *Journal of Management Studies.*

It is important to state that HR professionals should not limit themselves to purely HR-related journals because research findings relevant to HR can come from a variety of fields, including sociology, employment law and occupational psychology, to name just a few.

If you are studying at a college or university you will usually be able to access many types of journal through your library's online resources. If this is not the case, many can be accessed through the CIPD's website. To do this you need to click on the EBSCO link on the CIPD library pages at www.cipd.co.uk.

Textbooks can also provide good summaries of academic research, setting out key findings and often debating different interpretations. Some recent publications in the field of HRM include:

- *The Sage Handbook of Human Resource Management* edited by Adrian Wilkinson et al (2010).
- *The Oxford Handbook of Human Resource Management* edited by Peter Boxall et al (2007).
- *The Routledge Companion to Strategic Human Resource Management* edited by John Storey et al (2009).

Some of the websites that learners might find useful in continuing their learning are outlined in Chapter 1. Other useful statistics and reports are available.

Labour market data can be found by visiting websites such as the Office for National Statistics (www.ons.gov.uk) and UK National Statistics (www.statistics.gov.uk). The CIPD produces a number of very useful reports. From the CIPD's website HR professionals can access annual reports on issues such as absence management, reward management and recruitment. The CIPD's website also includes useful factsheets on a variety of topics, including performance management, employee engagement and dismissal.

Government department websites constitute another useful source of information. Examples of these departments include the Department for Business, Innovation and Skills (www.bis.gov.uk) and the Department for Work and Pensions (www.dwp.gov.uk). Here HR professionals are able to find valuable pieces of information, such as new government policies or practical advice.

Another website that is particularly useful to HR professionals is *People Management* (www.peoplemanagement.co.uk). This website provides a wealth of current HR news, case studies and 'how to' documents and is therefore useful to HR professionals at various stages of their careers. A similar website is *Personnel Today* (www.personneltoday.com). HR professionals can also access a wide variety of information through newspapers, such as:

- *The Times*
- *The Independent*
- *The Guardian*
- *The Daily Telegraph*.

HR professionals should be reading a broadsheet newspaper regularly. Periodicals including *Management Today* or the *Training Journal* are also very useful sources of information. Newspapers and periodicals (either printed or online) often provide case studies, benchmarking ideas, insight into new thinking in the HR community and practical tips. Further useful sources of information include specific trade journals that are relevant to different professions (for example, accountancy) or sectors (for example, construction).

Finally, ACAS (www.acas.org.uk) provides a significant amount of information, including guidance on employment contracts and disciplinary and grievance procedures. It is a very useful source of information. HR professionals can download a number of guides from the ACAS website free of charge or can call its advice line if they have specific queries or questions.

The key point to take from this part of the chapter is that there are many different sources of information that HR professionals can make use of when attempting to develop their skills and knowledge. Successful HR professionals will make sure that they review a wide range of material because it means that their final strategies, policies and/or plans are as comprehensive as they can be.

CONCLUSION

The purpose of this chapter has been to discuss, with tips and advice, the paths for your future learning and development and the means by which it can be accomplished. We hope this chapter has given you a sound understanding of the concept of continuous professional development (CPD) and its importance in the modern business world. You should be able to effectively argue the case for CPD to others and have a good understanding of the strategies that can help CPD be carried out effectively. You should be aware of the CIPD's membership criteria and HR Profession Map as well as the various sources of data that HR professionals can use to expand their skills and knowledge. We hope that you enjoy your learning.

FURTHER READING

CIPD (2012) *HR Profession Map [online]*. Available at: http://www.cipd.co.uk/cipd-hr-profession/hr-profession-map/. This website provides a wealth of information about the CIPD's HR Profession Map, including information on the key professional areas and the bands and transitions.

MEGGINSON, D. and WHITAKER, V. (2007) *Continuing professional development.* 2nd edition. London: Chartered Institute of Personnel and Development. This text provides an excellent guide to the concept of continuous professional development, highlighting its key principles and showing how professionals can effectively engage with it.

ROTHWELL, A. and ARNOLD, J. (2005) Continuing professional development: how has it worked for you? *People Management.* 8 December. This article discusses key issues around CPD, including the value that individuals attach to it and the implications of this for the CIPD.

WATSON, G. and REISSNER, S. C. (2010) *Developing skills for business leadership.* London: Chartered Institute of Personnel and Development. Chapter 1 is dedicated to skills for professional development and practice.

REFERENCES

BOXALL, P., PURCELL, J. and WRIGHT, P. (eds) (2007) *The Oxford handbook of human resource management.* Oxford: Oxford University Press.

CIPD (2012a) *CIPD and the HR profession [online].* London: Chartered Institute of Personnel and Development. Available at: http://www.cipd.co.uk/cipd-hr-profession [Accessed 28 April 2012].

CIPD (2012b) *CPD guidance and support [online].* London: Chartered Institute of Personnel and Development. Available at: http://www.cipd.co.uk/cpd/guidance/ [Accessed 28 April 2012].

CIPD (2012c) *CPD online [online].* London: Chartered Institute of Personnel and Development. Available at: https://www.cipd.co.uk/cpdonline/ [Accessed 28 April 2012].

MADDEN, C. and MITCHELL, V. (1993) *Professions, standards and competence: a survey of continuing education for the professions.* Bristol: University of Bristol, Department for Continuing Education.

ROTHWELL, A. and ARNOLD, J. (2005) Continuing professional development: how has it worked for you? *People Management.* 8 December.

SCHÖN, D. (1983) *The reflective practitioner: how professionals think in action.* New York: Basic Books.

SIMMS, J. (2005) High rollers. *People Management.* 14 July.

STOREY, J., WRIGHT, P. and ULRICH, D. (2009) *The Routledge companion to strategic human resource management.* London: Routledge.

WATSON, G. and REISSNER, S. C. (2010) *Developing skills for business leadership.* London: Chartered Institute of Personnel and Development.

WILKINSON, A., BACON, N., REDMAN, T. and SNELL, S. (eds) (2010) *The Sage handbook of human resource management.* London: Sage.

Glossary

Bachelor's degree with honours: Usually an academic degree awarded for an undergraduate course or major that generally lasts four years, but can range anywhere from three to six years. Undergraduate degrees are differentiated either as *pass degrees* (also known as *ordinary degrees*) or as *honours degrees*, the latter sometimes denoted by the appearance of '(Hons)' after the degree abbreviation. An honours degree generally requires a higher academic standard than a pass degree.

Benchmarking: The use of data that has been collected on current performance to compare performance, either internally or externally.

Best practice HRM: Best practice perspective of HRM of which adherents believe that there are certain HR policies and practices which will invariably help an organisation achieve competitive advantage, no matter which organisation applies them. There is therefore a clear link between HR activity and business performance, but the effect will only be maximised if the 'right' and 'best' HR policies are pursued.

Best-fit HRM: Akin to a best practice approach, an approach that also identifies a link between human resource management practice and the achievement of competitive advantage. In contrast to a best practice approach, HR practices are not applied universally to all; instead, all is contingent on the particular circumstances of each organisation. HR policies and practices are required to 'fit' the situation of individual employers. What is appropriate (or 'best') for one will not necessarily be right for another. Key variables include the size of the establishment, the organisation strategy and the nature of the labour markets in which the organisation competes.

Biotechnology: The bringing together of computing technologies and biology, leading to the manipulation of living organisms in order to create useful products such as drugs, biofuels and GM crops.

Black box studies: Research studies which were conducted by John Purcell and a team at Bath University for the CIPD and which examined the impact of people management on organisational performance. The study was conducted within a framework which claims that performance is a function of people's ability (knowledge and skills), their motivation and the opportunity they are given to deploy their skills.

Bureaucracy: In HRM a style of management and organisation design associated with Weber (1925) and Fayol (1949). Key features of bureaucracy include centralisation and unity of command, consistency of purpose, a widespread sense of order with a place for everything, the operation of 'equity', where management operates not just within the law but within the spirit of the law, treating employees both fairly and kindly, and long-term employment at all levels leading to a sense of order and stability.

Business cases: Documents which set out the reasoning behind projects and which detail key findings together with what they mean for future plans and strategies.

Centralised: Describing an approach to organisation structure whereby operational managerial decisions are made by a single overall controlling power. This type of structure is frequently associated with a bureaucracy. Decision-making is slower, but also more consistent.

CIPD HR Profession Map: An extensive and highly beneficial tool which can be used for many purposes, and which sets out in a user-friendly format eight 'behaviours', ten areas of professional practice and four 'bands and transitions' that provide a structure for the study and practice of professional HRM.

Collective bargaining: A method of determining pay and conditions in an industry or organisation that involves annual negotiation between trade unions and employers.

Continuous professional development (CPD): The ongoing learning and improvement related to the specific professional requirements of an individual's role. CPD is related to improving specialist knowledge, ensuring adherence to legislative and regulatory processes and a general awareness of developments within a given field.

Critical thinking: The systematic analysis of a document, process or system by an individual who possesses specific professional knowledge and expertise.

Decentralised: Describing an approach to organisation structure associated with flatter or divisionalised structures. Operational decision-making is delegated to individual units, away from centralised control.

Decentralised bargaining: A collective bargaining arrangement that involves negotiations which take place at the local level in business units. It represents a shift away from traditional national-level bargaining through which terms and conditions are established across a whole industry.

Differentiators: Aspects of people management which are able to encourage outstanding performance from a workforce and thus achieve superior results that exceed expectations. Part of becoming an employer of choice.

Ethics: Rules of conduct recognised as morally appropriate to a particular profession or area of life.

Evidence-based HRM: Form of HRM which involves taking HRM decisions, developing HRM policies and, when debating with colleagues, taking up positions all of which are informed by robust evidence.

Expatriates: Members of staff, mostly managerial, who are seconded by their companies to work in an overseas subsidiary or sister company abroad for a period of time. Assignments of three to five years are the most common.

Flexibility: In HRM, an integrated capacity for organisations to respond to change rapidly and efficiently. It is associated with part-time working, fixed-term working, flexible hours, multi-skilling and performance-based payment arrangements.

Foundation degree: A vocational qualification introduced by the UK Government in September 2001 similar in level to the higher national diploma but below the Bachelor of Science/Bachelor of Arts level of education. Courses are typically two years' full-time study or three to four years' part-time study and are offered both by universities and by colleges of higher education. Foundation degrees are intended to give a basic knowledge in a subject to enable the holder to go on to employment or further study in that field.

Globalisation: Process widely observed in recent decades whereby greater levels of international trade and international exchange are serving to bring diverse countries closer together.

HR business partner: A senior HR professional working closely with business leaders or line managers, usually embedded in the business unit, influencing and steering strategy and strategy implementation.

HR generalist: An HR professional who has knowledge of, and involvement in, all areas of the HR function.

HR Profession Map: Document produced by the CIPD which sets out the competencies that HR professionals require in professional practice.

HR specialist: An HR professional who has advanced knowledge of a particular area of people management (such as resourcing, reward or organisation development) and limits their focus to strategy development and operational activities in that particular field.

Humanist: In HRM, describing principles derived from the work of Elton Mayo (1933) in which the primary argument is that employees achieve higher levels of motivation, satisfaction and performance if the jobs they do are made more interesting and challenging. While it must be accepted that many jobs are never going to be highly enjoyable, it can be argued that the key to higher levels of performance lies in managers' designing jobs and managing people in such a way as to maximise the satisfaction, enjoyment and well-being that job-holders derive from their work.

Human resource management: A debated term formerly meaning a new way of managing people that was clearly distinct from 'traditional personnel management', but now used simply to refer to an overall body of management activities rather than any particular approach to carrying them out.

Infrastructure factors: People management activities which involve organising the work of other people and creating a working environment that can help a business or group to achieve its objectives.

'Knowing–doing gap': Jeffrey Pfeffer and Robert Sutton's (2006) term describing the challenge of turning knowledge about how to enhance organisational performance into actions consistent with that knowledge. Put simply, it is about converting knowledge about improving organisational performance into action.

Knowledge economy: Type of national economy in which most organisations are concerned with the production or manipulation of some form of knowledge. It is often argued that the UK economy is steadily evolving into a knowledge economy over time.

Leitch Review: Comprehensive government-sponsored investigation into the state of skills in the UK carried out between 2004 and 2006 which has informed government policy since. The final report is published on the HM Treasury website along with much of the research which informed its key findings.

MacLeod Report on Employee Engagement: Report commissioned by the Department for Business, Innovation and Skills (BIS) and produced by David MacLeod and Nita Clarke in 2009 to take an in-depth look at employee engagement and at its potential benefits for organisations and employees. The researchers found evidence of a clear correlation between engagement and performance – and most importantly between improving engagement and improving performance. They concluded that a wider take-up of engagement approaches could impact positively on UK competitiveness.

Nanotechnology: Technology which involves manipulating matter at the nano-scale to produce new materials. It has been made possible by advances in miniaturisation through optical magnification. The development of the material known as 'graphene' is a recent example.

Office for National Statistics: Publicly funded national statistics authority of the UK, which publishes a vast amount of data on employment matters on its website. This includes regularly collected statistics alongside articles and larger research reports on particular topic areas.

Outsourcing: Purchasing a service from an external source rather than performing it in-house. It can lead to cost savings and a better quality of service.

Personal development plan: A structured document that lists an individual's goals, relevant learning activities and the expected outcomes. Personal development plans can be used to build up a portfolio of evidence of CPD activity.

Pluralists: In HRM, people who believe that not only do employers and employees have different interests, but that they also have multiple different interests. What employees seek – for example, high wages, limitations on hours – is different from what employers are looking for: flexibility, low labour costs, a high degree of management control, improved productivity, and so on. The result, inevitably, is tension and an 'us and them' conflict.

Pragmatism: In HRM, a style of management whereby managers assess the usefulness of an approach as opposed to its 'rightness'. Pragmatic managers are therefore free to treat good performers more favourably than poor performers and manage their teams by 'gut instinct'. This can lead to problems associated with inconsistent practice.

Primary data: Information that has been collected specifically for the study in which it is to be used. In this sense, primary data is 'new' in that it has not been captured by previous research projects.

Privatisation: Process by which governments sell off public sector organisations – particularly publicly owned corporations – so that they become part of the private sector. Privatisation is associated with the creation of markets in which companies compete with one another for business.

Professional: Person who earns a living by the proficient use of expert and specialist knowledge, who exercises autonomous authority and who makes a commitment to a set of ethical principles.

Professionalism: Qualities or typical features displayed in a profession or by professionals, especially competence, skill, and so on.

Public–private partnership: Form of organisation increasingly common in recent years that represents a hybrid of the private and public sectors, often involving a private company operating part of a public service under some control by ministers or local authorities.

QAA for Higher Education: Quality Assurance Agency for Higher Education. Its job is to uphold quality and standards in UK universities and colleges. It guides and checks the quality of teaching, learning and assessment in UK higher education.

Qualitative data: Data based around words and meanings. It can usually show why certain things are happening in organisations.

QUANGO: Quasi-autonomous non-governmental organisation – a body that carries out functions on behalf of government and is funded by government. However, most quangos are independent of direct ministerial control.

Quantitative data: Data which usually contains numbers and can be analysed through statistical analysis software.

Reflective learning: Learning that involves sitting back and thinking carefully about past events, pulling elements together to aid future performance. Reflection involves 'deeper' learning which enables professionals to expand their personal understandings of concepts, applying theories and knowledge in a wide variety of situations.

Research design: Term used to refer to frameworks for the collection and analysis of data.

Resource-based view of the firm (RBV): A way of thinking about organisational strategy-making which focuses on building on existing internal strengths rather than on adjusting to meet the needs of the external environment.

Sampling: Method through which researchers select a proportionate number of individuals from a given population to participate in a research project.

Scientific management: In HRM, an approach historically based on the premise that the fully regulated organisation of the workforce and work methods improves efficiency. Work should be a co-operative effort between managers who manage and workers who work. Work organisation should be such that it removes all responsibility from the workers, leaving them only to carry out their particular task. By specialising and training in this task, the individual worker would become 'perfect' in its performance; work could thus be organised into production lines and items produced efficiently, and to a constant standard, as a result.

Secondary data: Data that has been included in or discovered through previous research projects or academic writing.

Shared service centre: A means of providing a common corporate service across a large organisation, or sometimes, across several partner organisations. There is a clear service focus, enabling each of the centre's customers to specify the level and nature of the service required.

SWOT analysis: Simple mental mapping tool which encourages managers to think systematically about their organisation's strengths, weaknesses, opportunities and threats. Traditionally, the S and the W relate to internal issues, the O and the T to developments in the external business environment.

Taylorist: Describing the tenets of **Scientific management**.

'Thinking performer': An HR professional who has relevant, theoretical knowledge and who, through reflection and application, can make sense of some of the practical complexities and ambiguities inherent in the management of people.

Three-legged stool model: Way of structuring the HR function in an organisation advocated by Dave Ulrich, making use of HR business partners, centres of excellence, and a shared service centre for routine transactional services.

Unitarism: In HRM, a perspective that assumes employers and employees share the same fundamental, long-term objectives as far as their relationship with one another is concerned. For example, both have an economic interest in the financial success of their organisation: the employer in order to maximise profit, and the employee in order to maximise job security and career opportunity. According to this view, harmonious relations between employer and employee are normal and conflict is abnormal.

Workplace Employment Relations Survey: Nationwide study carried out every few years into many aspects of employment practice in UK workplaces, including the very smallest. Summaries of the findings are published on the Department for Business, Innovation and Skills (BIS) website.

World Trade Organization (WTO): International institution that hosts near-continual international negotiations aimed at reducing formal and informal barriers to trade.

Index

Organisational Development

Sophie Mills, Amanda Lee, Krish Pinto and Kristen Stevens

CHAPTER CONTENTS

- Introduction
- What is OD?
- The historical basis of OD
- The role of the OD practitioner
- Understanding the OD process
- Practices, models and approaches
- The role and purpose of OD interventions
- Summary

KEY LEARNING OUTCOMES

By the end of this chapter, you will be able to:

- Analyse the underpinning history, theories and principles of organisation development.

- Describe and explain the organisation development process.

- Evaluate various organisation development practices, models and approaches.

- Discuss the value of organisation development interventions to business performance and productivity.

INTRODUCTION

This chapter introduces and examines the concept of organisational development (OD) and its role within the management of organisational change. It commences by introducing the concept of OD and includes definitions of its characteristics and those required of OD practitioners. The chapter then moves on to provide a historical insight into the emergence of OD, the role of the OD practitioner in greater detail and considerations relating to the place of ethics within OD interventions. Subsequently, the chapter offers a breakdown of a typical OD process, including contracting, issue diagnosis, intervention planning and evaluation. A series of theoretical approaches and models are included to help demonstrate the operation of the OD process. Finally, the chapter then reflects upon the overall purpose of OD and the importance of the incorporation of performance measurement methods to be able to gauge its overall impact.

Throughout the chapter there are questions and case studies. We strongly urge you to take time out to try to answer the questions. Only by doing so can you fully understand the complexity and relevance of organisational development.

WHAT IS OD?

Progressively, organisations find themselves needing to respond and adapt to ever-changing external environments, whether these changes are associated with customers, suppliers, competitors, legislation, challenging economic conditions, government initiatives/interventions, or a combination of any or all of these. OD can be used to support the management of organisations through change in order to enable them to introduce processes that will optimise their ongoing adaptability and flexibility.

OD, as defined by French and Bell (1999, pp25–6), is:

> a long-term effort, led and supported by top management, to improve an organisation's visioning, empowerment, learning and problem-solving processes, through an ongoing, collaborative management of organisation culture of intact work teams and other team configurations – using the consultant-facilitator role and the theory and technology of applied behavioural science, including action research.

Cheung-Judge and Holbeche (2011) used French and Bell's definition and those provided by a number of other authors – Margulies 1978; Beckhard 1969; Schein 1988; Lippitt and Lippitt 1975; Rainey Tolbert and Hanafin 2006 – to identify the following set of OD and OD practitioner characteristics (adapted from Cheung-Judge and Holbeche 2011, p11):

- OD practitioners are 'process experts' who aim to improve organisational processes.
- OD practitioners focus upon the total organisational system, even if only a specific issue has been identified.
- OD practitioners work towards improving organisational problem-solving and renewal processes.
- OD practitioners support organisational leaders.
- Applied behavioural science technology is used to help the organisation strive for healthy development.
- The OD process is 'theory based, process focused' and 'value driven'.

According to Cheung-Judge and Holbeche, the focus of OD is, therefore, on the support of organisational leaders in taking a holistic approach to organisational process improvement and renewal using behavioural science technologies. The incorporation of behavioural science technology is considered a key component of all OD interventions. 'Behavioural science' is a wide-ranging term used to describe the study of people's behaviour in the social sciences. It is often related to issues of management and organisations within a work context. The study of behaviour within behavioural science is predominantly considered using the disciplinary perspectives of sociology (the study of social behaviour), psychology (the study of human behaviour) and anthropology (the study of mankind and the study of social behaviour as a whole) (Mullins 2005, pp29–30).

THE HISTORICAL BASIS OF OD

The emergence of OD as a concept tracks back to the 1940s and 1950s. During this time, US psychologists began to focus their attentions on group dynamics. Exploring the interactions amongst group members, early researchers discovered that individuals responded favourably to participation, resulting in changes in attitude, positive interpersonal relations, increased performance and personal growth.

Stemming from research conducted in the USA in the late 1940s, Kurt Lewin developed a leadership workshop, known as the T-group (a form of sensitivity training), that provided participants with feedback on their behaviour. Lewin and his team of researchers discovered that the provision of such feedback resulted in a rich learning experience. Owing to the success of these initial T-groups, and with financial backing, national training laboratories (NTLs) were formed in 1947. The NTLs were expanded in 1950 to include business and industry, allowing individuals to learn more about themselves and their reactions to given situations. The term 'organisational development' began to emerge as internal professionals and academic scholars applied these participative techniques to organisations (McGregor 1960; Beckhard 1969) to change management styles and overall organisational performance.

Gaining a greater understanding of the impact of management styles on performance, McGregor (1960) discovered two different approaches to management. Based on assumptions made about employees, Theory X managers believe that employees have to be controlled because they avoid responsibility, are inherently lazy and cannot be trusted. In contrast, Theory Y managers assume that their staff will accept responsibility, are committed and will co-operate given the right conditions.

Blake and Mouton's (1981) managerial grid also focused upon management performance, asking managers to pinpoint on the grid their priority for employee or task needs (sometimes referred to as people or production needs). Blake and Mouton concluded that the most effective managers in their roles are those who do not favour production over people and vice versa. Paying the same level of high attention to each aspect (employee and task needs), effective managers inherently promote a higher level of employee participation because communication is greater and employees understand what is being done and why.

The need to be open with staff and provide opportunities for involvement and recognition also forms part of much theory on motivation, most notably

Maslow's 'hierarchy of needs' (1954). When designing jobs, working conditions and organisational structures, Maslow suggested, organisations should bear in mind the full range of needs detailed in his hierarchy – namely physiological, safety, social, esteem and self-actualisation needs. Maslow suggested that people seek to satisfy lower-level needs first (such as the need for food and shelter) before moving up the hierarchy to eventually reach 'self-actualisation' at the top. Maslow argued that as each need is satisfied, it is no longer a motivator. While Maslow's hierarchy was and still is held in high regard in management education, the theory has been criticised. Whetten and Cameron (2005, p318) state that 'The problem with the hierarchical needs theories is that although they help us to understand general development processes, from adult to child, they aren't very useful for understanding the day-to-day motivation levels of adult employees.' Other authors (Kogan 1972; Wahba and Bridwell 1976; Salancik and Pfeffer 1977; Rauschenberger *et al* 1980) concur with the view that there are some problems relating Maslow's theory to the workplace. The main criticisms are that people can satisfy their needs through other areas of their life, not just work; individual differences mean that people place different values on the same need; some rewards or outcomes may satisfy more than one need; and people on the same level of the hierarchy may not have the same motivating factors.

REFLECTIVE ACTIVITIES

1   To what extent do you agree with the contention that organisations spend too much time focusing on the lower-level needs of Maslow's hierarchy rather than providing employees with the opportunity to satisfy other higher-level needs?

2   Given the potential diversity of staff working within an organisation, what can HR practitioners do to ensure that they match job requirements with the individual needs of their staff?

Following concerns that traditional approaches to job design, such as Taylor's scientific management (1947), lacked attention to human needs, job design research evolved, giving rise to what became known as the quality of working life (QWL) studies. The QWL programmes worked with managers, unions and staff to design work that offered increased task variety and discretion, higher levels of involvement and the opportunity to gain feedback upon individual performance and contribution. Towards the end of the 1970s, QWL programmes increased in popularity as organisations began to realise the potential for redesigning work flows, reward systems and improved working conditions in order to improve worker productivity. Building on the initial features of QWL programmes, coupled with the emergence of a growing body of 'excellence' literature (Peters and Waterman 1992; Kanter 1983), and the emergence of total quality management (TQM) and human resource management (HRM) literature, many organisations started to support the notion that employees are an organisation's greatest asset. During this period, contemporary management practice, in post-bureaucratic organisations, sought to utilise more acceptable means of control as workers became more aware of their rights (supported by a plethora of legal instruments now regulating the employment relationship) and sought to fulfil their own needs from the employment relationship. Empowering staff, employers began to provide their employees with greater control over how they achieved their targets. Individual work activities were introduced that aimed to increase job satisfaction and loyalty while at the same time improving the profitability and performance of the organisation. In the early 1990s it was not uncommon for organisations to implement self-managing teams, whose members were responsible for determining their own ways of working within the boundaries set by management. As a consequence of this 'freedom', employers sought to improve job satisfaction, reduce absenteeism and reduce costs. However, Kunda's research (1992) demonstrates that the added pressure to conform to the rules of the team can become far greater and ultimately lead to employee burnout, which can arguably be considered somewhat self-defeating for management.

Continuing to concentrate on the potential value of involving staff in decisions at work, HR practitioners recently began focusing their attention on 'engaging' staff who then 'go the extra mile' and surpass the traditional levels of employee satisfaction and commitment. They have aimed to achieve this by introducing employee involvement schemes, improved communication strategies and a culture based on transparency and trust. These initiatives are some of the steps an organisation can take to actively promote high levels of employee engagement.

CASE STUDY

Department for Work and Pensions

In 2008, the Department for Work and Pensions (DWP) implemented an efficiency challenge that involved reducing 30% of its workforce over a period of three years while streamlining and modernising services to customers.

The DWP's 2008 employee engagement survey indicated that 18% of staff were 'disengaged'. This equated to approximately 20,000 employees, most of whom were holding junior grades in front-line delivery roles within Jobcentre Plus offices or contact centres. In response, DWP outlined a series of 'engagement priorities' which looked at increasing the capability, motivation and accountability of first-line and middle managers and the visibility and impact of all senior managers. These engagement priorities were aimed at putting tools in place to involve employees in discussing the vision of DWP and how it could deliver an excellent customer service.

In order to realise these priorities, DWP introduced a number of engagement initiatives, including the 'Making a Difference' programme for first-level leaders and the 'Back to the Floor' programme for senior leaders.

The Making a Difference programme was designed as the catalyst to enable participants to better engage with, lead and deliver business direction. It emphasises that leadership is not just about senior managers; it is about those who have the greatest influence on people within the organisation. Full implementation began in February 2009 and up to 10,000 people are expected to take part in the process. Stephen Hanshaw (Jobcentre Plus manager) believes his Making a Difference journey has better equipped him in engaging people in change: 'We had lots of opportunities to discuss the barriers which can affect our ability to lead our team through change, and share ideas for overcoming these.'

The Back to the Floor programme gives senior leaders the opportunity to experience a customer-facing role for up to a week, working with staff and discovering at first-hand the issues they face in delivering to the organisation's customers. Katherine Courtney (Director of DWP Customer Insight) believes the insights she gained from her Back to the Floor experience have enabled her to influence change for the better: 'In my role it is important for me to see things from the customer's perspective. I try to "walk in the staff's shoes". Seeing the real help we provide customers when they need it most reminded me why I joined DWP in the first place. I was able to influence issues arising from lone parent customers transitioning from Income Support to Job Seekers Allowance.'

The DWP's recent survey results show some positive movement in their engagement scores.

Source: http://www.bis.gov.uk/files/file52215.pdf

REFLECTIVE ACTIVITY

1 In an attempt to measure the levels of engagement amongst their workforce, organisations may decide to distribute an annual satisfaction survey. Compile five to 10 questions that you think would be appropriate to include in such a survey.

When thinking about the questions, remember to firstly consider what it is you are trying to measure, and why.

2 What can organisations do to maintain morale during challenging economic conditions?

THE ROLE OF THE OD PRACTITIONER

The OD practitioner can be a specialist, thereby concentrating solely on OD, or OD can form part of a more generalist management role. Cummings and Worley (2005, p450) suggest that 'many managers and administrators have gained competence in Organisation Development and therefore apply it to their own work areas'. OD practitioners can also be external consultants whose expertise is sought when this does not exist in-house. One distinct advantage of employing an internal OD practitioner is that they are very familiar with the culture of the organisation and the people working within it. However, there is an increased likelihood of bias because such practitioners may find it hard to detach themselves from their predetermined attitudes and assumptions. Conversely, an external OD practitioner may be better placed to make more objective judgements but take longer to form relationships with those with whom they will be working.

Challenging previous and existing organisational behaviours, the OD practitioner can sometimes face opposition because managers and staff may feel threatened or perhaps they may misunderstand the purpose of the OD practitioner's role and contribution. As with much of organisational life, it is essential that lines of communication are kept open and everyone is informed of the nature and likely duration of the OD practitioner's work, so as to optimise transparency and reduce resistance.

Adopting humanist principles, traditional OD practitioners promoted open communication, employee involvement and personal growth and development. However, criticised for sitting on the periphery of an organisation (Bradford and Burke 2005, p19), OD practitioners have since had to expand their skill sets to demonstrate an interest in organisational effectiveness and bottom-line results. Moving from a client-centred to a consultant-centred role, OD practitioners now seek to adopt a more central and strategic role as organisations face increasing change.

ETHICAL CONSIDERATIONS

The role of an OD practitioner is to promote the change that is needed within the organisation they work in or for. Accepting this professional responsibility, OD practitioners have to inspire trust and quickly identify and ascertain organisational norms and values. Needing to form close working relationships with staff, OD practitioners can potentially face myriad ethical dilemmas. Cummings and Worley (2005, p58) state that 'Ethical issues in organisation development are concerned with how practitioners perform their helping relationship with organisation members.'

In order to promote a positive working relationship and reduce the possibility of any misunderstanding, it is essential that both parties are honest with each other from the outset. When working with an organisation, the OD practitioner is responsible for clearly explaining, both verbally and in writing, what it is they will be able to deliver and the timescales to achieve it. Similarly, the client (or organisation) must ensure that it is completely honest with the OD practitioner about the current situation and how the OD practitioner is envisaged to be able to assist it. Under these circumstances it would be considered unethical for the OD practitioner to claim that the adoption of a particular intervention would solve all of the organisation's problems if it was not likely to be the case. The OD practitioner should be clear about the work they think they would be able to carry out within the specified time period and return to the client if this does not turn out to be the case.

Trust is an important aspect of the OD practitioner's role because they will invariably have access to confidential information. It is likely that employees may seek to elicit this information from the OD practitioner as they work on their assigned role. It is therefore imperative that confidentiality is maintained and agreements are made between the client and the OD practitioner in relation to any announcements that are made and access to any sensitive information being collected.

During the course of data collection, an OD practitioner may also obtain additional information which does not specifically relate to their initial brief from the client. For example, the OD practitioner could observe something that could be considered to be inappropriate behaviour at work and may therefore be placed in an uncomfortable situation as they decide whether or not to report this set of circumstances to management. Easterby-Smith *et al* (2008, p134) imply that it is difficult to establish hard-and-fast ethical principles and, consequently, that 'good practice will rely on considerable judgement on the part of the researcher'. Returning to a previous comment relating to the importance of communication in organisations, it is essential that both parties agree upon the information that should be reported, and how. During these initial meetings, both the OD practitioner and the client organisation are required to agree on the point at which the working relationship will cease, because in some situations the client can become totally dependent upon the OD practitioner and reluctant to 'let go' of their support. Paradoxically, the OD practitioner also needs to know when they are required to step back from the organisation and allow the client to take full responsibility of the OD intervention. The OD practitioner may wish to still be involved in the change process, even when their contract deadline has passed – that is, when they have completed the project and/or no longer work for that organisation. The ethics of their continued involvement should ideally be questioned and addressed.

REFLECTIVE ACTIVITY

Imagine you are an OD practitioner for a large multi-site retailer. You have been asked to oversee the relocation of the company's warehouse from Birmingham to a much larger facility in Manchester. The managing director has not yet announced that this move is going to happen and has therefore asked for your discretion as you undertake your preliminary investigations. You are asked to inform anyone who asks that you are doing a review of the health and safety worries within the warehouse. However, after work one evening you decide to join a group of staff that has gone to the pub for a drink. After several hours of chatting, one warehouse operative asks you the real purpose of your work at Birmingham and you let it slip that the Birmingham warehouse is likely to be closing down in six months' time.

Consider the potential consequences of your revelation to: a) the warehouse staff based at Birmingham, b) the organisation as a whole, and c) your role as OD practitioner.

UNDERSTANDING THE OD PROCESS

OD practice has evolved since the 1950s and yet maintained a conceptual core that is still relevant and applicable today. This includes a key focus on improving organisational effectiveness at an individual, group and organisational level, an emphasis on change and a preoccupation with the *process* of change (Schein 1999). The emphasis on *process* has been advanced by OD's humanist values promoting the ideology that *how* things are done between people and in groups is as important as, or more important than, *what* is done (Schein 1999).

Every organisation has its own context and issues, and therefore every OD programme is unique. Yet all OD processes have recognisable frameworks of phases, collections of activities and techniques or identifiable flows of interrelated events helping organisations move towards organisational and/or group and individual improvement (French and Bell 1999). Many authors have advanced slight variations on Kolb and Frohman's (1970) general framework for planned change outlining six basic stages. These include scouting, entry and contracting, diagnosis, action, and evaluating that action. French and Bell (1999) cite Warne Burke's description of the OD process, which outlines a seven-stage programme: entry, contracting, diagnosis, feedback, planning change, intervention and evaluation.

Although the OD process is described as a sequential, linear and logical progression of events, it is acknowledged that organisational change rarely flows in such a tidy way and in practice the phases are likely to overlap. The importance of paying due diligence to each phase cannot be stressed enough because each stage builds on the foundations for and has an effect on subsequent phases. It is also important to recognise the iterative nature of the OD processes. All organisational change and development programmes are complex and interrelated processes of goals → actions → redefined goals → new actions (French and Bell 1999). Change agents must therefore not only consider the steps required for one entire cycle of OD but also conceptualise and consider how multiple cycles of OD might develop. They also might need to consider how the end of one cycle, and subsequent evaluation, may lead to another iteration of OD (Neumann *et al* 1997). Each stage of the OD process has a set of activities that must be undertaken, and a preoccupation with the process does not negate the importance of the tasks within each stage of the process. It is important, therefore, to examine each of the stages of the OD process in more detail.

ENTRY AND CONTRACTING

Entry into an OD relationship usually starts when an organisational member identifies a problem within the organisation and seeks the help of an OD professional. This contact may come from a line manager, an HR professional or other stakeholders within the organisation that will be party to the client–consultant relationship. An OD practitioner may be someone from inside the organisation acting as an internal consultant, perhaps an appropriately skilled HR professional, or from outside, an external consultant.

The overall task during the entry phase is to decide whether there is a good match between the client and the consultant and to determine whether the two parties should enter into and establish an OD relationship. An understanding of the organisational problem, clarifying who the client is and understanding their objectives and motives, will help the consultant with this decision. Equally, the client may also want to gather some data about the consultant and be confident that they have the knowledge, skills and experience or the technical, interpersonal and consulting skills necessary to help the client with their problems.

The key purpose of the contracting phase is to reach a formal or informal, verbal or written but explicit agreement about how the OD process will be carried out. The goal of this stage should be clarity about the desired outcomes for the OD process, and the time and resources available, as well as agreeing the rules and boundaries for working together. It is essential that particular attention is paid to establishing a robust understanding of the terms of the informal psychological contract (PC) of mutual needs and expectations that the client and consultant have of each other. A misunderstanding of this could mean someone's expectations are unfulfilled, and a violation of the PC may have serious implications, not least the loss of commitment and support and possibly early termination and failure of the project. It is therefore a critical stage of the process and one that will need to be continually revisited and renewed throughout the life of the project.

DIAGNOSIS AND FEEDBACK

The diagnostic element of the OD process involves collaboratively collecting relevant information and data, analysing it and drawing some conclusions about the organisational client system. Consideration needs to be given to the possible courses of action that will address the problems or opportunities and bridge the gap between where the client organisation system is and where they would like it to be. These decisions, however, rely on and cannot be made without collecting and analysing valid information. The values and ethics that underpin OD encourage a collaborative approach to diagnosis as well as to designing and implementing appropriate interventions (Block 2011). Decisions about who, what, when, where and how information will be collected, and the appropriate course of action to be taken, must be arrived at jointly by the client and the OD practitioner. This philosophy is advanced by the belief that only the client owns the problem identified and understands the true complexity of their situation, and only they know what will work for them within their organisational culture (Schein 1999). The role of the OD practitioner is to facilitate the process. Furthermore, the stakeholders within the diagnostic process must not forget the developmental orientation of OD, and improving the overall effectiveness of organisations is as important as uncovering problems and reasons for these problems (Cummings and Worley 1996).

Once the information has been collected, the OD practitioner needs to deploy the appropriate skills and competencies in organising the data to a manageable number of issues. This may involve deductive, inductive and/or statistical techniques to organise and interpret the gathered information. The content as well as the way in which the information is presented will determine if the client is energised towards problem-solving and action. This may therefore involve producing large amounts of information that is properly analysed and presented in a way that the client will understand and find useful. Difficult and unpleasant feedback should not be minimised or avoided. As Block (2011) points out, the client has the right to all the information that has been collected. This will then enable the client to make some informed decisions about the best way forward for the organisation.

PLANNING CHANGE AND INTERVENTION

The purpose of the planning phase is to decide and agree on the action that needs to be taken to address the organisational issues. The OD practitioner's role is to facilitate an arrival at a common understanding of the issues and an agreement on the best way forward. The tasks during this phase may involve critically appraising a number of options and choosing, developing and agreeing a plan of action.

Schein (1999) observes that everything a change agent does is an intervention. You intervene the moment you enter a client system, and sometimes an intervention can be as little as asking a simple question. An OD intervention is defined as '... a sequence of activities, actions, and events intended to help an organisation improve its performance and effectiveness' (Cummings and Worley 1996, p141). Many interventions fail because they do not match the data and diagnosis, have unclear and/or overambitious goals, allow insufficient time for implementation, are poorly designed or because resistance to change has not been dealt with, the organisation is not ready for change and the organisation and/or the OD practitioner do not have the knowledge and skills required to motivate and lead the change process and sustain the momentum required to implement and institutionalise the change (Anderson 2010). For interventions to be successful they must be designed to meet the needs of the organisation, be based on valid knowledge, skills and experience and through active participation in the design and implementation of interventions develop and enhance the organisation's capacity to manage change.

CASE STUDY

Diagnosing issues facing a pathology department within a medium-sized NHS trust

The diagnosis of issues facing the Pathology Department in a medium-sized NHS trust was that it faced a number of problems with its location within the trust. There was, however, strong resistance to change and an equally strong desire to maintain the status quo from some key members of staff within the department. In response to a request for some help with this from the associate director, the internal consultant used Kurt Lewin's force-field model as a diagnostic tool as well as a process that may enable leverage for change.

● Key stakeholders were facilitated to identify and list the driving forces pushing for change on the left side of a page, and the restraining forces that were blocking change down the right side.

● These forces were then given weightings in terms of their power to enable or block the change.

● Totalling the driving and restraining forces showed the driving forces for the change were greater than the restraining forces.

● An action plan addressing the restraining forces and developing the power of the driving forces was developed through facilitation.

Using the force-field analysis had a twofold effect. It enabled the key stakeholders to understand the resistance to change, but also showed the department that the impetus to change was greater than the reasons to maintain the status quo and thus provided a leverage to change.

EVALUATION

Figure 2.1 Kurt Lewin's force-field model

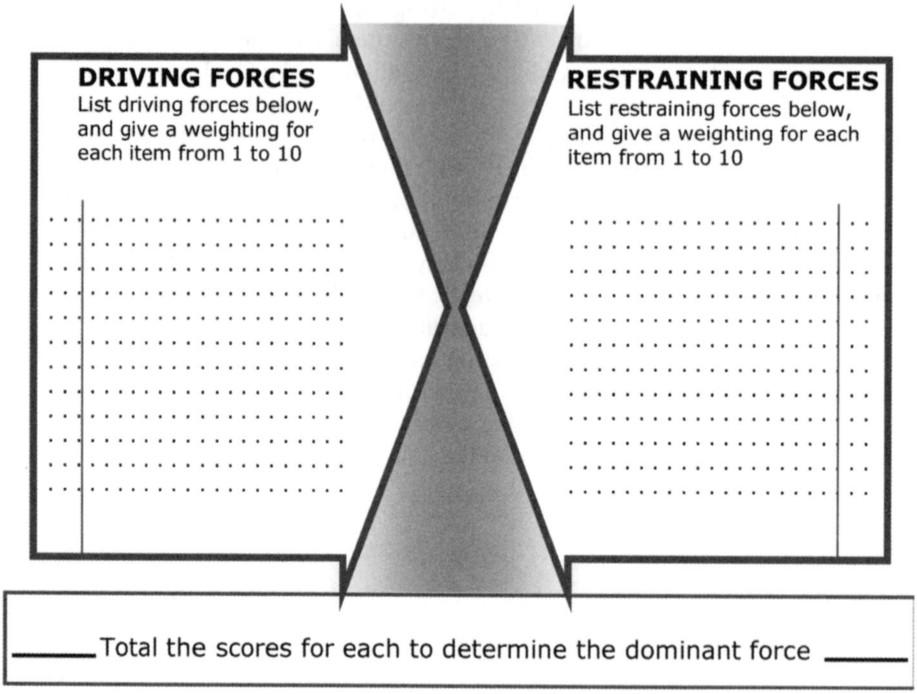

DRIVING FORCES	RESTRAINING FORCES
List driving forces below, and give a weighting for each item from 1 to 10	List restraining forces below, and give a weighting for each item from 1 to 10

_____ Total the scores for each to determine the dominant force _____

Evaluation represents assessing what has worked well, what needs further development, and if further diagnosis or intervention is necessary. Evaluation is also about learning from the process and deciding what happens next. It could be the stage at which the OD relationship is ended or a decision is made to enter another iteration of the cycle. In current financially difficult times, managers investing resources in OD efforts would be held to account for results. There are many challenges and barriers to evaluation and many practitioners fail to evaluate. Some of the reasons cited for this are lack of energy and resources, fear of the results, uncertainty about what to evaluate, lack of skills, knowledge and experience of evaluation, and some practitioners viewing it as an optional activity. Evaluation is, however, an essential part of the process and validates OD efforts and enables growth and development for both the client and OD practitioner.

REFLECTIVE ACTIVITY

Consider the collaborative and facilitative nature of the OD relationship. What do you think are the set of skills and competencies a practitioner needs to facilitate the OD process?

PRACTICES, MODELS AND APPROACHES

ORGANISATION DEVELOPMENT AND CHANGE MANAGEMENT TECHNIQUES

OD models tend to support the premise that in order for change to be successful it should be planned. Additionally, change management programmes should be continuously monitored to take account of internal and external influences. An early popular change model, still in use today, was first proposed by Kurt Lewin in the 1940s. Lewin put forward a three-stage model of change which involves 'unfreezing' the current state and mind-set to enable change to occur, 'change' or 'transition' to bring about and support the desired change, and finally 'freezing' or 'refreezing' to reinforce and anchor the change (Lewin 1951). Lippitt *et al* (1958) developed and extended Lewin's ideas into a seven-step planning model. In contrast to Lewin, Lippitt *et al* focused on the role and responsibility of the human players in the change process, rather than the change itself. Figure 2.2 shows the seven stages in the process aligned with Lewin's model of change.

Figure 2.2 Lippitt, Watson and Westley's change model incorporating Lewin's model of planned change

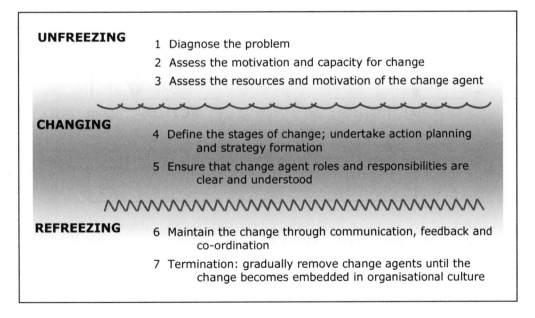

Source: Adapted from Lippitt, Watson and Westley (1958)

Similarly to Lippitt *et al*, Kotter (1996) proposed an eight-stage process for managing change, which can also be compared with Lewin's three-stage process. Kotter proposed: 1) establishing a sense of urgency; 2) creating a guiding coalition; 3) developing a vision and strategy; 4) communicating the change (unfreezing); 5) empowering action; 6) generating short-term wins (changing); 7) consolidating gains and producing more change; 8) anchoring and institutionalising new approaches (freezing).

REFLECTIVE ACTIVITY

The models above assume that successful change is planned change. How realistic do you consider this assumption to be in practice?

ACTION RESEARCH APPROACHES

Action research models are based on a systems approach and tend to be cyclical in design. In this way feedback is possible at each stage and planned actions and outcomes can be used to facilitate further change. It can be argued that models based on Lewin's approach to planned change take an action research approach in the sense that planned input requires 'unfreezing', action requires 'changing', and 'freezing' (or refreezing) requires embedding this change into an output (see Figure 2.3).

Figure 2.3 A simple action research model

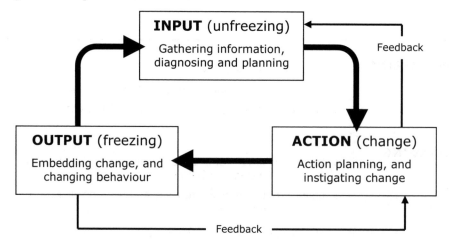

Writers such as French and Bell (1999) support this view and categorise OD as organisational improvement through the process of action research. Cummings and Worley (2008, p25) describe a cyclical eight-step action research model which expands upon the simple model outlined above:

1 problem identification

2 consultation with a behavioural science expert

3 data-gathering and preliminary diagnosis

4 feedback to a key client or group

5 joint diagnosis of the problem

6 joint action planning

7 action

8 data-gathering after the action.

Cummings and Worley argue that although these action research approaches are often associated with organisational change and development, they may not be applicable in all contexts and situations. Appreciative inquiry (AI) has been seen as a potential alternative approach and is outlined in the next section.

APPRECIATIVE INQUIRY AND THE POSITIVE MODEL OF PLANNED CHANGE

In contrast to Lewin's change and action research models, the positive model focuses on both challenges/problems (the negatives) faced by an organisation and the areas in which they are doing well (the positives). By identifying both, organisations can build on their strengths and eliminate or diminish their weaknesses. The process by which this type of planned change takes place has been described as 'appreciative inquiry' (Cooperrider and Whitney 2005). In essence AI examines what is going right within an organisation and uses this in order to address what is going wrong. Taking an AI stance towards OD enables a positive approach to change and the way it is managed and encourages wider employee involvement in the process. Cooperrider and Whitney initially proposed a 4-D model of AI but later models have added an initial 'define' stage, as illustrated in Figure 2.4.

Figure 2.4 The 5-D model of appreciative enquiry

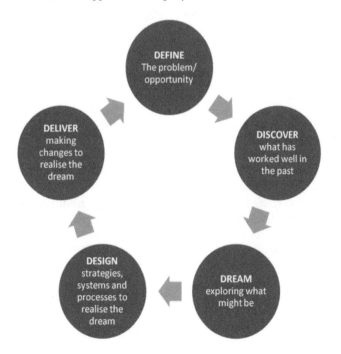

Source: Cooperrider and Whitney (2005)

EMOTIONS IN ORGANISATIONS

Many writers stress the need for employers to consider the role of employee emotions during organisational change (see Bartunek *et al* 2006), and many studies have shown a complicated relationship between employee emotions and behavioural responses to change (for example, Avey *et al* 2008). Positive employee emotions can be useful to drive change forward and increase trust, but by the same token, negative emotions can lead to fear, resistance to change and mistrust. Traditional approaches to OD assume that employees will fit in and respond to the required change and adapt to new practices, which ultimately become part of the overriding organisational culture (that is, frozen). Does such a view take account of the role of emotions during change? It can be argued that emotions are tied up with how employees adapt to or cope with change. How emotions evolve and develop during the change process must also be considered, and this is likely to vary from employee to employee. Moreover, change does not usually happen as a neatly isolated one-off event. It is more likely to encompass messy, multiple changes, which have the potential to further complicate the relationship between emotion and change. It therefore seems reasonable to surmise that in order to achieve successful, sustainable change, employee emotions should not be ignored.

REFLECTIVE ACTIVITY

Think about an ongoing or recent change that you have experienced.

1 How did you feel about this change?

2 What impact do you think your emotions had on the way you reacted to the change?

ORGANISATIONAL LEARNING

Organisational learning refers to the way in which the organisation as a whole adapts and responds to change as a result of internal and external influences. Many models have been developed to explain this process, one of the most popular being Argyris and Schön's (1978) theory of single-loop and double-loop learning. Single-loop learning is concerned with detecting and correcting errors within governing variables (that is, existing practices, procedures and processes), whereas double-loop learning questions the governing variables themselves (see Figure 2.5).

Figure 2.5 Single-loop and double-loop learning

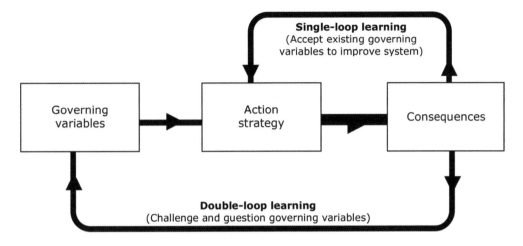

Source: Adapted from Argyris and Schön (1978)

Another influential writer in the field of organisational learning is Peter Senge. Senge (1990) proposed the concept of the 'learning organisation'. According to Senge (1990, p3), learning organisations are:

organisations where people continually expand their capacity to create the results they truly desire, where new and expansive patterns of thinking are nurtured, where collective aspiration is set free, and where people are continually learning to see the whole together.

Senge's theory uses systems thinking as a means of solving problems and focuses on five key disciplines, namely: personal mastery, which involves developing a personal vision; mental models, which involves developing awareness and reflection; shared vision with a focus on mutual purpose; team learning, which involves collective thought and discussion; and finally systems thinking, which brings the other dimensions together. However, many writers have challenged the assumptions put forward by Senge and there is ongoing debate around definitions, scope and what it actually is to be a learning organisation. One particular criticism of the model is the apparent lack of real-life organisational examples.

RESISTANCE, CONFLICT, DIVERSITY AND MULTICULTURALISM

The power of employee resistance should not be overlooked as a potential barrier to change. The CIPD (2011) defines resistance as: 'an individual or group engaging in acts to block or disrupt an attempt to introduce change'. The Institute identifies two main types of change: resistance to the *content* of change – in other words, *what* the change actually is, such as in the introduction of a new process or procedure – and resistance to the *process* of change – in other words, *how* the change is introduced and managed, rather than the focus of the change. Such resistance may be manifested in behaviours such as refusing to co-operate, withholding information, working to rule and strike action. A key factor here should be identifying the root cause of any resistance (other than the instigation of the change itself). Such causes could include lack of information, poor communication, fear, shock, perceived loss of control, threat to status, job uncertainty, and so on. Any successful change management programme has to address these causes in order to ameliorate or remove them. The CIPD (2011) suggests that it is essential that two-way communication is encouraged and active employee participation and involvement is used as a strategy for overcoming potential conflict and resistance to change.

OD initiatives should also take account of the multicultural and diverse nature of contemporary organisations and the wider national and international context within which many of them operate. Employers need to move away from Eurocentric and ethnocentric approaches towards developing an awareness of issues specific to wider multicultural and minority groups within the workplace. Strategies that actively encourage employee voice and inclusion have a part to play here. Diversity should be valued as an asset to the business and as a positive force for change.

CASE STUDY

Managing an ageing workforce: how employers are adapting to an older labour market

A survey published in 2010 by the CIPD and the Chartered Management Institute (CMI) examined the attitudes of HR professionals and managers to older workers, how equipped organisations are to cope with an ageing workforce, and the impact on HR policies and practices.

Findings from the survey suggested that employers acknowledge the invaluable contributions made by older employees and revealed that negative perceptions about older workers are generally declining. Nevertheless, the report concluded that there is a worrying lack of preparedness for an ageing workforce and recommended that senior teams must become strategically involved in promoting the age agenda.

(Full details of the survey can be accessed from: www.cipd.co.uk/ binaries/ Managing_Ageing_Workforce.pdf)

THE ROLE AND PURPOSE OF OD INTERVENTIONS

As stated earlier, the main purpose of any OD intervention is to introduce and develop processes designed to enable organisations to adapt to their changing environments. OD focuses on developing the organisations with the aim of improving overall performance. The purpose of OD is for sustainability and adaptability, with the utilisation of people to achieve this.

French and Bell's (1999, pp25–6) perspective of OD as a 'long-term effort, led and supported by top management [...] through an ongoing, collaborative management of organisation culture of intact work teams and other team configurations' highlights the importance of taking a longer-term focus in order to influence and impact upon organisation culture. It is argued that the values espoused by OD (those of employee empowerment, the creation of openness and awareness and shared ownership of change) can most positively impact upon organisational effectiveness if OD is able to permeate across the whole organisation, promoting a culture of collaboration and continuous learning. It is suggested that for any OD process to be successful it must be linked with business objectives and incorporated within performance management and measurement strategies.

An OD process can be introduced to address a specific organisational need within a part of the organisation or integrated throughout the organisation's processes and systems. The incorporation of OD processes as stand-alone initiatives could, for example, be effective as a pilot, before rolling out the process organisation-wide. This could cause less disruption to the organisation as a whole and take much less time, effort and resources. However, one of the potential difficulties with using OD in this way is that it risks misalignment with other activities and initiatives within the organisation.

A possible alternative would be to introduce a number of similarly focused OD interventions across the organisation. If this approach is adopted, care should be taken to ensure alignment across these interventions, so as to eliminate the potential for conflicting priorities and outcomes.

Another alternative would be to incorporate one overarching OD intervention that encompasses the organisation as a whole. The benefit of using this approach is that the OD process would be transparent and recognisable to all employees. However, the difficulty associated with this approach could be that if an organisation's functions are highly differentiated (different from one another), the approach might not be entirely suitable for each and every division.

MEASURING THE IMPACT OF OD

Arguably, one of the most important aspects of any OD intervention is to be able to ascertain how and when the organisation will know if the intervention has been successful and what impact it has made upon organisational effectiveness. It is therefore crucial to set and agree realistic and identifiable performance measures from the outset, as noted earlier. Important questions to be posed from the outset include:

- What is it that we want to be doing, and how do we know this? (Establish targets to meet organisational missions, visions and strategic objectives.)
- Who should be involved in these decisions? (This will make an impact on the level of buy-in or resistance demonstrated by organisation members, as discussed above under the heading *Entry and contracting*.)
- How will we know when we are heading in the right direction? (A combination of short-, medium- and long-term measures must be in place in order to identify the extent to which the organisation development intervention is on track and meeting its objectives.)

The three forms of organisational change outcomes OD should aim for, according to Golembiewski *et al* (1976), include *alpha*, identifying the difference between before and after measures (for example, enabling customer service quality improvement to be highlighted as a result of an OD intervention); *beta*, the identification of a shift in perspectives in assessment of the measure (for example, customer service quality might not have shown any dramatic improvements, but there is a greater awareness from those involved in the process of the need for customer service quality improvement); and *gamma*, a comprehensive reconceptualisation of the issue (for example, the focus may not be on before-and-after differentials, or on the greater awareness by employees of the need for customer service quality improvement; following the intervention, those involved in the process might conclude that changes are required in communications, roles and responsibilities, if organisation-wide improvements are to be realised). This outcome is concerned with more general organisational improvement.

A crucial aspect of OD is that it seeks to positively impact upon the organisation's flexibility to change and consequently its adaptability to future challenges. It is argued, therefore, that all three of these organisational change outcomes will contribute to the organisation's continued focus on process improvement and renewal.

QUANTITATIVE AND QUALITATIVE PERFORMANCE MEASURES

In monitoring effectiveness Carnall (2007) suggests that organisations should concentrate on the following four areas: the extent to which the organisation is achieving its objectives; the organisation's utilisation of its resources; how its internal system is maintained; and its adaptability to its changing environment. A range of measures can be utilised to identify these outcomes. Quantitative performance measures are those concerned with numerical analysis and measurement that help us establish past performance (for example, costs, productivity, wastage and turnover) in an attempt to make future predictions. However, solely relying on quantitative measures could mean that past experiences, judgement and intuition are missed. Qualitative performance measures are considered to delve more deeply into individual behaviours and perspectives, gaining insights into employee satisfaction, management style and development, corporate culture, etc. Even though the aims of these two approaches to measurement are very different, they can and arguably should be utilised in conjunction with each other to enable a comprehensive understanding of the extent to which performance outcomes have been achieved. Failure to do this could result in a narrow approach to measurement that misses key issues which have an impact on effectiveness. Table 2.1 lists some of the methods that are associated with each of these approaches to measurement.

Table 2.1 Quantitative and qualitative performance measurement methods

Measurement	Possible quantitative methods	Possible qualitative methods
Sickness absence	Analysis of absence figures to identify frequencies and trends	Return-to-work interviews identifying personal issues or gauging perspectives relating to absence Occupational health report analysis
Customer service	Number of complaints Frequency of product returns Customer feedback survey/questionnaire involving closed questions	In-depth customer feedback via interview or survey/questionnaire including open questions Observations
Employee satisfaction	Employee survey/questionnaire involving closed questions to gauge frequencies and inform trend analysis	Employee survey/questionnaire involving open questions Employee interviews or focus groups to gain an in-depth insight into employee attitudes and uncover the issues behind problem areas
Employee performance	Productivity rates Measurable performance target-setting and analysis	Employee interviews to gain an in-depth insight into employee attitudes and uncover the issues behind problem areas Performance review including the in-depth investigation of attitudes and behaviours Observation

Care must also be taken to ensure that a common language and common frameworks are used so that measurement structures can be transparent, easily understood and aligned throughout the organisation.

THE BALANCED SCORECARD

One method that incorporates a range of these OD measurement methods and is utilised by many organisations is the balanced scorecard (Kaplan and Norton 1996). The term 'balanced' is used because it places equal emphasis upon financial and non-financial measures. The four main perspectives of the balanced scorecard are:

- financial – the financial targets to be achieved
- internal processes – the processes that must be in place for the organisation to excel
- customers – how the organisation plans to provide value for its customers
- innovation, growth and learning – the ways in which the organisation can continue to learn and improve.

The measures selected to be used within the balanced scorecard then link these four areas with the organisation's business vision and strategy as a means of striving for continuous organisational improvement. This is usually achieved through the organisation's performance management processes.

SUMMARY

This chapter has provided a detailed overview of the origins, process, practices and measurement of OD. The history of the development of OD highlights human needs and group interaction as those areas that can hold the key to improvements in innovation, productivity and development. Accordingly, optimising transparency and employee engagement within the development of OD interventions is considered to be of utmost importance. Theoretical perspectives and models all place heavy emphasis upon the behaviours of the OD practitioners and organisational leaders as being crucial to the success of an OD intervention. In the evaluation of OD, considerations of combining both quantitative and qualitative performance measures offer the potential for analytical discipline to be supported by intuition in order to gain a holistic understanding of performance issues.

Organisational analysis and organisational development

CASE STUDY

Professor Les Worrall, Professor of Strategic Analysis, Coventry Business School, Coventry University

The context

Whether they are in the private, public or voluntary sectors, organisations exist in increasingly dynamic and unstable operating environments. Increasing instability requires organisations to be able to re-engineer business processes, restructure, re-skill, learn from change and redefine their own cultures. Organisations will need to become increasingly 'dynamically capable' if they are to succeed: this will have major implications for the leadership styles, behaviours and skills that senior managers will have to develop.

Managing strategic change is difficult because senior managers need to be able to trade off the pressures coming from outside the organisation against pressures coming from inside the organisation. While senior managers may see that competitive pressures in the private sector or budget reductions in the public sector are going to make the future problematic, it is difficult for them to respond to these pressures without causing significant negative effects on their workforce, especially if those changes require cost reductions, redundancy or organisational restructuring.

This case study describes an eight-year programme of organisational development in a local authority that had been created from the merger of two pre-existing organisations. The study shows how a succession of biennial employee surveys was used to develop the organisational development initiatives needed to build a new organisation, and how the implementation of these policies was evaluated over time.

The need for information and intelligence to inform the organisational development process

The organisation's senior management understood that building a new unified and cohesive organisation out of two pre-existing organisations was a long-term process that required a sophisticated approach to change management. To achieve this aim, the council appointed a long-term, independent, academic partner to advise them. The council also appointed a head of organisational development to work closely with the academic partner to design an employee attitude survey and to design and implement a communications process for feeding the results of the research process back to the entire organisation. At the outset, a transparent communications strategy and an open and honest approach to dealing with the results of the survey were seen as paramount.

The design of the questionnaire and the wider research process

The council encouraged a high level of transparency in the conduct of the survey. All key stakeholders (for example, councillors, trade unions and specific employee groups – for example, black and minority ethnic employees) were kept fully informed and involved. The head of organisational development facilitated several workshops to give employee groups the opportunity to raise issues that they wanted the questionnaire to cover.

After a long process of discussion, a questionnaire was developed which focused on the following:

To what extent do employees identify with the council?

How does the council treat its employees?

How do employees perceive the prevailing management and leadership styles in the organisation?

How good are employees' relationships with their immediate line managers?

How do employees feel about the work they do, the design of their jobs and the council as a place to work?

What are co-worker relationships like in business units/teams?

How satisfied are employees with their jobs and with facets of their job?

How effective is training, and how well is the personal and performance development process working?

Is there evidence of bullying, harassment or poor management behaviour?

Communicating the results

After each survey, feedback sessions were held for each department, with the academic adviser being given a relatively free rein to develop the presentations and deliver them. Occasionally, there were difficult messages to be communicated but on more than one occasion the chief executive expressed a wish to 'tell it like it is'. On occasions, senior managers had to listen to feedback that was not flattering to them or their management styles.

Experience revealed that a transparent communications strategy is essential if you are going to ensure that employees see surveys as worthwhile and honest. Employees are not stupid; they experience organisational life on a daily basis and they know when they are being lied to and when difficult issues are being glossed over. It became very clear that the managers who most tried to censor the feedback were perceived as having the worst leadership and management styles – it was their departments that were characterised by low reciprocal trust, managerial invisibility and inaccessibility, and poor upward and downward communications.

The survey revealed that the most potent driver of job satisfaction in the organisation was the quality of the working relationship that employees had with their immediate line manager. This finding encouraged the council to look hard at the management behaviours and leadership styles that it wanted to develop in the 125 people that had significant managerial and leadership responsibilities in the council.

What were the key issues that the surveys exposed, and how did the council react to them?

The research exposed and charted trends in a number of important issues. One of the key findings was that employees' experiences varied considerably within the organisation and, consequently, the survey was used to identify those areas where employee perceptions were at their worst. The data for these areas could then be analysed to develop an understanding of what was driving dissatisfaction and negative attitudes in these areas.

It was also possible to identify those areas that were performing well but had problems in specific areas – perhaps revealing concerns about how well a particular manager was performing in aspects of their jobs or with aspects of job design. It was also possible to isolate those areas where negative attitudes were most prevalent and link these attitudes to responses about the management and leadership styles of more senior council managers.

The survey had considerable value in helping the council develop actions targeted either on specific parts of the organisation or on specific issues within specific parts of the organisation. As a specific exercise, the chief executive asked the academic adviser to suggest measures and actions that could be included within the annual performance objectives of senior and middle managers. A detailed analysis of the data revealed that many of the issues raised in the surveys could be traced back to individual managers' leadership styles.

Implications for OD

While many organisations have conducted employee attitude surveys, few will have so systematically embedded their surveys into their organisation's wider organisational development process. The surveys were used to identify those parts of the council that were performing well and badly to identify where and how interventions could have the greatest effect. The surveys were used to test how well corporate initiatives on personal development and training were working; to expose patchiness in the take-up of development; and to expose the areas where some managers were being less than assiduous in responding to corporate drives to enhance the quality of all employees' working lives.

The surveys allowed the council to identify hot spots where employees were overloaded, where jobs were badly designed, where teams were not functioning well and where managers were displaying leadership styles and management behaviours which did not conform with how the council expected their managers to behave. The surveys also allowed the council to see which factors were reducing individual or collective job satisfaction.

Throughout the eight-year process, the council became far more adept at learning how to use the information the surveys provided. Initially, managers at all levels were fearful about what the surveys would reveal, but the more effective managers used the information to develop insights about how issues could be addressed and to learn about how they were being perceived as leaders and managers. These proved to be highly valuable insights.

Questions:

1 What were the main aims of adopting this approach to organisational analysis?

2 In what ways did this method support the organisation's OD process?

3 What were the main outcomes for the organisation of using this approach?

4 How does management behaviour contribute to the way OD

interventions are received by employees?

BOOKS

CHEUNG-JUDGE, M.-Y. and HOLBECHE, L. (2011) *Organisation Development: A practitioner's guide for OD and HR.* London: Kogan Page. A concise text offering clear guidance and support from a practitioner's perspective using a theoretical foundation.

COOPERRIDER, D. L. and WHITNEY, D. (2005) *Appreciative Inquiry: A positive revolution in change.* San Francisco, CA: Berrett-Koehler. A short, practical text giving insight into the theory of appreciative inquiry and its potential for collaborative change within organisations.

CUMMINGS, T. G. and WORLEY, C. (2008) *Organization Development and Change*, 9th edn. Cincinnati, OH: South-Western Cengage Learning. This book presents an examination of theory, models, practice and research in the field of organisational development and improvement.

ARTICLES

AVEY, J. B., WERNSING, T. S. and LUTHANS, F. (2008) Can positive employees help positive organizational change? *Journal of Applied Behavioral Science*. Vol 44, No 1. 48–70. This article provides an insight into the influence of employee attitudes upon the change process.

RAINEY TOLBERT, M. A. and HANAFIN, J. (2006) Use of self in OD consulting: what matters is presence, in JONES, B. B. and BRAZZEL, M. (eds) *The NTL Handbook of Organisation Development and Change: Principles, practices and perspectives*. 69–82. New York: John Wiley & Sons. This article presents a practical overview of the OD consultant's role in organisational change.

WEBSITES

CIPD (2011) *Change Management [online]*. Factsheet. London: Chartered Institute of Personnel and Development. Available at: http://www.cipd.co.uk/hr-resources/factsheets/change-management.aspx. CIPD factsheet offering guidance on the management of change within organisations and the role of HR.

CIPD (2011) *Organisation Development [online]*. Factsheet. London: Chartered Institute of Personnel and Development. Available at: http://www.cipd.co.uk/hr-resources/factsheets/organisation-development.aspx. CIPD factsheet giving an overview of OD, providing practical advice on OD initiatives and discussing the relationship between OD and HR.

FURTHER READING

REFERENCES

ANDERSON, D. L. (2010) *Organization Development – The process of leading organizational change.* Thousand Oaks, CA: Sage Publications.

ARGYRIS, C. and SCHÖN, D. (1978) *Organisational Learning: A theory of action perspective.* Reading, MA: Addison-Wesley.

AVEY, J. B., WERNSING, T. S. and LUTHANS, F. (2008) Can positive employees help positive organizational change? *Journal of Applied Behavioral Science.* Vol 44, No 1. 48–70.

BARTUNEK, J. M., ROUSSEAU, D. M., RUDOLPH, J. W. and DEPALMA, J. A. (2006) On the receiving end: sensemaking, emotion, and assessments of an organizational change initiated by others. *Journal of Applied Behavioral Science.* Vol 42, No 2. 182–206.

BECKHARD, R. (1969) *Organisation Development: Strategies and models.* Reading, MA: Addison-Wesley.

BLAKE, R. and MOUTON, S. (1981) Management by Grid® Principles or Situationalism, *Which? Group Organization Management.* Vol 8, No 4. 439–55.

BLOCK, P. (2011) *Flawless Consulting – A guide to getting your expertise used*, 3rd edn. Austin, TX: Jossey-Bass.

BRADFORD, D. L. and BURKE, W. W. (2005) *Reinventing Organization Development: New approaches to change in organizations.* San Francisco, CA: Pfeiffer.

CARNALL, C. (2007) *Managing Change in Organisations*, 5th edn. Harlow: Prentice Hall.

CHEUNG-JUDGE, M.-Y. and HOLBECHE, L. (2011) *Organisation Development: A practitioner's guide for OD and HR.* London: Kogan Page.

CIPD (2011) *Change Management [online].* Factsheet. London: Chartered Institute of Personnel and Development. Available at: http://www.cipd.co.uk/hr-resources/factsheets/change-management.aspx [accessed 25 April 2012].

COOPERRIDER, D. L. and WHITNEY, D. (2005) *Appreciative Inquiry: A positive revolution in change.* San Francisco, CA: Berrett-Koehler.

CUMMINGS, T. G. (2008) *Handbook of Organization Development.* London: Sage.

CUMMINGS, T. G. and WORLEY, C. (1996) *Organization Development and Change*, 6th edn. Cincinnati, OH: South-Western.

CUMMINGS, T. G. and WORLEY, C. (2005) *Organization Development and Change*, 8th edn. Cincinnati, OH: Thomson South-Western.

CUMMINGS, T. G. and WORLEY, C. (2008) *Organization Development and Change*, 9th edn. Cincinnati, OH: South-Western Cengage Learning.

EASTERBY-SMITH, M., THORPE, R. and JACKSON, P. (2008) *Management Research*, 3rd edn. London: Sage.

FRENCH, W. L. and BELL, C. (1999) *Organization Development: Behavioral science interventions for organization improvement*. New Jersey: Prentice Hall.

GALLOS, J. V. (2006) *Organization Development*. San Francisco, CA: Jossey-Bass Reader.

GOLEMBIEWSKI, R., BILLINGSLEY, K. and YEAGER, S. (1976) Measuring change and persistence in human affairs: types of change generated by OD designs. *Journal of Applied Behavioural Science*. Vol 12, 133–57.

KANTER, R. M. (1983) *The Change Masters: Innovation and entrepreneurship in the American corporation*. New York: Simon & Schuster.

KAPLAN, R. S. and NORTON, D. P. (1996) *The Balanced Scorecard: Turning strategy into action*. Boston, MA: Harvard Business School Press.

KOGAN, J. (1972) Motives and development. *Journal of Personality and Social Psychology*. Vol 22. 51–66.

KOLB, D. and FROHMAN, A. (1970) An organisational development approach to consulting. *Sloan Management Review*, Vol 12. 51–65

KOTTER, J. P. (1996) *Leading Change*. Boston, MA: Harvard Business School Press.

KUNDA, G. (1992) *Engineering Culture*. Philadelphia, PA: Temple University Press.

LEWIN, K. (1951) *Field Theory in Social Science*. New York: Harper & Row.

LIPPITT, G. and LIPPITT, R. (1975) *The Consulting Process in Action: Examining the dynamics of the client-consultant working relationship*. Washington, DC: Development Publications.

LIPPITT, R., WATSON, J. and WESTLEY, B. (1958) *The Dynamics of Planned Change*. New York: Harcourt, Brace & World.

MARGULIES, N. (1978) Perspectives on the marginality of the consultant's role, in BURKE, W. W. (ed.) *The Cutting Edge: Current theory and practice in organisation development*. La Jolla, CA: University Associates.

MASLOW, A. (1954) *Motivation and Personality*. New York: Harper & Row.

MCGREGOR, D. C. (1960) *The Human Side of Enterprise*. New York: McGraw-Hill.

MULLINS, L. J. (2005) *Management and Organisational Behaviour*, 7th edn. Harlow: Pearson Education.

NEUMANN, J. E., KELLNER, K. and DAWSON-SHEPHERD, A. (1997) *Developing Organisational Consultancy*. London: Routledge.

PETERS, T. and WATERMAN, R. (1982) *In Search of Excellence*. New York: Harper & Row.

RAINEY TOLBERT, M. A. and HANAFIN, J. (2006) Use of self in OD consulting: what matters is presence. In: JONES, B. B. and BRAZZEL, M. (eds) *The NTL Handbook of Organisation Development and Change: Principles, practices and perspectives*, 69–82. New York: John Wiley & Sons.

RAUSCHENBERGER, J., SCHMITT, N. and HUNTER, J. E. (1980) A test of the need hierarchy concept by a Markov model of change in need strength. *Administrative Science Quarterly*. Vol 25. 654–70.

SALANCIK, G. R. and PFEFFER, J. (1977) An examination of need satisfaction models of job attitudes. *Administrative Science Quarterly*. Vol 22. 427–56.

SCHEIN, E. H. (1988) *Organisational Psychology*, 3rd edn. London: Prentice Hall.

SCHEIN, E. H. (1999) *Process Consultation Revisited – Building the helping relationship*. Boston, MA: Addison-Wesley.

SENGE, P. M. (1990) *The Fifth Discipline: The art and practice of the learning organization*. New York: Doubleday Currency.

SENIOR, B. and SWAILES, S. (2010) *Organizational Change*, 4th edn. Harlow: FT/Prentice Hall.

TAYLOR, F. (1947) *Scientific Management*. New York: Harper & Row.

WAHBA, M. A. and BRIDWELL, L. G. (1976) Maslow reconsidered: a review of research on the need hierarchy theory. *Organizational Behaviour and Human Performance*. Vol 15. 212–40.

WHETTEN, D. A. and CAMERON, K. S. (2005) *Developing Management Skills*, 6th edn. Upper Saddle River, NJ: Prentice Hall.

Reward Management

Graham Perkins and Carol Woodhams

CHAPTER CONTENTS

KEY LEARNING OUTCOMES

By the end of this chapter, you should be able to:

- analyse the context of reward management, highlighting key internal and external factors that influence reward processes and systems
- critically discuss the most appropriate methods of gathering and analysing data relating to reward management
- analyse the various theories and perspectives that underpin the reward management field
- evaluate the concept of 'total reward', highlighting its overall aims and key benefits
- analyse various reward management practices, including grade/pay structures, job evaluation and the idea of 'contingent reward'
- critically discuss the role that line managers play in reward management systems and processes.

INTRODUCTION

When reward management is discussed and analysed within organisations, cash pay is often the first thing that comes to mind. It is very important to remember that cash pay is only one part of reward management and that there are many other factors and variables that must be considered.

The way in which employees are rewarded can provoke a great deal of controversy both within and outside organisations. The methods and reasons that sit behind reward decisions have strategic, practical and symbolic implications, so it is crucial to recognise that if firms stop paying people in ways that broadly match their economic value and expectations, they are unlikely to successfully recruit and retain staff. On the other side of the argument, paying in excess of market norms can significantly impact on the financial performance of organisations. HR professionals have a delicate balance to achieve.

This chapter begins by focusing on the business context of reward management, considering relevant trends and factors that can impact on reward decisions. Following this section attention turns to the various ways in which reward 'intelligence' (i.e. data) can be gathered and analysed. As we analyse reward at a deeper level in the chapter, various reward perspectives, theories and principles are covered, including the concept of 'total reward', before specific reward incentives and practices are evaluated. Towards the end of the chapter there is a section dedicated to the role of line managers in reward management, and a final section evaluates the impact of reward management.

DEFINING REWARD MANAGEMENT

The logical place to begin this chapter is by defining the term 'reward management'. There are countless definitions available, each with a slightly different slant or approach. One of the more comprehensive definitions is from Armstrong (2007: 3), who suggests that:

> Reward management deals with the strategies, policies and processes required to ensure that the contribution of people to the organisation is recognised by both financial and non-financial means. It is about the design, implementation and maintenance of reward systems (reward processes, practices and procedures), which aim to meet the needs of both the organisation and its stakeholders. The overall objective is to reward people fairly, equitably and consistently in accordance with their value to the organisation in order to further the achievement of the organisation's strategic goals.

This definition highlights the intricacies of reward management and demonstrates that it is not solely concerned with financial issues. Armstrong (2007) specifically states that reward management involves both financial and non-financial elements, and that the overall objective of reward management is to reward people fairly, equitably and consistently.

It is notable that Armstrong suggests that reward management aims to meet the needs of both the organisation and its stakeholders. This is a point that is sometimes missed. It is important to remember that the territory of reward management is as concerned with the needs of organisational stakeholders (such as shareholders and line managers) as it is with the needs of employees. Imagine a situation in which an HR professional managed to put through a 20% pay increase for all workers at a particular company site. No doubt the employees affected would be delighted – but shareholders on the other hand might be very disappointed because their earnings from organisational profits would drop. It is crucial to recognise that HR professionals have a delicate balance to achieve in order to satisfy the many different stakeholders of reward.

THE PRINCIPLES OF REWARD MANAGEMENT

Now that the basic concept of reward management has been defined, its underlying principles must be briefly discussed before the concept as a whole can be related to the wider business environment.

As hinted at above, a key principle of reward management is that individuals in organisations are rewarded for their contributions fairly, consistently and transparently. It is important to recognise that pay itself is a very emotive issue – that is to say, that individuals can have very strong feelings about what is 'right' and what is 'wrong'. As a result of this, reward practices that are thought to be unfair can quickly break the psychological contract between employer and employee. Clear and effective communication about reward practices and decisions is therefore essential to maintain employee engagement and commitment.

A further key principle of reward management is that rewards can be either 'intrinsic' or 'extrinsic'. *Intrinsic rewards* come from work itself and can include a sense of meaningfulness, a sense of challenge and opportunities for advancement. *Extrinsic rewards* by contrast include pay, status, non-essential training and even the working environment (i.e. a more comfortable office). It is important to understand that organisations can use a combination of intrinsic and extrinsic rewards to motivate their employees, although there is no 'one best way' because the effectiveness of strategies depends to a large extent on organisational context and culture.

This introductory section of the chapter has defined the concept of reward management and introduced basic principles that underpin it. In order to arrive at a greater comprehension of where reward management 'sits' in organisations it is important to understand the business context that it operates within.

THE BUSINESS CONTEXT OF REWARD MANAGEMENT

The business context of reward management can be split into the following three broad areas:

- the international context
- the national context

- the corporate context.

This section explores these three areas before other specific contextual issues – such as those around the political environment – are examined in greater detail.

THE INTERNATIONAL CONTEXT

Global competition has demanded that organisations revise the ways in which they deliver services and products in order to produce the 'exceptional' performance that must be delivered to compete in the global marketplace. Armstrong (2002: 28) argues that the 'impact of global competition on pay systems has been to focus attention on a number of specific areas'. These include:

- flexible approaches to pay to help businesses react swiftly to new demands and pressures
- paying for performance and competence to provide competitive edge
- broad-based structures to reflect the 'lean' de-layered organisation and facilitate flexibility in the delivery of pay
- the emergence of globally mobile executives and the challenge of how they should be rewarded.

A key theme running through the list above is the need for flexibility. It is important to recognise that globalisation has an impact on the way in which organisations reward their employees, and that maintaining intransigent, outdated or inefficient models may compromise the competitiveness of firms. A further point to highlight surrounds the fact that reward management strategies and policies must be compatible with the structures of organisations. Without this link it is arguable that HR professionals will have difficulty in aligning reward management with the overall strategic goals and culture of organisations.

THE NATIONAL CONTEXT

Armstrong (2002) suggests that alongside international issues there are a number of variables at the national level that impact on reward management. For the United Kingdom these include:

- the introduction of the national minimum wage from April 1999, which affected an estimated 2 million workers
- structural change in the demand for skills. This started in the 1980s with an emphasis on high levels of attainment and expertise. Reward structures have been under pressure to adapt to encourage skill development
- structural changes in industry: a continuing shift from manufacturing to service industry, with greater complexity in associated reward practices
- fragmentation in the labour market. There are more flexible working patterns, a greater proportion of women in the labour market, a more ethnically diverse workforce, and so on. This has, for example, made it more difficult for trade unions to engage in collective bargaining, which has traditionally been applicable to blue-collar, full-time, permanent male employees in the manufacturing sector

- the lowering of inflation rates, which means that the double-digit pay awards seen in the 1970s are a thing of the past, and the view that everyone is entitled to a base pay increase each year has been challenged
- the huge gap between remuneration at the top and lower levels of the organisation, which has led to both social and legislative pressure on reward practice
- social and political trends to create new jobs in a low-inflation environment and to improve the skills of the workforce.

Perhaps the key point to draw from the list above is the structural changes that have occurred in the economy. It is vital to recognise that as the UK's economy has moved from an industrial base to a service base, reward management strategies and approaches have been adapted to fit the new context. Alongside these important changes there has also been fragmentation in the labour market. More and more individuals work part-time or have some other form of flexibility in their contractual arrangements, and this too has an impact on reward management practices. Again, reward management strategies have been adapted to take account of these changes and, as mentioned above, there is now less collective bargaining by which pay is set through negotiations between employers and trade unions.

Alongside the issues discussed above it is also important to understand that reward management in organisations is significantly influenced by politics and legislation. The following sections consider the influence that New Labour and, more recently, the Coalition Government have had on reward management practices.

New Labour

Although traditionally closely allied to the trade unions and advocates of collective bargaining, the New Labour Government elected in 1997 was reluctant to return to its 1970s policies – policies that had seen it spend nearly two decades out of power. As a result of this decision it advocated a 'third way' – one that lay between market-driven approaches and the highly interventionist approaches of previous Labour administrations. These policies contributed to the decrease in collective bargaining in organisations and encouraged public sector organisations to introduce what was called 'performance-related pay'. These pay systems included bonus elements that were tied to the achievement of specific objectives and were thought to be key ways to improve performance and increase efficiency.

The Coalition Government

During 2010 the on-going recession and presence of a large budget deficit divided electoral opinion on economic policy. The election held in 2010 reflected these divisions in that no one party was clearly re-elected. A change of government took place and a coalition was formed between the Conservatives and the Liberal Democrats. Once elected, the Coalition took action to reduce public borrowing and imposed strict cuts in government spending. In essence, the government is arguing for a much-reduced role for government and an increased role for ordinary citizens, particularly in the delivery of public services.

What implications does this shift in policy have for reward management? The government has argued for a reduction in regulation, built on its position that this constrains business and economic growth. Examples of this are the delaying of the implementation of certain provisions in the Equalities Act 2010 and the suggested extension of the qualifying period for unfair dismissal to two years. The government has committed to keeping the national minimum wage, although its level may not now increase as much annually as has hitherto been the trend.

THE CORPORATE CONTEXT

Armstrong (2002: 31) highlights the most significant aspects of the corporate environment that affect reward management:

- the impact of organisational change, particularly on corporate structures
- the impact of corporate environmental change on pay systems
- employer and employee expectations
- organisational culture
- corporate values.

Many of the factors listed above are internal to organisations but nevertheless have a substantial impact on reward. It is important to understand that these internal factors are also influenced by the external context. Employee expectations, for example, are formed within the organisation but are influenced by external variables such as education levels and comparisons that are made with family and friends who work in other organisations. Even at the corporate level, the range of influences brought to bear on reward constrains the ability of management to determine outcomes (i.e. final pay settlements, and so on) on their own terms.

REFLECTIVE ACTIVITY

In what ways does the corporate context inside your organisation (or in one with which you are familiar) shape reward management practices or systems?

Hopefully, the Reflective Activity above caused you to reflect on the specific elements of corporate culture impact on reward management. Perhaps your organisation has developed a reward system that encourages specific behaviours or attitudes. Alternatively, you may have noted that your organisation is trying to minimise costs and find efficiencies, in which case you may feel that pay systems are being tightened up or reward packages are becoming less generous overall.

Reward in the public sector

There are often substantial differences in reward practices between public and private sector organisations – not least because governments of whatever political persuasion have a role as a model employer and thus attempt to offer favourable terms and conditions of employment. This has also led to most of the public sector continuing to recognise trade unions and to collective bargaining being dominant in wage determination. We continue to see, for example, incremental pay scales, a limited emphasis on contingent pay and generous benefits in the form of flexible working, holiday entitlements and final salary pension schemes. While the *quid pro quo* for this was often argued to be lower base salaries and higher job security than the private sector, economic recession and government spending programmes have led to the erosion of salary differentials. Indeed, there have been recent claims that public sector salaries are in many instances now comparable with or superior to private sector equivalents. This has led to considerable hostility around the issue of public sector reward. Gillian Hibberd (2010), however, argues that much of this hostility is based around myths on levels of reward in the sector.

Reward in the public sector: fiction or reality?

Hibberd (2010) sets about exploding some of the myths she believes have arisen about public sector pay in recent years. She includes:

Myth 1: Public sector pensions are gold-plated. Final salary pension schemes do still exist but take-home payments from them are not, in most cases, excessive. Average salary is £13,000 and average pension £4,000.

Myth 2: The taxpayer meets the cost of all public sector pensions. There are both funded and unfunded schemes in the public sector. For example, the Local Government Scheme is funded, employer and employee contributions are invested, and pensions paid from the returns – not by the taxpayer. Employee contribution rates also vary widely – e.g. 0% for the armed forces and 11% for the police.

Myth 3: Public sector workers are paid more than their private sector equivalents. A recent Institute for Fiscal Studies (IFS) report has concluded that public sector workers are paid in line with their private sector counterparts. Raw data may not indicate this, but it needs to be adjusted to account for the often highly skilled labour that is employed in the public sector – for example, in the NHS.

Myth 4: The public sector has grown out of all control. A perception has emerged that the public sector has expanded hugely in the past decade. The IFS report suggests that public administration jobs rose by 1% and other public sector jobs by 4% in the period 2000 to 2005. These figures are now predicted to decline sharply.

Myth 5: Many public sector workers are paid more than the prime minister. Around 300 senior public sector executives earned more than the prime minister out of a workforce of over 5 million. Hibberd argues that the salaries of chief executives of public bodies are commensurate with the responsibilities they take, and less than those of most private sector senior executives.

Source: Hibberd, G. (2010) HR Column 'Fiction or reality?', *People Management*, 12 August

INTERNAL AND EXTERNAL FACTORS THAT SHAPE REWARD MANAGEMENT

Many sources, including Hatchett (2008), outline a number of pressures on reward management including inflation, rates of economic growth, labour market issues and increases in individual domestic expenditure, such as Council Tax. Alongside these issues there are a number of other factors that HR professionals need to keep in mind when setting reward strategies, including:

- the desire to maintain purchasing power: this is eroded by inflation, and workers will seek pay increases to compensate for it in order to maintain or to improve their living standards
- talent management: there has been a long period of tight labour markets in the UK, and skills shortages continue even in labour markets where there are larger numbers of unemployed individuals
- transparent pay structures: there is a greater demand both legally and socially for transparency and equity both internally and externally, and reward practices must respond to this
- equal pay issues: there have been a number of successful claims in the public sector with substantial financial implications. There is consequently a need for reward processes to support equal pay structures
- market-related comparisons: economic difficulties mean that there will be modest (or no) rises for some while others will receive higher rises in the face of skills shortages. This can create tensions within the workforce and highlights the need for transparency in pay decisions.

Alongside the issues outlined above it is important to understand that employers have a range of mechanisms for establishing job and grading systems – for example, job evaluation systems and internal labour markets – to which they attach pay structures. All of these terms are explored later in this chapter, but at the moment the key point to keep in mind is that a key justification for imposing pay and **grade structures** is to ensure that pay processes are seen to be fair.

Having said that, however, the external labour market can create problems for attempts to standardise internal systems, especially where they are applied at a national level. The price of labour in the external market may, for example, vary by geographical location. Living costs and thus wage expectations are very different in the north-east from what they are in the south-east of the UK. Similarly, there tend to be surpluses of labour in the north-east and skills shortages in the south-east. Such factors have implications for the way that pay levels are set within organisations. This discussion introduces the issue of how pay is determined in organisations. The following subsection defines the term 'pay determination' and briefly considers how organisations go about setting pay levels in practice.

PAY DETERMINATION

'Pay determination' may appear to be a complex term at first glance but the concept is a relatively simple one. Pay determination is simply the process of making decisions about how much employees should be paid for their work. Druker and White (2009: 23) believe that:

the method and level at which decisions are taken and criteria used to determine pay levels are key issues in reward management.

This statement highlights crucial components of pay determination – the level at which decisions are made and the criteria used. Some organisations devolve pay decisions to individual managers whereas others keep control at higher levels. In the public sector, for example, salaries are often pegged against national frameworks and there is little, if any, room for manoeuvre. In the same way different organisations use different criteria to determine pay levels. In some settings skills and competencies are used as ways to set pay levels while in other environments pay may be set by reference to specific achievements against set objectives. These issues are debated in more detail a little later in this chapter.

A key external factor that impacts on the reward management decisions made by employers is legislation – notably the national minimum wage and equal pay.

THE NATIONAL MINIMUM WAGE (NMW)

The National Minimum Wage Act was passed in 1998 by the Labour Government in office at the time. It marked a shift away from a reliance on market forces to determining wages effectively, and established the first national pay rate in UK history.

From April 1999 all employers in the UK have had to pay at least the national minimum wage to their employees. Opponents of the legislation argued that an NMW would lead to higher unemployment because employers could no longer afford to employ as many staff. Opponents also suggested that inflation would increase as higher wages fed through into the economy. There is, however, very little evidence that the NMW has led to increased unemployment and inflation. Indeed, employment in traditionally low-wage sectors such as hospitality and retail has continued to grow since the introduction of the NMW.

In April 1999 the NMW was set at £3.60 per hour (£3.00 for 18- to 21-year-olds). By 2011 the headline rate had increased to £6.08 per hour for individuals aged 21 or more, although there were separate rates for those aged 18 to 20 (£4.98 per hour) and those aged between 16 and 17 (£3.68 per hour).

Alongside the introduction of the NMW employers also have to contend with equal pay legislation.

EQUAL PAY

There are several pieces of legislation that impact on reward decisions, including those around equal pay and discrimination. The Equal Pay Act 1970 (as amended by the Equal Pay (Amendment) Regulations 1983) now incorporated into the Equality Act 2010 was needed to address pay discrimination on the grounds of gender. For example, as noted by Perkins and White (2011: 77), until the passing of the Equal Pay Act in 1970 it was perfectly legal to pay women less than men for doing the same job. Legislation now prevents this from occurring.

Equal pay legislation defines pay as wages and all other contractual entitlements, including holiday and sick pay, for example, as well as any discounts offered by the employer and 'benefits in kind'. The specific provisions of the legislation around equal pay now provide for the right for men and women to be paid the same in the following three circumstances:

- for like work (where two employees are doing exactly the same or very similar work)
- for work rated as equivalent (how this rating should be arrived at is not specified in law but is often informed by **job evaluation**)
- for work of equal value (where jobs are very different in terms of their skills and abilities but contribute a similar amount of 'value' to the organisation).

CASE STUDY

Equal pay, or more-than-equal pay?

Gemma Cartwright and Steven Garth work in the same organisation doing work of equal value. At present she earns £20,000 and Steven earns £21,000. A job evaluation exercise is conducted, but the results are not communicated because they are considered too politically sensitive. No changes are made to salaries. Gemma learns via the organisational grapevine that her post was evaluated 25% above

Steven's. She takes the organisation to an employment tribunal and wins her case. What should her new salary be?

- £25,000?
- £26,000?

or

- £21,000?

GATHERING AND ANALYSING REWARD INTELLIGENCE

There are many sources of reward management data that HR practitioners can take advantage of. The CIPD, for instance, produces an annual reward management survey, which examines issues such as pay positioning, pensions and benefits and performance-related bonuses. Alongside reports produced by professional institutions such as the CIPD there are also various industry benchmarking reports and surveys, including those produced by the local government group for the public sector and private sector organisations such as Croner (www.croner.co.uk) and Incomes Data Services (www.incomesdata.co.uk).

Together with the data sources listed above, national statistics also have relevance within reward management. Before making pay decisions HR professionals often need to take account of the following factors:

- inflation
- unemployment rates
- the number of vacancies
- average working hours

- average earnings.

Information relating to factors such as inflation, unemployment rates and average earnings/working hours can be found from government websites such as www.statistics.gov.uk. By examining these sorts of data sources HR professionals can quickly identify trends in particular areas and can adapt their reward management strategies and decisions as a result. When thinking about the number of vacancies, it is important to recognise that positions that are particularly difficult to fill generally command higher reward packages. Vacancies that attract many applicants, by contrast, can usually be given lower reward packages – although this is not always the case.

When examining reward management data it is important to recognise that statistics can be influenced by issues occurring at a variety of different levels. The previous section of this chapter considered the international, national and corporate contexts of reward management, and it is important to understand that these factors shape the ways in which organisations make their final decisions. Alongside these considerations, as we saw above, HR professionals must also take the effect of legislation into account when gathering and analysing reward data.

Before moving on to examine the various theories of reward management, it is important to consider the ways in which reward data may be presented to various stakeholder groups. The primary consideration here is the level and type of data that is going to be relevant to each group. Whereas senior managers might want to see detailed benchmarking data from comparable organisations or data that allows them to gauge how factors such as inflation or the number of vacancies are affecting reward management, other stakeholders may have different requirements. Employees, for example, are unlikely to be concerned with specific comparisons between particular roles but they are likely to want to know how their earnings compare to the average across an industry. It is important that HR professionals can provide appropriate information for each specific stakeholder group.

From the discussions in this section it should be clear that there are a variety of internal and external factors that influence reward management in organisations. To add greater complexity to the lives of HR practitioners there are also several underpinning theories that inform the reward management field. These theories shed more light on reward management decisions. However, their positions frequently contradict. It is important to understand that there is not necessarily one theory that is 'right' or one theory that is 'wrong' – they are simply different interpretations that may or may not be relevant in given contexts.

THEORIES OF REWARD MANAGEMENT

It is important to understand that there are a variety of perspectives and theories that exist within the reward management field. This part of the chapter outlines and discusses the main theories and perspectives:

- economic theory
- institutional theories of reward

- human capital theory.

Please do not be put off by the terminology in the bullet list above. The theories are relatively straightforward and the key principles of each are explained in detail.

ECONOMIC THEORY

Economic theories broadly consider wage rates to be determined by a combination of the supply of labour and the demand for that labour from employers. Wage rates are therefore arrived at to try to achieve a balance between supply and demand. If labour is in short supply, the value of the labour increases and wages go up. Conversely, where labour is plentiful, its value drops. Key assumptions of economic theories are firstly that both employers and employees are rational actors who have all the information they need to make informed choices, and secondly that employees are fully mobile – that is, they will move to where there are jobs available.

There are, however, complexities within these theories. Firstly, of course, not many employees are really 'fully mobile' because they are constrained by family and social circumstances. So the opportunity to maximise their reward is limited. Secondly, economic theories focus only on forms of financial reward to attract labour and achieve organisational goals. Within these theories the 'worth' of the potential employee and the state of the labour market are the features that determine wage rates. A criticism of these assumptions has been provided by individuals who are more disposed towards what are termed social psychological theories. Social psychologists emphasise, instead, the long-term nature of the employment relationship and suggest that economic theories that focus only on pay rates do not accurately reflect reality. They suggest that it is more important for employees to experience job satisfaction and a sense of fairness in relation to reward. It is important to understand that tensions in the employment relationship can lead to the adoption of different perspectives on reward.

INSTITUTIONAL THEORIES OF REWARD

Perhaps unsurprisingly, given all the above criticism of economic theories, there are a number of other economic theories that seek to explain how wage rates are established. These have all influenced thinking in different ways, rather than one being superior to or replacing another theory. This is an important point to keep in mind.

Institutional theories of reward introduce a more 'open systems' approach to setting wage levels. They recognise the role of institutions within reward systems – in other words, context or environmental factors are recognised as influencing wage levels. An open systems approach allows for the possibility of an employer's actions in the use of wages to influence employee attitudes and behaviours. An example of an employer action might be if an employer offered a wage premium in order to attract labour. Such a decision might motivate workers to focus their efforts on achieving organisational strategy. In addition to this point it is important to remember that workers do not necessarily 'sell' their labour as individuals: they may act collectively (most obviously through a trade union) and such activity will affect wages. The sizes of organisations or of industry sectors are also thought to influence pay-setting.

Institutional theorists argue that recognition of these factors helps to explain why wage levels rarely appear to fall. Classical economic labour market theories such as those explored above suggest that wages will be lower when there is a surplus of labour, but in reality wages are often described as 'sticky' – that is, they are resistant to being reduced. It can certainly be argued that trade union activity may well achieve this outcome, because workers operating collectively often prevent any reduction in their pay. There are a number of competing explanations for the 'stickiness' of wages, and it is important to understand that this issue is not generally well understood.

HUMAN CAPITAL THEORY

Human capital theory (Becker, 1975) is one of the founding theories in understanding reward. This theory suggests that workers 'invest' in themselves via education, training and development to increase their own capital (or value to employers). Different levels of reward are used to attract workers dependent upon their skills, experience and qualifications. In other words, the higher an individual's capital, the higher is the return on it in terms of pay and benefits as organisations compete for skilled labour.

REFLECTIVE ACTIVITY

Which of the theoretical approaches outlined here do you think best fits with the reward management practices and systems inside your organisation (or one that you know well)?

THE CONCEPT OF 'TOTAL REWARD'

The term 'total reward' is often used in modern reward management systems, but what does it actually mean? The CIPD (2009) states that total reward is:

> the term that has been adopted to describe a reward strategy that brings additional components such as learning and development, together with aspects of the working environment, into the benefits package. It goes beyond standard remuneration by embracing the company culture, and is aimed at giving all employees a voice in the operation, with the employer in return receiving an engaged employee performance.

This definition demonstrates that total reward considers far more than just base pay and that it 'embraces the company culture'. It highlights the holistic nature of total reward, and this is a key point to keep in mind. Within this interpretation the basic elements of a total reward package include:

- financial compensation
- benefits

- work–life balance
- performance and recognition
- development and career opportunities.

The key learning point in this section, then, is that a total reward approach involves both extrinsic and intrinsic elements. An example in practice can be seen in the case study below, which has been taken from *People Management*.

CASE STUDY

Charities use total reward to make work staff's own Eden

Third-sector organisations can achieve success with a total reward approach to make up for their inability to offer high salaries, delegates at this month's CIPD Reward Forum heard.

Leah Brewer, organisational development manager at the Eden Trust, explained how the environmental charity had pioneered a range of innovative benefits, including on-site yoga, podiatry and massages. High-performing employees are nominated for one-off bonuses, vouchers for the Eden Project shop, or a one-to-one lunch with Tim Smit, Eden's chief executive. Workers are also entered into a draw to take an extra week's annual leave.

'Working for Eden is rewarding, and not only for the pay packet,' said Brewer. 'It's important to make sure it works for the organisation as well as the individual.'

Firms should not be afraid to try new things when it comes to reward, and while pilot schemes are a good way of getting management buy-in, not everything will work, she said.

'Sometimes knock-backs can be good – you have a reason why [a scheme didn't work] and you can deal with that,' Brewer told *PM*.

Joe Bennett, HR director at Scope, told delegates that performance-related pay had proved a success at the charity, although it concentrated on senior staff.

'HR can add value by focusing its attention on that particular group of people and really getting them to excel,' said Bennett. 'To help get a feeling of clarity and consistency, you have to get the messages right. You need the top team banging out those messages.'

Source: Chubb, L. (2007) 'Charities use total reward to make work staff's own Eden', *People Management*, 29 November.

REFLECTIVE ACTIVITY

Does your organisation (or one that you used to work in) use a 'total reward' approach? Do you think that this has/would have any effect on your level of engagement with your organisation?

THE AIMS OF TOTAL REWARD

Although there are many different models of total reward that organisations can adopt, the CIPD states that 'the principle of viewing a range of non-financial factors as part of the rewards package' is the same. Many organisations are now looking at the experience they offer in a more holistic manner when deciding how best to attract, retain and engage existing and potential employees. The broad aim of a total reward approach is to achieve a better balance between the needs of the employee and the needs of the organisation.

Looking at the fundamental purpose of total reward a little more closely, Armstrong (2007: 31) believes that the central aim is 'to maximise the combined impact of a wide range of reward initiatives on motivation, commitment and job engagement'. There is a broad view that total reward should aim to increase employee satisfaction and ultimately business performance. To this end the CIPD (2009) maintains that the aim of total reward should be to obtain 'more positive employee commitment without incurring open-ended operational costs'. This statement confirms the view that total reward aims to balance the needs of the employee with the needs of the employer. Having now understood the broad aim of total reward, let us consider its benefits in an organisational setting.

THE BENEFITS OF TOTAL REWARD

The CIPD Factsheet on Total Reward (2009) states that there are four key benefits of such strategies. These are thought to be:

- the easier recruitment of talented staff
- reduced wastage through staff turnover
- better business performance
- the enhanced reputation of the organisation as an employer of choice.

Whereas these points may seem appropriate from a theoretical stance, how might they translate to operational practice? Empirical evidence gathered from Buckinghamshire County Council, where total reward was introduced in 2006, displays evidence of the benefits listed above being realised in practice (Hibberd, 2009). The results from this particular study included the following findings:

- Confidence in the leadership of the authority rose by 21%.
- 80% of staff felt 'well recognised' for the work they did (an increase of 3%).
- Those who felt 'valued' increased by 7%.
- 91% of employees enjoyed being part of a team (a rise of 13%).
- 76% of staff enjoyed working for the Council.

Hibberd (2009) believes that total reward sends a strong message to the workforce. The findings above arguably demonstrate that the organisation in question is perceived to *care* about its employees, which is an important factor when using reward to foster engagement. Hibberd (2009) suggested at a later conference that the public sector needed to communicate the value of total reward in a more effective way in order to retain top talent. Hibberd pointed out that if this could not be done, talented members of staff might be tempted to

move to the private sector once it emerges from recession and starts to create
large numbers of jobs once again.

REWARD INITIATIVES AND PRACTICES

The focus of this part of the chapter is on specific reward initiatives and practices.
In broad terms this territory incorporates:

- grade and pay structures
- job evaluation
- market rate analysis
- 'contingent' reward.

Please do not be put off by the terminology above. The text explains and discusses
the concepts in detail in order to convey a detailed understanding of reward
initiatives and practices.

GRADE AND PAY STRUCTURES

Grade and pay structures are important parts of reward management. When they
are designed properly and fit effectively within the wider context of the
organisation, they provide a logical framework within which an organisation's
pay policies can be implemented. Grade and pay structures help HR professionals
work out where jobs should be placed in a hierarchy, define appropriate pay
levels, and demonstrate how pay can be progressed over time.

In simple terms, a grade structure is made up of a number of grades, bands or
levels into which groups of comparable jobs can be placed. Organisations may
choose to operate a single-grade structure into which all jobs are placed, or they
may choose to group jobs into job or career 'families'. Either approach can be
appropriate: suitability is determined by contextual variables such as the size and
complexity of the organisation.

Along similar lines to the thoughts outlined above, a pay structure defines the
different levels of pay for jobs or groups of jobs by reference to their relative value
to the organisation. Relative value can be determined in a number of ways
including job evaluation and market rate analysis (both of these concepts are
discussed shortly). As with grade structures, an organisation may decide to
implement one pay structure for all employees or it may choose to operate
different structures within different occupational groups. Armstrong (2006)
points out that organisations are increasingly looking to harmonise terms and
conditions of employment, so that single pay structures are becoming more and
more common.

Broadly, there are several different types of grade and pay structures that
organisations may choose to operate. The most common are:

- narrow-graded
- broad-graded
- job family
- career family

- pay spines.

As you may imagine, narrow-graded structures have many different pay and grade levels (more than 10 and sometimes as many as 18) whereas broad-graded structures have fewer levels. It is important to understand that within broad-graded structures there may be reference points placed within each grade or level, perhaps splitting each into two or three segments.

By contrast to the approaches above, job family structures seek to group jobs functionally or operationally – in other words, splitting the IT roles from the finance roles or production roles from research roles. Along similar lines, career family structures seek to split roles into different career paths but try to ensure comparability between different families. In other words a 'junior' finance role is pegged at the same level as a 'junior' administration role, and so on.

Armstrong (2006) tells us that pay spines are often found in the public sector and in organisations that have adopted a public sector approach to reward management. These systems consist of a number of different pay 'points' extending from the lowest- to the highest-paid positions in an organisation. Increments can be placed at regular intervals – perhaps 2% or 3% of salary – or organisations may choose to widen the gaps between jobs towards the top of the hierarchy. It is very important to understand that there is no 'one best way' to set up a grade or pay structure. An approach that may be appropriate in one organisation may be unworkable in another, and *vice versa*.

JOB EVALUATION

At its most simple, a job evaluation scheme is a systematic process for defining the relative worth or size of jobs within an organisation. The main reason why HR professionals undertake job evaluations is to assess which jobs in an organisation are similar in order to plot their position within grade or pay structures. Job evaluation schemes aim to:

- establish where jobs in an organisation are of similar size or value
- allow for the development of equitable and defendable pay and grade structures
- help practitioners make market comparisons about specific roles
- provide internal transparency for all stakeholders
- ensure that organisations meet equal pay obligations.

Broadly, job evaluation schemes can be either 'analytical' or 'non-analytical'. Analytical job evaluation is by far the more common approach and revolves around analysing specific factors such as competencies and making objective decisions about the relative value of specific roles. Whereas analytical job evaluation seeks to compare and contrast different factors within roles, non-analytical job evaluation seeks to compare whole jobs and place them into a grade or rank order. It is important to understand that non-analytical job evaluation schemes do not meet the requirements of equal value legislation although they can still be useful exercises to broadly assess jobs within an organisation.

Although job evaluation can be a useful method of comparing jobs internally, it is not suitable for making comparisons between organisations. In order to make comparisons of jobs or grades between organisations, a process known as market rate analysis must be used.

MARKET RATE ANALYSIS

It is very important to understand that pay levels within organisations are subject to external as well as internal pressures. Whereas job evaluation schemes can be used to determine internal relativities, HR professionals can only determine external relativities by using a technique called market rate analysis.

Armstrong (2006) points out that the concept of the market rate is an imprecise one. He argues that there is no such thing as *the* market rate, and that there are a variety of rates paid by employers even where jobs appear to be identical. Organisations do this for a number of reasons – perhaps a skill shortage in a particular geographical location has pushed up the salary for a particular position, or maybe an organisation has adopted a cost-minimisation model and consequently pays below the market average.

In order to conduct a market rate analysis HR professionals must gather and analyse data related to the salaries and reward packages offered by similar organisations. It is very important to understand that data can often be misleading or incomplete, and HR professionals have to be very careful to make accurate comparisons. When making market comparisons the aim should be to:

- acquire accurate data that correctly details base pay, bonuses and benefits, as was analysed above
- compare like with like – in other words, compare rewards attached to jobs of similar size and importance
- ensure that collected information is up to date
- interpret the information with an eye on the organisation's current needs and circumstances
- collate and present the information in such a way that actions become clear.

CONTINGENT REWARD

At first glance the concept of contingent reward looks confusing, but it is essentially focused around two basic questions: what do we value, and what are we prepared to pay for? Armstrong (2006) points out that there are many different contingent reward strategies that firms can adopt, including performance-related pay, competence-related pay, skill-based pay and team-based pay. All of these approaches link pay to some form of variable (such as job performance or personal competence), but organisations can take different approaches to the structure of their reward offering.

Most firms that operate some form of contingent reward strategy provide employees with an element of base pay and a bonus related to whatever factor they deem to be important. Within performance-related pay systems this might be individual performance against a set of objectives, whereas within skill-based pay a bonus might be linked to the acquisition of new skills. There are many terms for this bonus element, including 'variable' pay or 'pay at risk'.

Contingent pay systems are popular in organisations because many individuals see them as the best way to motivate people. They assume that linking an element of pay to the achievement of a particular goal will encourage employees to achieve that goal. Having considered the topic of total reward at an earlier point of this chapter, it can be argued that this view of contingent pay is perhaps a little simplistic. Within total reward systems individuals are thought to be motivated by intrinsic factors as well as extrinsic factors. It is important to remember that pay itself is an extrinsic motivator whereas the satisfaction derived from work can often be an intrinsic motivator. HR professionals must ensure that they strike the right balance between extrinsic and intrinsic motivators in their policy frameworks.

REFLECTIVE ACTIVITY

What benefits might contingent reward offer organisations? Do you think the use of contingent reward improves organisational performance?

The Reflective Activity above should have made you think about the applicability of contingent reward. In broad terms it may be argued that contingent reward systems can help to support improved organisational performance because they focus individuals on certain activities and can be used to highlight particularly important goals or targets. But you may think that they are potentially divisive and too subjective in their measurement. Both would be partly true. The use of contingent pay has to be carefully managed and fit with the organisation's goal and culture. Below is a case study that illustrates how an organisation made changes to its contingent reward scheme on the basis that the scheme did not match its strategy.

CASE STUDY

Nationwide

Nationwide Building Society operates over 700 branches, within which there are around 450 senior financial consultants (SFCs). They sell many products that are regulated by the Financial Services Authority. The pay and bonus scheme for SFCs required an overhaul for several reasons: it focused on volume rather than value; it was not cost-effective; and it didn't differentiate sufficiently between low and high performance. Because any changes to the reward schemes were contractual, they required full union negotiation. As a result a new total reward package

that met all the outlined criteria was launched four months after the project was started in January 2009. Following a comprehensive communication programme asking SFCs how they should be rewarded, the reward team gained full union support. Staff feedback was also positive. Sales performance in the quarter following launch increased to 184% of target.

Source: *People Management* (2010) 'CIPD People Management Awards

2010: Performance and reward
category', 12 August.

LINE MANAGERS AND REWARD MANAGEMENT

As with many areas of HR practice, line managers play an important role in reward management systems and processes. Line managers are the individuals who have most contact with employees and are normally responsible for making pay decisions within the frameworks set out by HR professionals. For this reason line managers have a crucial dimension in maintaining fairness, consistency and transparency across organisations. It is important to understand that these individuals need to be trained in how reward systems work and how decisions should be arrived at.

Towards the beginning of this chapter the fact that reward management consists of both extrinsic factors (such as pay and benefits) and intrinsic factors (such as work itself being meaningful) was highlighted. Line managers have a crucial role to play in enhancing intrinsic rewards and can do it by designing jobs so that employees can feel a sense of purpose at work and by providing praise as and when necessary. Reward management does not revolve solely around monetary pay and benefits, as was shown earlier in this chapter when the concept of total reward was investigated.

Despite the points outlined above, line managers often do not feel involved in reward management – and this can consequently affect employee commitment and engagement. HR professionals must take time to ensure that line managers are consulted about reward management decisions and must make sure that their views are taken into consideration. HR professionals must explain grade and pay structures to line managers and indicate where and when rewards, whether financial or non-financial, might be distributed. If organisations operate some form of contingent pay system, line managers are a vital source of information regarding performance, competence and/or employee skill. Again, it is vital that HR practitioners provide line managers with the necessary training so that they can make objective judgements about relative levels of performance, competence and/or skill – otherwise, final reward decisions may not be consistent or even fair.

Throughout this chapter it has been shown that reward management is an area of practice that is deeply affected by both external and internal variables, including the business context as a whole, legislative decisions and organisational strategies. If line managers are not supported in making effective reward decisions, reward systems and processes will be redundant. No matter how much thought has gone into grade or pay structures, if line managers do not know how they apply in practical ways, there will be no consistency of reward across the organisation.

EVALUATING THE IMPACT OF REWARD MANAGEMENT

Organisations must take time to assess the impact of reward management to ensure that strategic decisions are having the desired effect. Evaluation is often an overlooked area but it is important to understand that it need not be a laborious process.

In previous sections it was noted that HR professionals might benchmark their reward strategies or packages against those of their competitors. Although this might be an easier task in public sector environments where information is perhaps more freely available, there are surveys such as those conducted by the CIPD that HR professionals might find useful. By analysing organisational performance against these benchmarks broad trends can be found and reported back to senior managers. In addition to external benchmarks HR professionals can also make use of tools such as staff surveys to attempt to spot any correlations between reward management and both employee commitment and engagement. By examining trends over several surveys HR professionals may be able to highlight the impacts of certain decisions and policies, and produce convincing evidence to support their business cases or proposals.

In addition to the measures outlined above, it is quite possible that HR professionals will be able to link employee performance with reward decisions. By taking time to analyse data emerging from staff appraisals or performance management processes, HR professionals will be able to indicate where specific reward practices are having an impact. Perhaps a team-based bonus might be found to be contributing to more effective teamworking in a particular department, or perhaps a higher starting salary in another department might have attracted a more skilled workforce. Of course, findings always differ between organisations, but if accurate data is collected, HR professionals should be able to make a judgement about the effectiveness of reward strategies and policies.

CASE STUDY

Merit based pay versus yearly rises for all

Please take some time to carefully read through the article from *People Management* presented below, which discusses the idea that organisations prefer 'merit-based' pay increases as opposed to yearly rises for everyone. Once you are happy that you understand the key points from the article, see if you can answer the three questions that appear at the end.

Firms prefer merit-based pay to yearly rises for all

Almost half (46%) of organisations no longer award employees an across-the-board annual rise or cost-of-living adjustment, the Reward Management 2008 survey has revealed. Manufacturing, production and private sector firms were the least likely to provide such a pay rise. An increasingly popular alternative is to allocate pay budgets to departmental heads to distribute among staff based on their contribution, the survey of 603 organisations found. 'The decline in the yearly traditional pay rise seems to be spreading throughout employment sectors,' said Charles Cotton, CIPD adviser, reward and employment conditions. [...]

David Conroy, principal of the human capital business at HR consultancy Mercer, said that 20% of pay deals now have a long-term nature. While this helps employers by making planning more predictable, sweeteners are often needed to overcome union reservations, said Conroy. 'Sometimes there are other benefits bundled in as a way of encouraging the workforce to agree to a deal, such as improvements to annual leave and to maternity and paternity provision,' he said.

Cotton warned that any changes to pay and benefits needed to be effectively communicated by line managers to their teams to avoid leaving staff 'confused, demotivated and in the dark about what they need to do to achieve reward and recognition'.

Paul Ryan, HR operations manager at consumer brands firm Henkel, told PM that across-the-board pay increases in the private sector run counter to the principle of basing rises on merit.

'High-potential staff won't find it motivating if they are told their pay will progress at a mediocre rate whatever they do,' he said. Ryan, who is responsible for compensation and benefits for the company's 1,150 UK staff, added that most people in the

private sector were 'conditioned to be more flexible' but admitted that multi-year pay deals might be more commonplace in highly unionised environments.

Meanwhile, unions in the public sector have expressed concern that the government's new longer-term pay deals, which will initially focus on teachers, nurses and the police, may amount to pay cuts in real terms. They have demanded 'escape clauses' if economic conditions change during the three-year period.

Source: Phillips, L. (2008) 'Firms prefer merit-based pay to yearly rises for all', *People Management*, 24 January.

Questions

1   Why might firms prefer merit-based pay increases rather than standard annual pay rises for all?

2   Evaluate the role that line managers play in communicating pay decisions to employees. Why are they such important individuals in this process?

3   In what ways might the external context facing organisations influence decisions related to pay increases?

FURTHER READING

Armstrong, M. (2010) *A Handbook of Reward Management Practice*, 3rd edition. London, Kogan Page. This is a useful resource, which covers both theory and best practice in the reward management field.

Churchard, C. (2010) 'Reward professionals go "back to the drawing board"', *People Management*, 23 February. This *People Management* article discusses reward strategies and priorities in the wake of the recent recession.

Churchard, C. (2011) 'Creative non-cash rewards "drive key staff behaviours"', *People Management*, 1 November. This *People Management* article discusses how employers might be able to get more value for their money by investing in 'non-cash' rewards.

CIPD (2012) *Reward Management* Information Page. [Online] Available at: http://www.cipd.co.uk/hr-topics/reward-management.aspx. This website provides factsheets, podcasts and survey reports on the subject of reward management.

E-Reward (2012) *E-Reward: The online guide to reward management.* [Online] Available at: http://www.e-reward.co.uk/. This website provides practical guidance, 'top tips' and links to other websites which contain reward management content.

Hall, J. (2012) 'Hundreds of gold-plated final salary pension schemes close', *The Daily Telegraph*, 31 January. This article discusses the move from final salary to 'defined contribution' pension schemes.

Perkins, S. and White, G. (2011) *Reward Management*, 2nd edition. London, Chartered Institute of Personnel and Development. This CIPD text discusses the overall context of reward management, explores key conceptual frameworks and discusses the various elements of pay- and benefit-setting in detail.

REFERENCES

Armstrong, M. (2002) *Employee Reward*. London, Chartered Institute of Personnel and Development.

Armstrong, M. (2006) *A Handbook of Human Resource Management Practice*, 10th edition. London, Kogan Page.

Armstrong, M. (2007) *A Handbook of Reward Management Practice*, 2nd edition. London, Kogan Page.

Becker, G. (1975) *Human Capital: A theoretical and empirical analysis, with special reference to education*, 2nd edition. Chicago, University of Chicago Press.

CIPD (2009) *Total Reward*. Factsheet. June. London, Chartered Institute of Personnel and Development.

Croner (2012) Croner. [Online] Available at: www.croner.co.uk [accessed 11 February 2012].

Druker, J. and White, G. (2009) *Reward Management: A critical text*, 2nd edition. London, Routledge.

Hatchett, A. (2008) 'Area of high pressure as cold front approaches', *People Management*, 10 January.

Hibberd, G. (2009) 'Engage staff through total reward', *Employee Benefits*, 16 January.

Hibberd, G. (2010) 'Fiction or reality?', HR Column, *People Management*, 12 August.

IDS (2012) *IDS: Employment Information and Analysis*. [Online] Available at: www.incomesdata.co.uk [accessed 11 February 2012].

Office for National Statistics (2012) UK National Statistics: Publication Hub. [Online] Available at: www.statistics.gov.uk [accessed 12 February 2012].

Perkins, S. J. and White, G. (2011) *Reward Management*, 2nd edition. London, Chartered Institute of Personnel and Development.

Phillips, L. (2008) 'Firms prefer merit-based pay to yearly rises for all', *People Management*, 24 January.

Also from CIPD Publishing . . .

International Human Resource Management:

A Cross-cultural and Comparative Approach

Edited by Paul Iles and Crystal Zhang

International Human Resource Management offers balanced coverage of international, comparative and cross-cultural HRM.

- This title is ideal for students taking international HRM for the first time or studying in their 2nd language.
- A cohesive co-authored text, with contributions from experts on specific countries and regions.
- A title grounded in theory but balanced with cases and examples.

Order your copy now online at cipd.co.uk/bookstore or call us on 0844 800 3366

Paul Iles is a Professor of Leadership and HRM at Salford Business School, the University of Salford, and was previously Running Stream Professor of HRD and Course Leader of the DBA at Leeds Business School, where he provides academic leadership in HRD , leadership, talent and change management.

Dr. Crystal Zhang is a senior Lecturer in Human Resource Management and Organisational Behaviour at Leeds Business School, Leeds Metropolitan University.

| Published March 2013 | ISBN 978 1 84398 300 2 | Paperback | 340 pages |

Student resources

Your dedicated online area giving you all you need, when you need it. Helpful factsheets to guide you in revision and preparing for exams, practical tools, online journals and much more can be found at **cipd.co.uk/studyresources**

Students can **save 20%** on textbooks

Plus **save 10%** on CIPD training, online subscription products, conference tickets, publications, DVDs and Toolkits.

To find out more, call us on +44 (0)20 8612 6208 or visit cipd.co.uk/memberbenefits